DRIFTING LIGHT

Kendall Clarke

ISBN-13: 9798369903568
ISBN-10: 9798369903

Cover design by: Kendall Clarke
Library of Congress Control Number: 2018675309
Printed in the United States of America

For my fifteen-year-old self, and every other teenager who is navigating through this strange, ever changing world with hope and an open mind.

"I like songs about drifters, books about the same. They both seem to make me feel a little less insane."

MODEST MOUSE

CONTENTS

PART 1: THE JUNGLE

CHAPTER 1

Lirah sprinted, effortlessly avoiding every shrub and root covering the jungle floor. Her bare feet had memorized the network of the ground below as if they had minds of their own. She picked up speed, and the breeze pushing against her face grew stronger. Tingles of adrenaline shot down her spine and through her legs.

When she could no longer hear Au's footsteps tracking behind her, she slowed to a halt and leaned against a wide tree trunk to catch her breath.

Noises of the jungle surrounded her. Silver theetles buzzed in tight packs like clumps of floating crystals, followed by a pudgy blum bee that jingled as it flew by in zig-zagged patterns and intoxicating loops.

Lirah squinted. In the distance, two speckled chara cats lounged in the center of a flower so huge that it overshadowed every bush around. The charas' pointed ears stretched two feet high as their golden speckled eyes, peering through the shadows of the petals wider than pillows, locked onto hers.

More feet stomped closer.

Frightened, the chara cats uncurled themselves and darted off.

Lirah turned.

There was Au. He was gasping and grinning, his shaggy brown hair a wild mess piled on his head.

"I think that's the farthest," he inhaled deeply, "you've outrun me yet."

Lirah smiled. She was tall and toned, though in comparison, Au's muscular body towered over hers. But it didn't matter, she always ran faster.

"You're ... *definitely* the fastest in the whole Pride now ... All the other men ... *have* to be jealous ... that you're my partner," he rasped.

Running was the most praised skill in their Pride, besides being able to quickly detect hiding creatures. When it came to hunting, Pride members had to run faster and longer than the creature they were trying to chase down. Or they had to outrun beasts trying to take *them* down. And on rare occasions, they had to chase away unwelcome strangers that crossed over the boundary markings and into the Pride's territory.

But none of that fazed Lirah. She loved being out in the wild jungle where she could be herself. Alive and alert, without feeling overly anxious. She felt significantly less anxious out here than she did in her Pride's Treetop Society, where everyone ate and slept and socialized. There were way too many rules. Knowing how much to eat, how to chew, who to look at in the eye, when to reply to an elder, when to stay quiet, when to give thanks, when to laugh. It was *exhausting.*

Lirah wasn't a mischievous adolescent; she just liked adventure. She loved climbing trees, capturing bugs, and finding fruits and whacking them with a branch to watch them soar. Many of the elders, and *all* of the Pride leaders, frowned upon these activities. Everyone in the Pride had to stay safe, first and foremost.

Lirah attempting backflips off a twenty-foot tree branch was *not* what her elders considered safe. After that stunt, an elder went out of their way to tell a Pride leader about it, which resulted in Lirah's harshest punishment yet. She couldn't roam with Au, her partner and mentor, for fifteen days.

Finally, today, she got to run free. "Free" meaning anywhere in the bounds of the Pride's territory.

"Ready to head back home?" Au asked her, having fully regained his breath.

His honey brown eyes looked back and forth into each of Lirah's, as if trying to decipher her thoughts.

Lirah shrugged and squatted on an outstretched root. She placed her fists against her cheeks and planted her elbows on her knees. She contemplated the Pride while the insects hummed and the birds returned to the trees. She knew the birds were settling down for the night, that they could sense the light dropping from the sky along with the temperature. She wished she could join them.

"I feel more at home out here," Lirah said, picking up a stick and brushing it back and forth through the dirt between her feet. "I mean ... it's obvious I don't fit in with the other women in the Pride. Because I don't act *exactly* how I'm expected to." She groaned. "They're all so boring. And we could go *anywhere*, but we just keep running the same paths across our territory."

Her glassy amber eyes peered up at Au. He was leaning against the same tree that possessed the roots beneath her. He gazed into the jungle, watching the glowing light beams slowly dip down and filter through each crack between the branches.

When it became clear to Lirah that Au wasn't going to respond to her for one of two reasons—he had heard these complaints *hundreds* of times and was bored of entertaining her fantasies, or because he admired and respected his leaders in a way she would never identify with—she pressed him further. "We're so isolated it hurts. Wouldn't it be safer if we all moved? Created allies with another community? Built a larger, *stronger*, society? No one could hurt us again. After the last attack we just rebuilt, right? The Pride just fixed the damages, moved everything up into the treetops, and forgot about it."

Au sighed. "I can tell you that no one *forgot* about the last attack. And we can't just walk right onto another community's territory and expect them to let us in. We don't even know of any communities with as much technology as us. But even if someplace did, it could be dangerous. They could attack us and take all our resources. And, who *knows* how far away this imaginary place might be? Most of the jungle is still unclaimed; you know that. We're best off staying where we're at. We already established our own territory that we can guarantee is safe." He was just repeating what his elders had drilled into his head during his adolescence training.

Lirah appreciated he was at least debating with her. But she hated that his replies were all the same. Why couldn't he understand her perspective?

She stood and leaned against the trunk, pressed her shoulder against his, and assessed the trees surrounding them. "Trees live all around each other, tangling up their roots and sharing water from the sky. If they can intermingle with other groups, why can't we?" She leapt up and grabbed hold of the lowest branch of the tree, pulling herself up before continuing to the one above that. "We've never met anyone outside of the Pride before. I'm sure they're not *all* bad."

"We're also fifteen. The leaders are triple our age at *least*," Au said, and she could feel him watching her climb higher. Her long legs and arms nearly blended in with the tree's golden-cream leaves, but her auburn hair gave her location away. It coursed down to her hips and the light amplified its auburn tint, a hue which perfectly complemented her amber-brown eyes. "They're more knowledgeable than you think they are. You should trust them."

Lirah grimaced.

Au shook his head. "We need to head back before it gets too dark. Whether you believe it or not, our Pride genuinely cares for you, and I don't want them to worry. I'm in charge of you now anyway. So, get down … now." He pointed a hesitant finger down at the tree roots. "And don't flip!"

"You're just my mentor temporarily. You're my partner indefinitely. So, we're equals. However," Lirah slipped down the branches just as smoothly as she climbed up, reaching the ground without a sound, "I know how much *you* care for me. So, let's go!"

She bolted through the jungle, giggling like she hadn't just questioned her society and all of its principles.

Au's footsteps didn't join hers right away. He must be admiring her. Lirah knew he secretly loved their debates, that they were the most entertaining part of his days too. She slowed down and turned her head just as Au started running to catch up, passing her. They raced over roots, rocks, and streams, all the way back home.

CHAPTER 2

Home. Up in the sky. In the jungle canopy.

Hundreds of spherical rooms dangled from massive, sprawling branches interconnected by ropes and wooden bridges. It looked like giant blum bees inhabited the area instead of people. The hives were constructed out of clay, wood, and straggly branches, and they weren't actually shaped much like beehives at all; Pride members just named them that.

During the day, the hives looked much more like hollowed walnuts. But during times like now, when the small rooms glowed brightly and their round windows cast golden beams against the darkness outside, the society looked like a radiant dreamland from the jungle floor. Especially with the rare and translucent moss Pride members hung over branches, which absorbed light during the day and sparkled dimly through the night.

Au called up a series of clicks and hollers to two small specks above, the nightshift guards. Moments later, a rope came hurtling down before his and Lirah's feet.

Lirah grabbed the rope, positioned her feet flat on the tree trunk, and began climbing. Au latched on and ascended behind her, moving swiftly and carefully, making sure nothing was trailing behind them.

Once they reached the top, they silently nodded to the guards and performed a short series of hand gestures to identify themselves, their Pride's greeting symbol.

The guards waved them through.

Lirah and Au walked across the spider web of bridges—left, right, then left again—until they reached Lirah's hive. They rubbed noses, and wished each other pleasant dreams. Partners were only allowed to sleep in the same hive once they were officially Always and Forever mates. Lirah watched Au as he sauntered away to his room, her gaze full of longing.

She swung open the curtain to her hive, and was immediately taken aback.

A body-shaped lump lay beneath the covers of her cot.

She crouched down, grabbed for the sharpest spear on her floor, and slowly inched toward the poorly-hidden figure. She reached out and poked it with the wrapped handle of the spear, making the lump lightly squirm.

It went still.

She poked it again.

It sprang forcefully upright, letting the covers fall from its form.

A petite, fifty-year-old woman with laugh lines, beaded black hair, and a cute button nose revealed herself. Lirah's mother.

"Mala!" Lirah half-shouted, half-whispered, tossing her spear onto a pile of dirty dress cloths. "What are you *doing* here? You know I'm too old for a guardian to be in my room after hours."

Lirah's mother attempted to smooth down her hair and wipe away the sleep from her eyes.

Lirah's wind chimes lightly jingled as wind rushed in through the small window of the dangling treehouse.

"Hush, now. Listen to me." Mala lifted Lirah's hands and cradled them in her own. "I needed to see you, and this is where I knew you'd come back to. I'm staying with you tonight."

"Why do you need to see me *now*? Are you alright?" Lirah looked into her mother's sunken eyes. Oh, how she knew the depths they could reach. Tonight, they looked cloudy, like navy whirlpools.

"I saw something. You know..." Mala's eyes dashed around the candlelit hive before dropping to the floor.

Lirah did know.

Her mother had a special gift. Short glimpses of the future spontaneously flashed beneath her eyelids. Visions.

Mix this ability with well-established connections with spirits, and you've got a mother who *always* knew when great changes lingered over her family and Pride. Who *always* knew when to start preparing, often months before anyone else noticed anything unusual. But Mala never warned anyone else about her visions. The only living members who knew about her gift were Au and Lirah.

While contacting spirits was considered a dark practice in the Pride, possessing the power to predict the future topped the list of prohibited behavior. Claiming that you could see the future meant, to the Pride leaders, that you thought you personally had more power than they did, rather than thinking your bizarre assertions came from a realm outside of yourself.

If anyone in the Pride found out about her visions, Mala would be tortured until the darkness was beaten out of her soul. Mala knew this for a fact because it happened to her own grandmother. And while Lirah knew her mother could sense wonderful changes, this one did not feel positive.

"Are they returning?" Lirah whispered, releasing her hands from her mother's and letting herself fall back onto her cot.

She was just a baby when the last attack occurred, but Mala remembered it vividly and told her the story years ago. Back then, their society was planted firmly on the jungle floor. After the attack, the leaders decided to rebuild in the sky. It was a foolproof solution for any future attacks, or so they thought.

"Yes. But I saw more than that barbaric cult with their crooked arrows and knives. I saw balls of fire and hives falling to the ground." Mala shuddered. "Clay and ash exploding in all directions, and laughter echoing from behind those *horrible* masks." She sat down beside her daughter.

"What ... what do we do? When will this happen?" Lirah asked, her lips trembling.

"I wish I could tell you more, my light. I wish I knew myself. I'm still translating these images inside my mind, but they're ... confusing." Mala shut her eyes tightly and placed her fingers against her temples, as if concentrating hard enough would materialize the answer in this very room. "More guidance from the spirits would also be helpful." She sighed and dropped her hand. "But for now, I don't want you sleeping alone. If we need to flee, we need to be together. Au, too."

To flee ... to be together, Lirah thought.

Her mind drifted to her last memories of her father, Bue. Mala had predicted his death six months before it occurred.

During those months, Mala did everything in her power to keep him by her side. She came up with every excuse she could for him to stay home from the hunt, no matter how flimsy the reasoning.

"Lirah's only an infant. She's been whining for you. She needs her father around today."

"The knots around our hive are loosening again. Can you fix them?"

"I think I've come down with food poisoning from the bronaya rolls last night. Could you watch Lirah today?"

Mala didn't want to tell Bue the real reason that he shouldn't leave. In her mind, she didn't want her Bue to spend his final days worrying about his own fatality.

And while Mala may have postponed her Always and Forever mate's death with her excuses, that dreaded day surely came. In the middle of winter, when the rain ran silver, Mala broke down and told Bue the actual reason she didn't want him to leave.

But Bue, being the fearless hunter that all the other men idolized, told his mate that her vision was a common concern for *all* families in the Pride.

"This is my duty," he told her, calmly stroking her cheek as her tears seeped into the skin of his fingers. "I can't stay home and sit around forever. I must bring home food. Death is a worry for all hunters. I don't need a vision to warn me of that possibility."

After the hunt that day, two solemn, muddy men approached Mala in the dining area. When Bue wasn't there beside them, she already knew what they were going to say. She told Lirah, years later, that she started bawling before they even opened their mouths to tell her the news.

Now, in the peach glow of her candlelit hive, Lirah tried to fight back the tears forming in her eyes. She scrunched up every one of her facial muscles and pulled her hair up from the roots. But the tears came anyway. It was inevitable that the Pride would collapse ... even in the safety of the jungle canopy ... even if it went down two years from now. Just like her father, the Pride would fall. Her mother's visions always reigned true.

Tears streaming down her face, she yelled out, "I wish you just didn't know! Then I wouldn't have to worry. Now I'm just as uncertain as to when and how, but I know something *awful* is on its way to *destroy* us! I feel helpless here, and I'm certain that I will *always* be uncertain about everything!"

"Lirah..." Mala hesitated. She tried lifting Lirah's chin, but Lirah didn't want to look into her mother's eyes.

Lirah knew she shouldn't have yelled so loudly. She knew she was actually very thankful for her mother's ability. She also knew her mother sensed these emotions in her too.

"Is something else bothering you?" Mala asked, stroking Lirah's hair. "I know this is scary. But I'm only trying to keep you safe by warning you. We don't have to take any action yet, except, of course, we can try and warn the leaders. We can tell them you saw an odd figure out in the jungle today."

Lirah shot her mother a nasty look. She didn't want her jungle privileges revoked right when she got them back.

"I doubt they'll believe it ... but we can try, I guess." Lirah sent a deep breath down through her tense body and wiped her tears. "But you had a vision of the future. Which means, even if we do warn them ... it's ... it's going to happen. You *saw* what will happen. I just—"

Lirah was interrupted by a grunt. A shadow appeared at her curtain and knocked on the side of her hive. Her eyes darted to Mala, who shot her eyes towards Lirah's blanket. Lirah threw the blanket over Mala and sat in front of her.

"Er ... come in." Lirah crossed her legs and sat up as straight as she could to block Mala's body.

The curtain swung open. The shadow turned into Jeero—a tall, gangling man only one year older than Lirah. He thought this was a large difference, however, since he was just a year away from reaching full maturity and moving up a rank in the Pride.

He grunted again. "I know someone's in your hive, Lirah, and I know you just got relieved from your last punishment. So, stop making so much noise or I'll go tell the nightshift guards." He crossed his arms and stuck his smushed, rutapuga-like nose into the air. "Some of us need to wake up early."

"What are you talking about? No one's in my hive. Haven't you ever talked to yourself before?" Lirah asked with impudence, while also knowing how unbelievable she sounded. But she was too annoyed that he had threatened to snitch on her to care.

No wonder his last two partners left him, she thought. *He's bound to have his own hive for the rest of his life.*

Jeero arched his neck up even further to get a better look at the lump behind Lirah. She stretched her body up in reply, like a reared snake guarding its kill.

Jeero sneered. "I'm not a *child*, Lirah. I don't talk to myself. I also don't hide others beneath blankets to play hide-and-seek."

"Good to know, Jeero. I'll try my best to grow up and talk to myself more quietly. Bye, now." Lirah aggressively waved him out.

Jeero rolled his eyes and closed the curtain. She could hear him grumbling to himself as he entered his hive next door.

So much for not talking to himself.

She tapped Mala, letting her know she could come out of hiding. Mala dropped the blanket from her head and whispered, "What were you saying before that foul-spirited man walked in?" She gave a light smile.

But Lirah didn't smile back. Instead, her heart sank.

Jeero had distracted her from their conversation, and what they were discussing came rushing back—destruction, uncertainty, and helplessness. She sighed; she might as well tell her mother what else was on her mind. "Earlier, I told Au that ... well, you *know*, I don't fit in here. I told him I feel isolated and that we'd all be safer anywhere else ... and now, I'm even more confused. Why can't we flee right this second, Mala? You know we're destined to suffer here, so why would we stay? Like when ... when you knew Bue's destiny for months." She adjusted herself so she could clearly see her mother's face. It was filling up with frustration and shame.

"I just don't know, my light. I can't explain my visions. I know I said we might need to flee. But I don't know when ... or where we would go," Mala whispered. "I said those things halfheartedly. You had just woken me. But the more I think about it, the more I realize wandering out in the jungle would be even more dangerous."

Lirah scoffed. "How do you know? You've never been out there."

Mala didn't answer.

They sat in silence for what felt like hours, until Lirah spoke again. "Well, I'm not waiting around to *die*. You don't even want me sleeping alone. You haven't requested that since I was first assigned my own hive, *five years ago*. Let's leave tonight.

I'll leave a picture to warn the Pride. When members come searching, they'll find it on my cot. But I'm through with being told what to do. No one is going to give me permission to save my own life."

Without waiting for a reply, Lirah stood from her cot and started rummaging through her hive. She pulled out a small sack and threw in the essentials—clean dress cloths, water skins, berries, herbs, sharpened rocks, her miniature spear. She knew her mother could hear what she was doing. But Mala stayed stock-still on the cot. She had her eyes closed, reciting mantras to herself, hurriedly trying to connect with the spirits.

Lirah fumbled with a thin slate of wood and an old container of crushed berries, huffing as she opened it. She knew she was wasting her time. A guard would find her painting and bring it to the leaders. From there, the leaders would convince themselves that living in the trees provided the best protection and whoever doubted them surely deserved to be abandoned. Lirah hastily began wiping the dark liquid on the wood anyway.

Her painting didn't look detailed, but someone would be able to decode it. It resembled an angry group of brutes standing below a smeared tree and a collection of ovals that were supposed to be hives.

Lirah wiped her hands on her blanket and tossed the slate of wood next to Mala. "I'm going to wake up Au. You should pack a bag too," she whispered, harshly.

She cracked open her hive curtain and looked left, right, and left again (directly at Jeero's hive to make sure he had stopped snooping). She knew she would get reprimanded *again* if she got caught walking around this late. And she knew the punishment would be far worse than the last one. But she already felt herself caring less about the rules. Those rules were about to become non-existent.

CHAPTER 3

Out on the wavering bridge, in the breeze of a typical winter's night, Lirah's dilated eyes scanned around for signs of other members up past curfew. She knew the only guards stationed in this section of the Treetop Society were by the entry ladder, which was currently blocked from her view by two rows of clay hives.

She tiptoed to her right. The rocking wooden bridge creaked slightly.

Luckily, she could see where she was stepping by the dim glow of moss and torches attached to each corner of the bridge. She just had to move slow and stay low. She rounded both rows of hives with ease before peering around the final corner at the guards.

Au's hive was located directly in their line of sight. But they were both dozing off. She looked ahead at Au's lightly swaying curtain and couldn't help but giggle.

This is almost too easy.

She slunk into Au's small hive and crawled over to a shape that looked like his head.

It was pitch black inside and he slept like a rock. She didn't want to startle him and wake up other Pride members, so she whispered, "It's Lirah—wake up." She repeated this about twenty times until he showed signs of stirring.

"Lirah?" Au mumbled longingly, as if he heard her voice in a dream.

Lirah brushed his wild hair out of his face in reply.

Au half smirked, half yawned, then rolled over so that his back was facing her.

She rolled her eyes and shook his shoulders lightly. "Yes, it's Lirah. Wake *up*." She helped him roll back over to face her.

His eyes fluttered open. "Couldn't wait to see me again, huh? Or did you know I was dreaming about you?" He leaned toward Lirah and pulled her up onto the cot with him.

She settled down next to him, her head on his shoulder. They rested like this for a few moments. Lirah let her thoughts wander. She pictured Mala sitting in the same spot that she left her in, speaking with spirits and deciding if they should leave or not.

"Au, are you still awake?" Lirah whispered.

"Yes."

"We need to leave the Pride."

"*Er* ... what?"

"I can explain more later, but Mala had a terrible vision. It's not safe here anymore. Our Pride is being targeted." She sat up.

"Is this about earlier?" he mumbled and rubbed his eyes, speaking more clearly now. "I know you want to explore the jungle, but I told you why we have to stay."

"No, Au." Lirah groaned. "I did *not* instigate this. Mala was in my hive tonight. She didn't want me sleeping alone. She said that she saw balls of fire and hives crashing to the ground. We need to leave."

"Can't we talk about this in the morning? Why do we have to do this now?"

"Why would we wait another second if we know we'll die here?" she asked in a volume far louder than she knew was acceptable, but she was growing too irritated to care.

"I think this is exactly what you wanted to hear so that *you* would have an excuse to get out of here," Au said, sitting up, raising his voice too. "You don't have *any* idea what leaving the Pride would mean, Lirah. It's one thing to talk to me and your mother about your feelings, but actually acting on them? You're crazy."

"No, Au, seriously," she dropped her voice and murmured into the darkness, "Mala is in my hive right now. She'll tell you."

"Okay, great. Then go and tell her that I'd love to talk about this. Tomorrow."

Lirah stood up, fists clenched, but kept her voice low. "Fine, I'll leave you alone. I guess I came over here for nothing. I really thought you'd come with us. I guess I am crazy."

"Come on, you wouldn't actually—" Au shut his mouth tight.

Lirah's adjusted pupils could see his eyes grow wide even in the darkness of his hive. "What are you looking at?"

Au's silhouette of an arm pointed past her face. The last thing she wanted to do was turn around. He looked petrified, and she could feel warm air blowing down onto the back of her head.

Slowly, she took a deep breath and turned around.

Muhu, the third-in-command Pride leader, peered down at her, his nostrils flaring. He was quadruple her size and had arms the width of tree trunks.

Lirah gulped.

"Did I interrupt something?" Muhu asked in a voice so deep it rattled Lirah's insides. She was petrified now too, stuck still like a clay statue even though her heart was beating rapidly.

"Jeero came to me and woke me up. I *hate* being woken up." Muhu growled. "He told me that you were hiding someone in your hive, Lirah, and that he saw you sneaking down the bridge after he confronted you. Is this true?"

Jeero popped his head out from behind him.

Lirah managed one nod.

"I presume you both moved from Lirah's hive to this one for more privacy, taking turns crawling from one hive to the other. Do you think you can get away with sneaking around like this?" Muhu paused as if waiting for an answer. But before Lirah or Au could manage to move their lips, he answered for them. "*No.* Also, the nightshift guards will be punished for allowing you to sneak past them. I hope you are happy about that."

Jeero thought Au was the one under the blanket? So, they hadn't checked her hive? Where was Mala now? These questions flew through Lirah's mind as she stood facing her giant leader.

"How long has this been occurring?" Muhu asked, his voice growing deeper and more agitated with each word. "How many more guards do I need to punish?"

Au opened his mouth and managed a confused "uh" sound. But Lirah cut him off in fear that he would reveal he was never in Lirah's hive tonight. She didn't want Mala to be punished too. It was already too late to save Au, or herself. "Just tonight, Leader Muhu," she sputtered.

"Likely story. You will both come with me now."

Before either one of them could blink, Muhu grabbed Lirah and threw her over his shoulder, drawing the breath out of her. Then he grabbed Au out of his cot and tossed him over his other shoulder. He turned around to face the exit, which Jeero was blocking.

"Move," commanded Muhu.

"Yes, leader. Any time. I'm happy I could help." Jeero squirmed out of the way to give his leader room.

Muhu had to duck down and turn sideways to fit himself and his two captives through the hive opening. "Get back to your hive now," Muhu said.

Jeero scurried off.

Muhu made his way down a long stretch of hives, stomping hard enough to shake everyone awake and swaying Lirah and Au with every move. They stayed completely silent, not even looking at one another. Their upside-down faces were flushed red as their blood rushed toward their cheeks.

Both Lirah's body and mind felt numb as she lay helplessly over Muhu's shoulder. She could hardly imagine where he was taking them or what Mala must be thinking of her long absence.

* * *

Given that her entire perspective had been flipped upside down, and there were no torches lighting the bridges in this area of the Treetop Society, Lirah couldn't recognize where Muhu finally stopped.

She heard the creaking of an opening door rather than the usual flimsy curtain.

Muhu ducked down and entered a musty hive, shrugging both Lirah and Au off his shoulders and casting them to the cold floor.

Lirah felt momentary relief that she wasn't upside down anymore until Muhu walked forward and ignited a single candle on the wall, faintly lighting the room.

Horror rushed through her. This creaking, damp, moldy hive was packed with many oversized wooden cages, and there were no windows.

Clearly, Muhu noticed Lirah's petrified facial expression because he quickly approached her, then shoved her into the cage closest to the entrance and slammed it shut before she could run. He grabbed Au by the wrist and dragged him into another cage on the opposite end of the hive.

"Wait!" Lirah sputtered and, unable to think of anything else, decided to spill out a warning as an excuse for being in Au's hive. "This really was the only night this has happened. We saw something out in the jungle today!"

Muhu ignored her. He headed back towards the only lit candle in the room.

Frantic, she started speaking faster, “It looked like a brute was running across our territory! It scared me, so I didn’t want to be alone tonight. We were discussing it, right Au? We were planning on how to warn you. The brutes are back!”

Muhu shook his massive head. “Lies will never protect you. How dare you mention brutes as a tactic to save your skin.” He spat at her.

She whimpered.

He blew out the candle and left, closing the door and locking it behind him.

Too stunned and too scared to speak, neither Lirah nor Au said another word.

The hive was pitch-black, and very cold. *Probably due to the damp floors*, Lirah thought.

After a while, her heart rate slowed, and her mind cleared. Thoughts of how much she hated this place consumed her. Forget Mala’s vision; she had to leave regardless.

She promised herself that no matter what, she would escape. Right after she got out of this cage.

CHAPTER 4

A screeching sound woke Lirah, who was sprawled out in her wooden cage. She opened her eyes as the blinding light of day burst through the door as it opened.

Six muscular men ducked into the hive one after the other.

Lirah sat up in a haze. After looking all around, her focus leveled out and she remembered where she was ... and the events that had unfolded last night. Mala's vision. Her attempt to warn Au. Getting busted by Muhu. Being forcefully locked up.

Three men silently swarmed around her cage, keeping their eyes down, refusing to look at her directly. The other three went to surround Au. Lirah tried to catch a glimpse of him, but he was completely blocked from view. Her heart started thumping violently again. What was happening? Whatever it was, Au certainly didn't deserve it.

All at once, as if they had been silently counting together, the six men squatted down and lifted both cages from the ground, sending Lirah and Au sliding around within them.

The men marched out the door and lifted the cages above

their heads in sync.

Out in the natural light, Lirah could see it was mid-morning. Pride members roamed around with sleepy eyes until they had to leap out of the way, jolted awake as the six men passed by carrying Lirah and Au. In her wake, Lirah saw their worried, angry faces as they made way, squeezing against the sides of the narrow bridges and steadying themselves against the ropes.

Lirah wanted to apologize to everyone, but she felt like hands were wrapped around her throat. So many Pride members could see that she was a culprit of some wrongdoing, along with Au, who never did anything wrong. And she had no idea where they were being taken.

The Pride is always constructing. It's no wonder the leaders got defensive about outside threats; they put too much effort into building this society to believe that something could destroy its never-ending progress. They'll never move away.

Lirah almost felt thankful when the men stopped. But she quickly remembered what followed after her temporary relief last night when Muhu threw her down from his shoulder. A moldy room full of cages.

One of the men holding Lirah's cage released his grip and knocked on a massive black door twice. She knew this place. The Pride leaders lived and worked here. Their hive was eight regular hives long, and five hives deep. The largest hive in the Treetop Society.

She couldn't help but wonder how a structure this dense could hang sturdily in the treetops. She had wondered this since she first started breaking Pride rules and exploring off-limit areas. That was before she was old enough to roam the jungle floor.

The Pride leaders' hive looked freshly painted. Red and silver with black accents made it the only clay hive in the whole canopy that wasn't its natural shade of rusty orange. Detailed designs of flowers and trees surrounded the door and trailed across the front of the structure, almost making it appear inviting. But Lirah sensed something sinister lying behind its artificial appeal. She didn't dare look back at Au. He probably hated her and blamed her for his humiliation and the punishment that was surely coming.

Maybe she would have a chance to explain the situation to the leaders—leaving out the part about Mala's vision and wanting to flee the Pride, of course—but maybe she could persuade them to spare Au. She didn't care if she received a worse punishment in return. She was leaving the Pride. She didn't forget her promise to herself. Of course, she would still try and convince Au to come along, but after this stunt, she figured he would never want to come with her. The thought brought her to tears.

She was devastated.

After what felt like a lifetime of waiting and crying, the lock in the door turned with a click. The door slowly opened, revealing another muscular man who kept his gaze down at his feet. Lirah wiped her eyes and sucked up her snotty nose. She perched up attentively in her cage, her sweaty hands gripping firmly onto its wooden bars. She looked up and beyond the man. She could make out the shadowy figures of the five Pride leaders across the empty room, easily spotting Muhu's colossal form. They sat behind a long wooden table pressed against high-backed chairs.

As the six men entered the room and walked forward with the cages, Lirah kept her eyes on the many burning candles lining the edges of the open area, comprising the room's only light source.

The men dropped the cages side by side with an echoing bang in the center of the empty room. The impact sent Lirah's head knocking against the bars of her cage. The men then bowed to their leaders and left, closing the door and taking all of the natural light with them.

The cold room went silent. Lirah didn't know if she should look up at the leaders' table or down at her legs, but she couldn't look at Au. She set her gaze on a quivering candle in front of her and waited, trying to steady her shaking breath.

Qualisiun, the main Pride leader and first in command, pushed back his chair and stood at the center position of the table. He cleared his throat. Lirah looked up at him, then reflexively jerked back like a startled animal. Everything about him was ominous. He wore a long black cloak with his face covered by a hood, his crooked nose just peeking out from under it. And his eyes looked like menacing black holes, mostly hidden by shadows.

"We do not tolerate indecency in this Pride," Qualisiun said, his voice calm. "Adolescences are to sleep alone, might I remind you, since you seem to have forgotten."

Lirah shook in her cage. She was cold, hungry, and thirsty. She dared to look over at Au. He was shaking too. She wondered if they looked like terrified, captured prey about to get slaughtered to the leaders.

"Lirah," Qualisiun purred. "You have been acting out quite frequently. I am afraid that you have lost the meaning of what this Pride represents. We are a unit. We work together to provide safety and comfort to every inhabitant equally. When one piece of the unit steps out of line, the whole unit is thrown off balance. Have you ever seen a blum bee hive?"

Lirah bobbed her head.

"Then you understand what I mean," Qualisiun said.

He turned his pointed hood and shadowed eyes towards Au's cage. "Au, you are one of the top-performing men in your age group. Unlike with Lirah, I am shocked by your behavior. I can only speculate that Lirah has been swaying you in the wrong direction, which would mean two pieces are now out of line." The leader shook his crooked nose in disappointment. "I highly advise that you select a new woman at the partner matching coming up next month if you would like to maintain your respectable status. That is all I ask of you."

Qualisiun directed his attention back to Lirah, pressing the tips of his fingers together as if a hot meal was being carried over to him. Lirah swore she could make out a glimmer of pleasure in one of his black, shaded eyes. "As for you, I will make sure that you don't shame your Pride anymore and never again reject the rules that keep us all safe." Qualisiun turned and nodded at a woman draped in a red hooded cloak sitting directly to his left. Her position at the table signified that she was the second in command. Lirah didn't know anything else about her, not even her name. She rarely left the leaders' hive.

The mysterious leader pushed her chair back, the scrape echoing throughout the domed space, and walked over to the candle on the ground that Lirah had been staring at earlier. She bowed down to pick it up and then glided over to Lirah's cage.

Lirah's whole body turned to soup. Her heart, which had somehow relaxed during Qualisiun's speech, now pounded out of her chest and up her throat. What was happening?

The woman extended her free arm and motioned at Lirah's shaking one.

Hesitantly, Lirah extended her arm through the bars of the cage without looking up at the leader's shaded face.

The woman grabbed onto it with a falcon-like grip.

Lirah twitched at the feeling of her icy fingers and squeezed her eyes shut. "Please don't hurt me," she whispered.

She scarcely heard the leader as she whispered back, "I am helping you." Then, she slowly pulled Lirah's wrist down over the candle flame so that it hovered in the fire but not low enough to extinguish it.

Lirah screamed in pain. She tried to jerk her burning arm back through the bars, but the leader held it firmly in place. Lirah started sobbing. Tears streamed down her cheeks. Au yelled out too, telling the leader to stop.

The leader ignored him. She rotated Lirah's arm and continued to burn the entire circumference of her wrist like she was roasting skewered meat over a fire.

She was creating a burn bracelet.

Lirah kept straining to tug her arm free, but the woman was too strong. She maintained a tight grip on Lirah's arm, holding the flame at just the right level, despite Lirah's desperate pulling, until she had completely singed off a layer of Lirah's skin and completed the burn bracelet. Then she calmly released Lirah's arm and placed the unbothered candle back down, leaving Lirah at the bottom of her cage, weeping. She turned and bowed to Qualisiun, reclaiming her seat at the long table.

Au's yelling ceased, but his mouth hung open like he had been stunned mid-shout.

Qualisiun cleared his throat. "That is all."

Lirah could hardly hear him over her cries and moans.

Muhu paced over to her cage and bent down to unlock it. Au had already been released from his. He wobbled where he stood.

Muhu pointed to the door and said, "Go now."

Lirah scrambled from her cage, gripping her injured arm above the wound. Au managed to help her up, and they made their way shuddering and swaying across the dim room and out the door.

CHAPTER 5

In the bright daylight, Lirah's burn hurt even worse, like the candle was still searing away at her skin. She ran for the closest water bucket hanging beneath an unlit torch on the corner of a bridge, opened the lid, and shoved her arm into it.

Other members of the Pride stared. Surely they had heard her screams and cries, so no one stopped her from contaminating the drinking water with her open wound.

Once her pain reached a bearable level, she released her arm from the bucket and dumped the tainted water out. Then she and Au walked back to the area of the Treetop Society that they knew best—the small, shabby area of hives for the lowest-ranking members and adolescents.

Lirah looked around as she walked, paying extra attention to everyone's wrists while tearfully gripping her own. A handful of members had scars in the same shape and place as hers. She had noticed members with these scars before but never knew what they were from. Now, she wondered what these members had done to earn their burn bracelets. Had they been locked up in cages beforehand too? Qualisiun made it seem like no one else ever stepped out of line in the Pride. Only her. But it was becoming clear that this was a common way the leaders punished their members.

Members they care oh-so-much about, she thought, scoffing.

When they arrived at Au's hive—muddy, sweating, and exhausted—Lirah was nervous to be alone with him even though she knew it was allowed during light hours. Surely, Qualisiun intended for her to feel this way, so she forced herself to shake away her fears and step inside.

Au closed the curtain behind them.

"I'm so sorry, Lirah." He cast his gaze down at her enflamed, bubbling wrist.

Lirah was taken aback. *He* was sorry?

Earlier, she was sure that he despised her. She was the one who should be apologizing. Still, she was relieved that he said it.

He really does care about me, no matter what.

"No, *I'm sorry.* You did nothing wrong." She sniffled. "But it doesn't even matter now. I'm leaving this demented place. I'm never being tortured like that again. And for what? Being in my partner's hive? They acted like I tried to hurt someone."

"I know, I know. And I can't believe that Qualisiun told me to choose a new partner at the next matching." Au shook his head. "I won't do it. Don't worry; I'm coming with you."

Lirah's sunken heart began to soar. She jumped on him for a quick hug. When she pulled away, she beamed up at his eyes. They only contained affection. "Let's find Mala. She can tell you about her vision."

After Au put on clean dress cloths, they made their way to Mala's hive. She wasn't there.

Lirah's heart sank again. "I hope the leaders never found Mala in my hive last night," she whispered.

"Oh yeah ... I was so confused when Muhu accused us of sneaking from your hive to mine for more privacy. It took me a minute, but then I remembered you saying that Mala was in there. I would have never given her away," Au reassured her.

"I know you wouldn't have," Lirah leaned in to rub his nose. "And it's still early. I shouldn't worry yet. Let's go check my hive."

Here, they found Mala curled up peacefully on Lirah's cot.

They lightly shook her awake.

Mala sat up right away, looking up as if she had been expecting them. "Oh my! It's so light out. You never came back last night!"

"You've been here this whole time?" Lirah asked, thankful her mother had been safe. Her emotions had already run through every possible combination today.

"I stayed awake as long as I could, waiting for you to come back with Au. I must have fallen asleep. You both look like you haven't slept ... at all." Mala's eyes examined them from head to toe. Their scraggly hair, worn-down faces, and dirty legs.

"Lirah, my light! A burn bracelet? How did you get that?" Mala stood from the cot and embraced her daughter, concern painted over her face.

Lirah explained the events that unfolded last night and earlier that morning while Mala listened with silent tears falling down her cheeks. Once Lirah finished, ending her story with Muhu unlocking their cages and casually telling them to "go now," she asked Mala to explain her latest vision to Au.

"Let's move to my hive for that discussion," Mala requested.

Her hive was in the elder's section. Only members who were fifty or older could live there. The oldest elder was pushing ninety-five years, but Mala had just moved in. The area was designed to provide an oasis for older members to escape from the younger ones who had too much energy and made too much noise while elders napped.

While it was still natural for older members to enjoy eavesdropping on others (like Jeero did), their ability to hear wasn't nearly as efficient. So it was here, huddled in a close circle on Mala's cot, where Mala told Au everything she saw. She told him about the disturbing masks, laughing, fire, and crashing hives. Afterwards, he sighed deeply. The air felt tense.

"Okay. We need a plan," said Lirah. "And I'm sure that after last night, the Pride leaders will warn the nightshift guards to keep a closer eye out for anyone wandering around. Muhu said he was going to punish the guards who let me pass them last night." She winced, thinking about what their punishments could be.

"Or they won't worry with the other guards. The leaders might think your burn bracelet is enough to put you back in your place. They wouldn't want to give other members any ideas, either. They don't want it to seem like they can't keep us in order," Au pointed out. "And anyways, the nightshift guards are more concerned with what's *outside* the community, not what's going on inside. Unless there's an emergency. Muhu knows that. He was probably bluffing about punishing the guards."

Lirah wasn't convinced. She was sure the leaders would take some measures against them. But she decided there was no sense in arguing. "What should we do to sneak past them?"

"I'm glad you asked." Au smirked. "I've been thinking of ideas ever since we got locked up in those cages. I couldn't fall asleep, so I decided to make use of that time so I wouldn't go crazy. I knew you wanted to escape, so I planned out how we could make it happen." He shrugged. He was always one step ahead. "The leaders aren't who I thought they were. You were right to always be questioning them, Lirah."

Lirah beamed at him. Everything he said today only made her like him more. Finally, he understood her. Relief washed over her like rain.

He grinned back. Then his expression grew serious and he dropped his voice to a whisper. "You both know that I have to go through the guard rotation too. So, I already know Riel and Riggul are assigned the second shift tonight for our exit."

The three started giggling. This was the best news they could have received. Everyone in the Pride knew Riel and Riggul were dimwitted in most ways. There were even theories floating around that because they were twins, they had split their intelligence between the two of them. They would be the easiest of all the guards to get around. Their shift would definitely be the best time to escape. Lirah wondered why the Pride leaders would be foolish enough to pair the twins together. But then again, the leaders isolated themselves from the other members and didn't know anyone's personality very well … unless a member caused trouble.

Lirah knew there were always eight guards patrolling at a time during the night. And with two different shifts, that totaled up to sixteen different guards each night. Two were always stationed by the entry ladder in Lirah's section, where the lowest-ranking members and adolescents lived. Two more patrolled the only entry ladder to the hives of the higher-ranking members. Two patrolled the elders' section, and two guarded the leader's massive hive. Lirah was grateful that out of all the men in the guard rotation, Au didn't get assigned a shift tonight.

"Feel free to reject my idea but consider this," Au continued. "We'll all meet up in my hive since it's the closest to our exit. Then while you're both watching from my hive window, I'll run and tell Riel and Riggul that while I was up getting water, I saw a vipra bird wandering towards the dining area and scratching at hives on its way over. I'll say I would've tried capturing it myself but couldn't because I hurt my leg out running yesterday. I'll offer to stand guard while they check it out. Since, you know, I go through the guard rotation too." Au winked at Lirah.

"We get it, Au; you're a guard too," Lirah playfully shoved his shoulder. "But you also *just* said that the guards are only concerned with what's going on *outside* the society."

"Yes, but this is what I meant when I said, 'unless there's an emergency.' If I tell them that there's a vipra bird up here, at least one of them would have to investigate. Come on; you've seen vipra birds."

Mala nodded.

Lirah shrugged. "I know they're dangerous, but I've never

seen one."

"They're all black with beady red eyes and a crooked underbite," said Au. "They only come out at night. Usually alone, but sometimes in pairs. They're nasty to chase off. They'll tear up anything with their arched claws to reach food." He shuddered. "They keep their talons tucked in so they can walk silently. Then they shoot them out on command!" He curled his fingers into his palms and then opened them wide in Lirah's face for emphasis. "They've shredded ropes here before, making the bridges fall so they couldn't be followed. Luckily, they don't usually come here to look for food. There's too many of us. But a desperate mother vipra bird will come around every now and then."

"All right. All right. Nice description," said Lirah. "That's a valid reason for guards to leave their post. But what if only one twin goes? And leaves the other left standing by you and our only exit?"

"Well ... you'll be watching from my hive," said Au. "If you only see one leave, run up to the other and tell him that there's a vipra bird scratching through your hive, and you barely got away from it. But make sure he's looking out into the jungle before you run over so he doesn't see you coming from my hive. Tell him that you won't go back inside until it's gone. Then, when I'm the last one standing guard, and both twins are out of sight, you can both get a head start climbing down the exit rope. I'll stand guard and block the exit until you make it down safely. After that, wait for me at the bottom, and we'll get out of the Pride's territory and run until we can't anymore."

Au looked at them with wide eyes, hopeful for feedback.

Lirah liked his plan. But at the same time, there were so many things that could go wrong. She hoped that if the twins reacted differently to anything during their escape, they could adapt to the new situation.

Good thing Au problem solves best under pressure, she thought. *He must've gained those skills over the last few years of joining the hunt.*

After all, you have to learn how to think fast while chasing down a meal—or even more vitally, think fast if something is trying to make a meal out of *you*. Convincing a couple of foolish men to step away from their post for a few minutes sounded a lot easier in comparison. And the other six guards would be stationed too far away to hear what was going on from their section.

"Yes, this could work," she finally said. "But we also have to hope the twins aren't smart enough to figure out that we're trying to lure them both away. Or smart enough to question you for being out so late for water."

"I don't think it should be a problem. Riel and Riggul respect me. Even though they're older, they always copy what I do during our all-man practice drills. Anyway, I doubt they'll put too much thought into it since I'm a guard too." Au winked at Lirah again.

Lirah rolled her eyes.

Mala laughed. She seemed satisfied with the plan too. She hadn't said much, but she nodded along the whole time Au was explaining his idea.

Lirah's confidence grew. Her head felt like it was floating, though this could partially be from not eating for so long. Her heart jolted hard into her ribs as she imagined their plan in action.

"We'll meet in your hive, then, Au? And how will we know when it's time to go there?" asked Mala.

"How about you both wait in Lirah's hive? It's much closer to mine. I'll come to get you when the guards have switched shifts."

"That's risky," Lirah groaned. "We'll have to be completely silent … since Jeero's out to get me." She gazed down at her blistering wrist.

"We won't make a sound. I'll peek my head into your hive, and you'll get up and follow. Simple," Au reassured her.

"All right," said Mala. "Now, let's go to lunch. Today's my day to serve. I need to be there early." She wrapped her thick, beaded hair up on the very top of her head.

* * *

The trio kept their distance from one another for the rest of the day. They all wanted to nap anyway, and during lunch and dinner they made minimal contact but still enough to not look odd. They rubbed noses and hugged when they crossed paths in the dining hall. But while they ate, Au stayed with the men in his age group, Lirah with the women, and Mala with the elders.

When daylight faded into a smoky dusk, Lirah went to her hive. This was earlier than usual for her, as, typically, she waited until the last possible moment, when it was completely dark. But she was sick of the other women staring at her tarnished wrist as if it were contagious. It already hurt enough.

She lay down on her cot beside her packed bag. She lit only one candle. She stared at the patterns of dried clay on her hive ceiling and allowed herself to reminisce on the Treetop Society—everything it had provided her and everything from which it had been holding her back.

She was most grateful for the Treetop Society as it allowed her to meet Au. They had known each other their whole lives. They never talked much at first, though Lirah always had a liking for him since they'd been children. He was always the sweetest and bravest one in her age group, climbing to the very tops of trees to retrieve the loveliest flowering plants and fruits for his elders. When they'd both entered adolescence and had to choose a trial partner, which was more like a mentoring friendship, Lirah had decided to take her chance and selected Au. When he'd accepted, she had been ecstatic.

At the beginning of each spring, by tradition, all five Pride leaders gathered up every member in adolescence ranging from age eleven to sixteen. They would line up the young women and men separately, then have the lines turn and face each other. Older members always gathered around to watch.

It was traditional for the women to select their choice for a trial partner and mentor. Then, the men had to accept or decline the offer. After an offer was accepted, the man—who had already been thoroughly trained on Pride rules and skills throughout his childhood—was instructed to guide his partner through a similar training so they would learn how to work together as a cohesive unit. Every spring, the adolescents had the chance to switch trial partners or keep the same one. But they couldn't end up alone. When there was an uneven number of men and women, there had to be groups of three. Luckily, Lirah and Au had always chosen to stay together and never had a third member with whom to compete.

The partnering process continued on like this until a couple officially decided to announce their bond and become Always and Forever mates in a ceremony monitored by all Pride leaders. The first leader-in-command had to approve and unite the bond by pricking each partner's nose. Once both partners' noses were bleeding, they rubbed them together to seal the bond. Everyone watching would clap and cheer. Then, the new, red-nosed, Always and Forever mates would lead everyone to a bonfire to celebrate. There was always dancing, drums, and vibrant fruit arrangements.

It was customary for members to be in an Always and Forever bond by the time they reached full maturity. If not, they would end up alone for life, which usually happened to members who were constantly thrown into a group of three and voted out the following spring. But there could only be one man and one woman together by the end of the process.

Lirah and Au were only a handful of seasons away from discussing the possibility of sealing their own Always and Forever bond. But now, they would be long gone before they could decide if they wanted this ceremony.

Actually, Lirah recalled, *Qualisiun told Au today that he didn't approve of our relationship.* So that wasn't even an option anymore. Pride leaders had to approve all bonds.

Guilt bubbled up and churned in her stomach. Why did she think it was a good idea to sneak over to Au's hive last night with no escape plan? Oh, right. She hadn't been thinking at all. She tried provoking him to leave everyone he loved right then and there without even giving him time to think about it. His parents had died when he was a baby. He couldn't even remember what they looked like, so Mala described them to him the best she could. The Pride had collectively been his provider and family for his entire life.

Although, Muhu hadn't hesitated to lock him in a cage. And what else were they supposed to do about Mala's vision other than flee? Lirah had made the painting for the leaders and already warned Muhu verbally. What more could they do?

Lirah's thoughts were still circling when Mala swung open the drape to her hive. She strode in, gripping the strap of a bag that hung over her shoulder.

Lirah smiled at her mother and placed a finger to her lips. Mala gave her a wrinkled grin. Her tangled black hair was pulled up with colorful beads strung throughout, her navy eyes glowed with mischief, and carved wooden bracelets made their way halfway up her forearms. She smelled like eucalyptus, mint, and adventure.

Without speaking, Mala opened her bag to reveal a bandage cloth and essential oils. She motioned for Lirah to raise her blistering wrist and began tending to it in the dimly lit hive.

Once Mala patched Lirah up, she blew out the candle and rested by her daughter, grasping her hand and squeezing tight. She cupped her free hand around her lips and whispered in Lirah's ear, "An idea came to me before dinner. When Jeero walked up to be served, I secretly dropped some potent chomomull oil in his food. It usually takes hours to kick in. But once it does, it makes full-grown men fall into a deep sleep for a *whole day*. I watched Jeero eat it all. By now, he must be in another world. I thought about doing the same for the twins, but I didn't want to risk different guards being called in to take their place."

"Wow ... you're amazing." Lirah giggled, gripping her mother's hand even tighter.

They stayed like this and stared at the ceiling in the darkness. As time went on, they didn't grow tired. Their anticipation only rose.

Outside, the sounds of other members settling down and saying their final goodnights shifted into total silence. Besides the chattering of insects, which Lirah had learned to tune out long ago, she could only hear her pulse pounding in her ears.

* * *

Lirah didn't know how much time had passed. Her heart nearly exploded when a shadow appeared against her curtain. A hand reached to grab at the corner.

Au pulled it open slightly, inching into the hive. He tapped on Lirah and Mala's shoulders, assuming they had fallen asleep. When they sat up, Au left the hive and closed the curtain. No one spoke.

Carefully, Lirah and Mala stood from the cot and picked up their bags. Lirah peered through a crack in her curtain to ensure their path was empty. Then, without turning back to look at her hive one last time, she crawled down the bridge just the same as the night before.

Mala followed her closely, gripping the ropes holding up the bridge, moving as slowly and prudently as a dying snail. Lirah waved for her to move faster, but instead, Mala stopped.

Somehow, a strap of her bag had gotten caught under a wood plank. She pulled and pulled, and the bridge swayed.

Lirah swore under her breath. They would get caught before their plan even began.

But before she could assist her mother, the bag freed itself. Mala started moving again. Thankfully she went faster this time—about the speed of a larger, not dying, snail.

They slowly but surely reached Au's hive, where their plan could be brought to life.

Lirah's heart thumped so frantically that she fooled herself into believing she could hear Mala and Au's heartbeats echoing out of their chests too.

CHAPTER 6

"Here goes nothing," Au whispered. He gave Lirah's sweating hand one final squeeze and headed over to the guards. They were Riel and Riggul, as expected.

After Au disappeared through the curtain, Lirah and Mala rushed to his small hive window and watched him. They kept their heads low, pressed together, with only their eyes peeking above the opening.

Au looked strong and poised as he sauntered down the bridge. He had his chest puffed out, and his chin held high.

But Riel and Riggul didn't even notice him. They looked distracted and bored, pointing off into the jungle and poking one another in the ribs. When Au reached them, both twins jumped back in surprise.

Lirah and Mala couldn't help but snicker. They couldn't hear him, but they watched Au's body movements as he greeted the twins and identified himself with hand gestures. Au pointed in the direction of the dining area and motioned down at his leg.

Probably telling them the lie about injuring it yesterday.

The twins exchanged confused expressions while Au talked

and scratched at the air with his hands. Eventually, one of the twins handed over his spear and Lirah let out a faint, excited gasp. Both twins slowly walked away from Au, whispering to one another with furrowed brows. Lirah and Mala ducked down before the twins passed Au's hive. They were discussing what to do about facing the mother vipra bird.

The plan was unfolding better than Lirah had ever expected. Not only did one of the guards agree to leave post but *both* left without question. Now they just had to scale down the exiting tree.

Lirah and Mala waited until the twins vanished around the corner before dashing down the bridge. When they reached Au, Lirah wanted to ask him exactly what he said to convince both twins to leave, but they had no time. Au kicked down the rope and instructed them to "*Go, go, go.*"

Except ... gaping down at the misty blackness below, Lirah realized she forgot to account for the extra time it would take her mother to scale down the exiting tree. And it was a *long* way down.

Lirah knew her mother lacked athleticism compared to herself. She got her long legs and running abilities from her father, not her petite mother. But for her age, Mala's health was pristine. Lirah never considered her physical state an issue before now. But there was no other way out.

"I'll go first," Lirah said, trying to remain composed. "Give me your bag. I'll carry both. You don't need the extra weight." She swung the other bag over her shoulder. "Now, watch how I place my feet and move down the rope."

Lirah reached for the thick rope and gulped, peering down at the dark abyss they were about to descend into. She hoped with all her heart that her mother wouldn't fall. It would be a deadly drop, and it was too late to turn back now. If they got caught here, blatantly trying to abandon their Pride, the punishment would be death or life imprisonment. So, either way, death was a possibility. Lirah took a deep breath and started her descent.

A few paces down, Lirah looked up into her mother's terrified eyes. "Come on," she urged.

Mala grabbed hold of the rope, positioning herself with trembling hands.

"You'll be fine; you can do this," Lirah whispered.

Mala placed her small shaking feet against the trunk and inched downwards.

A torch fastened at the top of the exit allowed them to see where they stepped, but not clearly. With every stride, the torch grew further and further away and, eventually, they could no longer rely on their sight. This posed a challenging task even for Lirah, who only climbed during the day.

"Slow and steady, slow and steady," Lirah whispered.

The ground was so close, yet so far.

She tried to remain optimistic. They were halfway down, and she still couldn't see or hear the twins. She gazed up at Au guarding the bridge. He was looking off into the distance and acting natural, as if he didn't notice Pride members escaping right next to him.

"I can't see anything, Lirah. I'm *slipping*!" Mala squealed.

Lirah felt the rope shaking from her mother. "You don't need to see! Just close your eyes and feel, like you always do."

Just then, Au shouted, "*Go! Go! Go! Fast! Fast! Fast!*"

He threw the guard's spear over his back and grabbed the torch by the exit.

Lirah glanced up, her palms sweating. Riel and Riggul sprinted down the bridge at full force toward their hijacked post. Au grasped the rope and scaled down.

The twins took turns yelling questions at Au as they ran, their feet stomping hard against the swinging bridge.

"What's going on?!"

"Where are you going?!"

"Where's the vipra bird?!"

Au ignored them and focused on scaling down the rope, using only one hand, the other clutching the torch. Even under these conditions, he quickly caught up with Lirah and Mala.

The twins straddled the rope and started climbing down too.

Once Lirah, Mala, and Au hit the ground, the twins had already descended a quarter of the trunk.

Lirah was shocked by their speed.

"Run! Hurry!" Au yelled.

Mala's shaking legs gave out on her first step, and her tired arms failed to break her fall.

She faceplanted into the dirt.

Au didn't hesitate for a second. He handed Lirah the torch and scooped Mala into his arms. "Run!" he yelled again, and Lirah sprinted in a random direction of blackness. She had no idea where they would end up. And she never expected to be rushed by guards following them out into the gloom of the jungle either.

What have I gotten us into? Lirah derided herself.

Once they exited the only area of the jungle they had ever been allowed to roam, the Pride's territory, they would be at the mercy of their new surroundings. How was this any safer than a well-lit community in the sky? Maybe Mala's vision was predicting this—this reckless decision to run away and fulfill their own self-destructive prophecy.

But the pain of her burn bracelet told her to shut up and just run.

* * *

Once Lirah, Au, and Mala had travelled a fair distance and could no longer make out the luminosity of torches in the sky, Lirah panted for them to take a rest and plan out their next move.

"I sense danger," Mala whispered through light sobs. She looked like a baby, the way her petite body was cradled in Au's sprawling arms.

Lirah's pupils were so wide they took up the entirety of her eyes. She stared at Au for advice. Thinking logically through fear was harder for her.

"We need to find a hallowed tree with large roots for shelter," he said, gasping for air.

His chest heaved in and out, and his face had beads of sweat forming under the torchlight. He readjusted his slippery hold on Mala. "I've seen lots of trees like that out here, but I have no idea where we are now."

They gazed around but could hardly rely on their sight. They tuned in to the sounds of the night—the creaking trees and rustling bushes. Pungent soil and decaying plants filled Lirah's nostrils with smells she didn't quite recognize. A crawling sensation spread across her foot, as if a million little feelers were running over it.

"Who's there?!" a deep voice called from yards away. It sounded like one of the twins.

Lirah waved the torch flame in the direction of the voice. It was too late to put the light out and hide now.

"Aha!" One of the twins jumped out of the shadows.

Au impulsively whipped around and punched him square in the eye while keeping a firm hold of Mala with one arm. Lirah was impressed with him but couldn't help but cringe at the sound of that blow.

"What did you do?" the other twin screeched, ambling up like he wasn't in any danger himself. He didn't even attempt to help his brother.

"He came up from behind. I wasn't sure what jumped at me. It was a reflex." Au shrugged, as if he were sorry, but not too sorry. "Why did you follow us?"

"What?! We can't just let Pride members leave under our watch whenever they want," the uninjured twin said, crossing his arms and puffing out his chest.

Lirah had never been this close to the twins before. They were much shorter and stockier than she imagined, and had deep voices. They looked like identical malvor monkeys with their thick hair and oversized teeth and feet.

"Isn't it a guard's job to keep trespassers *out*? And not members locked *in*? The rope is still down, but who's guarding for intruders? I'd say that you both failed at your jobs. Good luck explaining yourselves when you return," Au snapped.

"No one will be blaming *us* after we bring *you* back. You'll be the ones with some explaining to do." The uninjured twin pointed at Au like a defensive child.

"But sadly for you, we're not going back," Au spat. He threw back his shoulders and repositioned Mala against him. She looked down, as if very uncomfortable being so close to the middle of this argument.

Lirah looked at the stolen spear on Au's back, then at the spear lying next to the injured twin. She started to wonder where this conversation was headed.

While Au and the uninjured twin were locked in a stare-down, Lirah inched over to the fallen spear and slid it toward herself with her foot. The injured twin was too busy moaning and cradling his face to notice. She slowly bent down and scooped it up, keeping it low, at hip level. Now that they had two extra spears and the twins had nothing to threaten them with, they needed to find shelter somewhere in this tangled maze.

She tapped on Au's shoulder and whispered in his ear, "I took their other spear. Let's keep moving."

Without breaking his intense eye contact with the standing twin, Au said, "Sorry, dimwits. But you shouldn't have followed us out here. We're leaving now, and I'm warning you not to follow us again."

The twin on the ground stood up with one hand pressed against his eye where Au had punched him. "Riggul?" He groaned loudly. "Let's leave these traitors. They can *rot* out here. I don't care anymore. They wanted this. Let's go home."

Lirah and Au ignored his insults. They turned to strut away, Mala still in Au's arms.

But Riggul didn't appear to want to depart from this drama yet. "Wait!" he said. "Why did you backstabbers run away, huh?

Planning a retaliation? Mad you didn't get fed first at dinner or something?" He scoffed.

Unexpectedly, Mala replied to his sarcasm, her voice soft. "I had a vision."

Both twins stared blankly back at her. She took a deep breath and motioned for Au to let her stand. Once she was back on her feet, she repeated, "I had a vision of the future. I saw destruction, falling hives, and fire. The rest is blurry."

Lirah grabbed hold of her mother's shoulder. "What are you *doing*? Why would you tell them that?"

"I believe they have the right to know why we caused a commotion. It wasn't to retaliate or out of evil intentions," Mala said calmly, brushing off Lirah's hand. "We wanted to leave the Pride for our own safety, though we left a painting behind as a warning."

The runaway guards didn't say anything. They stood motionless like dolls. Mala was an elder, so Riggul wouldn't dare speak to her as he had spoken to Au. Lirah knew this. But it also seemed like they actually believed Mala.

In the awkward silence that had descended, Lirah arched her neck up. Warm light beams began streaming through the dense foliage, revealing a misty network of twisted vines and colorful plants in an area she didn't recognize.

Surely, Pride members are awake by now. A leader will check on the guards at their post soon. Where there are none.

She felt bad for the twins, picturing the sinister, hooded faces they would have to return to. But with no one left arguing or even speaking, Lirah knew it was time to move forward. She cocked her neck, signaling for Mala and Au that it was time to go.

The trio turned and walked away.

Lirah couldn't help glancing back at the confused twins. She saw them huddled together, whispering. Riggul was scratching his head, and Riel's eyebrows were creased in panic. Then they nodded in unison.

"Wait!" Riggul called out again.

Au whispered to Lirah and Mala, "Keep going."

Riggul ran after them, leaving his brother behind, and overtook them, turning to block their path. "Stop. Okay, you were right. We shouldn't have left our post to chase you, even though we were scared and didn't know what to do. I mean, you're Pride members, after all. We care about you." He smiled sheepishly. "And ... after hearing about Mala's vision... we can't go back. We'll come with you."

Lirah, Au, and Mala stared silently. They never expected other members to tag along. That meant two more bodies to feed, keep warm, and keep hidden. But at the same time, that meant two more bodies to help hunt, build a shelter, and keep watch at night.

Riel staggered over to meet the group, his eye swollen and red from Au's punch. "Yeah, Au, you're the one who said we failed at our jobs. We left the rope down. How are we going to explain that to the leaders? And on top of that, explain that we *still* managed to let you get away?"

"I apologize." Au sighed. "But I'm sure they won't be too mad. Just say we ran too fast, and you got lost."

"No, please," Riggul begged. "We aren't even respected in the Pride as it is. And I'm not going to be punished, watch my home get burned down, *and* possibly die."

Maybe they aren't as stupid as other members say they are, Lirah thought.

"Everyone, calm down," she said. "Au, you know the leaders would severely punish them. And it was our actions that caused all of this. It wouldn't be right to leave them stranded." She paused, directing her attention to the twins. "You two can come with us. But you need to follow any and all orders that we give you and contribute however you can. Our lives depend on one another now. Also, we have no idea where we're headed, so no complaining." She lifted her chin and held her new spear up high.

Riggul and Riel nodded furiously.

Lirah looked to Au and Mala, "Anything you want to add?"

"Welcome to the club of runaways." Au reached out to shake each twin's hand. "I hope you don't snore."

CHAPTER 7

Water. Food. Sleep. All three of life's basic necessities were on Lirah's mind. Finding cures for the first two would be more challenging without the last.

Everyone was sleep deprived and dragging their feet. No one in the club of runaways had a sharp mind.

Out in the open jungle, appearing weak and exhausted was the last thing you wanted. Especially now when invaders could be on the prowl, coming back for redemption over established territories.

"We need to stop wandering aimlessly and find somewhere to take turns sleeping and collecting resources," said Lirah. "Two of us can sleep while one guards. The other two can look out for a river or try to find food nearby. Then we'll switch off. Almost like the guard rotations."

The group collectively agreed. They trudged through brush and weeds until they spotted a resting place that captivated them all.

It was a massive curtain tree that towered above every plant around. Vines coiled around the top of its golden trunk and all the way down to the dirt like hundreds of snakes. Countless more vines draped freely over the tallest branches and hung down like a curtain, hence the name. This tree would be perfect for keeping them hidden and would provide a decent water supply.

Lirah and Au used their spears to slice through its thick vines to reach the fresh water inside. It trickled out slow, cool, and steady.

After they collected enough water to fill up half of one of their water skins, Lirah handed it over to the twins along with one spear. They offered to search for food and another water source while Mala and Lirah slept against the roots, and Au offered to stand guard first.

"Don't wander too far," said Au. "We don't know this area."

"We couldn't miss this monster of a tree if we tried," Riel hollered as they sauntered away.

Lirah and Au stared at their hairy backs until they shrank into black dots in the greenery.

"I think you made the right call about letting them come along. I'm glad they offered to hunt first. I don't want to move." Au slouched against the tree to take his guarding post and smiled lazily up at Lirah. His eyes brimmed with admiration.

Lirah couldn't help but blush. She looked away and observed their great protector of a tree. Its twisted vines looked the same as the veins running through her arms. "My two great protectors," she whispered. She pressed her hand against the tree trunk and rubbed her nose against Au's. Then she crawled through the draping vines to rest.

* * *

When Lirah emerged from her slumber, she found Au struggling to keep his eyes open. She reached for his spear to take over his position, and, without hesitation, he crawled through the vines and passed out.

Lirah sat alone in the jungle, which was silent except for the singing insects. This was the first time she'd been able to relax and re-experience their escape. She couldn't believe they pulled it off.

Her whole outlook had changed after resting. She felt like she was ready for anything. Being free in the jungle felt like a dream.

Questions flew through her head: What would they do next? Would they build a shelter here? Would they build a shelter anywhere? Would they find a luxurious, accepting society to call home? One that would allow her to fully express herself? One where she could feel safe, and where the leaders would listen to her concerns?

If the others wanted to make a temporary home here, Lirah wouldn't argue. But she knew in her heart that she wanted to keep moving forward. She had a strong feeling there was something much greater beyond everything she had grown up around, maybe even beyond the jungle itself. It couldn't go on forever, right? Lirah pondered all the possibilities of what the unknown might look like. All of the different creatures and plants she might discover, like this magnificent, golden, curtain tree. Butterflies fluttered in her stomach, and her head grew airy. The feeling of the unknown. She craved more of it.

The unknown ... Riel and Riggul had gone into the unknown. Lirah had been in such deep thought that she just noticed they still hadn't returned. Where did they go? Weren't they exhausted? It was their turn to sleep in the rotation, and based on the light, many hours had passed since they left.

Lirah didn't know what to do. She knew it wasn't her responsibility to worry about them, but she couldn't help but think something bad might've happened. She hoped the rumors about their intelligence wouldn't prove to be true. She sighed.

She needed to distract herself from these negative thoughts. She picked up a thick and sharp rock from her sack and started piercing the thicker vines wrapped around the trunk to collect more water.

Over the sound of her chopping, she swore she heard footsteps approaching from behind, softly crunching against the carpet of leaves.

Lirah froze as her heart picked up speed.

She was facing the curtain tree. She had no idea if the alleged steps belonged to the twins or something else.

The sounds stopped. Then she heard them again.

She whirled around as fast as she could, lifting the sharpened rock overhead.

"Hey!" she called to her empty surroundings.

No one replied.

With sweating palms, Lirah reached for her spear propped against the tree,

keeping her eyes forward and her rock ready to throw.

"No need for that," a woman's voice called from the trees.

Adrenaline rushed through Lirah's veins like fire, hitting every point in her body. She gulped and squinted up into the canopy.

She couldn't see anyone. There were too many branches shaded by moss and leaves.

"Who's there?" she managed to choke out.

"Toodle-oo," the voice teased.

Leaves rustled above her.

"I'm over here," the voice echoed from a new location.

Lirah grabbed her spear and aimed it at the sky. She spun around in an attempt to pinpoint the stranger's location before they moved again.

"Don't get dizzy," the woman's voice giggled.

"This isn't a game! *Come out.*" Lirah's fear morphed into anger.

"Oh my, nobody *ever* wants to play with me," the voice said, much closer now. It sounded calm and smooth, like fresh sap.

Feeling pathetic compared to the teasing voice, Lirah dropped her spear and stopped circling with her chin up. She decided to keep her attention evenly distributed in all directions by leaning against the tree.

She scanned her surroundings. There could be other threats. Maybe this voice had accomplices.

She heard rustling in the leaves again but ignored it. Then she heard a sigh. "You're no fun. But you sure are beautiful."

Lirah brought her gaze forward, and the owner of the voice revealed herself.

A long, golden-tanned body was sprawled out on a low-hanging branch in Lirah's line of sight. She had shining black hair that stopped at her torso, and she wore a small cream-colored dress cloth. It started at her chest and stopped at her upper thighs. The cushy moss branch she was lying on curved against her body perfectly. And she appeared to be glowing from the way the light radiated through the leaves behind her.

Lirah merely stared as the beautiful stranger twirled her silky locks in between her fingers. She blinked. A long tail dangled beneath the stranger's branch. Lirah had never met anyone from outside the Pride before, let alone someone with a tail. She was at a loss for words.

"Well, what's your name?" the woman asked, jaded.

"I'm ... uh ... Lirah. What's yours?"

"Suki," she replied. She sat up and swung off her mossy branch, landing on the dirt without a sound. She turned around and scooped up her tail, or what Lirah had *thought* was a tail, and hung it around her neck like a scarf. Lirah now recognized it as a long furry creature with two large ears on its head that resembled green leaves, and three more that were clustered on the end of its indigo body. A trealea.

Suki swayed over to Lirah with her hands open, expressing that she had no weapon. Lirah stood with her back pressed against the tree, her sweating palms gripping the spear. Suki stared directly into Lirah's eyes and drew very close, grasping onto a lock of Lirah's hair.

"What are you doing?" Lirah whispered, thinking of Au and Mala fast asleep on the other side of the tree trunk. Then she looked at the trealea again. She had never seen one up close.

They were poisonous. This one looked like it was sleeping and smiling at the same time. Its eyes were slits, but its mouth was curled up and it wiggled its huge leafy ears.

"I always thought I had the nicest hair. But you might have softer. Here, feel mine," Suki said, drawing Lirah's attention back to her.

Lirah hesitantly released a hand from her weapon and reached for Suki's hair. They stood inches apart, locks of each other's long hair crossed over one another. Lirah could feel Suki staring into her soul while she tried to keep her focus on Suki's hair, but the piercing feeling brought Lirah's eyes up to meet hers. They were golden and sparkled behind thick black eyelashes.

Lirah blushed. She dropped Suki's hair.

"Your eyes look like the precious stones I used to trade with the Guzols in the jungle," Suki said, dropping Lirah's hair and stepping back.

"What are Gu-zols?"

Suki laughed. Clearly, Lirah had pronounced the name wrong. "Guzols are loners. They aimlessly walk around the jungle in search of valuable items ... Maybe I'm a Guzol." Suki smirked.

Lirah blushed even harder.

"Are *you* a Guzol?" Suki batted her thick eyelashes.

"No, I don't think so."

"Then what are you doing out here all alone? I've been watching you sit by this tree for at least an hour. I had nothing better to do."

Lirah tried to ignore the fact that she had been watched without her knowledge. She had no idea why she trusted this stranger, but she did. Maybe it was because she looked roughly the same age, fifteen. And it didn't seem like a bad idea to make a new friend, especially one who undoubtedly knew this area of the jungle.

"I'm not alone," Lirah said. "I'm guarding while others sleep. A small group of us left our Pride in the canopy. It wasn't safe there anymore."

Suki laughed. "And you think the jungle floor is safer?"

"I don't know." Lirah shrugged. "At least now we aren't attached to anything. We can move as we please. Isn't that what you do?"

"I used to, but I have a home now. A community called Airis. It's by a waterfall nearby if you'd like me to take you there. There's plenty of fish and sumara to eat," Suki coaxed.

Lirah didn't know what a sumara was.

Suki strolled back over to the low-hanging branch and jumped straight up. Her toned arms grabbed onto the branch and pulled the rest of her body up with ease. She lay down with a big yawn before Lirah had time to blink.

"Well," Lirah paused, thinking over Suki's offer. "I've never seen a waterfall before. That would be—" Footsteps approached from behind again. This time, she reacted without hesitation. She lifted her spear and whipped around.

It was Au, scratching his head and stretching.

Lirah sighed deeply, dropping her weapon. "Oh, hey."

"Who are you talking to?" he asked, mid-yawn.

"This is Suki," Lirah motioned over to Suki then looked back at Au.

He suddenly looked wide awake, his bulging eyes locked onto Suki's figure.

Lirah elbowed him and continued her introductions. "Suki, this is Au. He's my partner, mentor, and a part of the group I ran away with."

Au waved and gave Suki an awkward half-smile.

"Hello ... partner." Suki narrowed her eyes to thin slits.

Suki's pet trealea seemed to sense its owner's energy shift because it turned back its ears and dropped its smile. Confused by Suki's attitude change, Lirah interjected to end the tension.

"Um ... Au, Suki told me that she lives in a community by a waterfall. She offered to take us there and—"

"Actually, I said I could take *you* there," Suki said, filing her nails with her pointed teeth. "Men aren't allowed where I live."

Lirah immediately thought of the twins. They had been gone for so long. What if they stumbled into Suki's community?

She turned to tell Au about the missing twins, but he seemed preoccupied. His face looked contorted with bewilderment, as if he was trying to imagine an all-woman community. She turned back around to face Suki. "What if men *did* somehow end up by your waterfall?"

"They'd be imprisoned ... or possibly decapitated," Suki replied, not looking up from her nail filing.

Lirah and Au stood motionless, blood rushing from their faces.

"Ha. Just kidding. First, they would be told to leave and escorted away from our boundaries. If they refused, *then* they'd probably end up headless."

"Well ..." Lirah stumbled over what to say. "Maybe we shoall go check it out. Au could wait close by. Outside of your boundaries, of course. But two of our male members aren't back yet, and I'm afraid they might have gotten into trouble with your community. We aren't used to travelling through different territories yet."

"Men? Not understanding boundaries? What a shock." Suki rolled her eyes. "*Fine*, you can both come. But *he* has to stay unseen." Her golden eyes locked onto Au, nearly piercing through him. Her trealea's tail thrashed back and forth around her neck.

Au rolled his eyes back at Suki. He whispered to Lirah, "I don't like the sound of this. Why should we trust her? She probably wants to make a meal out of us. She clearly hates me because I'm a man."

"But Riel and Riggul ..." Lirah murmured.

"Yes. What if they're totally fine and return here? But instead of waiting, we decide to go off. Then they would think *we're* the ones in trouble. I don't think leaving would be a good idea."

"Well then ... I guess you can stay, and I can go." Lirah raised her chin in defiance.

"Lirah," Au pressed his fingers against his temple, "you're too trusting. You just met her, and you've *never* met anyone outside of the Pride before."

"We're out in the middle of the jungle. We're bound to run into others! She's offering to show us a resource and help us find the twins. She even said you could come. Not everyone is out to hurt us. Even if they have different views. Right, Suki?" Lirah looked over at the branch Suki was lounging on.

She wasn't there anymore.

In the midst of their argument, Suki must have gotten fed up and left. "*Suki*? Where did you go? Come back!" Lirah shouted.

A few birds flew away, rattled by the noise. Other than that, silence.

"Suki! I'll come with you!" she shouted again.

Nothing.

Lirah threw her arms into the air. "See, Au? We lost our chance. And now we're creating enemies instead of allies. She could have *helped* us! We have no idea where to go out here. She used to wander around the whole jungle. She told me. That sounds like a valuable friend to have."

Au shrugged.

"You don't want to admit that I'm right! You know—"

A blurry figure leapt in front of her, causing her to jump back, trip over a root, and fall to the ground.

Suki stood before her, having dropped from the canopy, and landed on all fours directly in front of her. She stood calmly, fallen leaves floating down and drifting around her head.

"Let's go," she commanded. She turned to walk away, not giving Lirah another moment to change her mind.

Au bent over to help Lirah up. He rubbed his nose against hers.

"Fine," he whispered. "Go. Make allies. I trust you more than anything. I'll stay with Mala and wait for the twins. But if you're not back after the jungle grows dark, I'll come searching.

I don't care how dangerous it is. I'll listen for a waterfall."

CHAPTER 8

"Do you really think your man friends wandered onto my territory? Or did you just want to get away?" Suki asked Lirah. "I saw how aggravated you got with your partner, *Au*."

So far, their surroundings looked similar to the Pride's territory. They passed towering green, yellow, and orange trees with colorful blossoms and prickly vines tumbling down their branches like dangerous rainbow waterfalls. Giant fungi grew up their sides like massive steppingstones.

Some shorter trees had furry branches extending straight up toward the sky. Others had sticky branches wilting down in long, spindly threads. But most were covered in rough dark bark. Lirah loved spotting rare wonders like translucent leaves with vibrant pulsing red veins, or neon blue trees with braided trunks that glowed during the night. But the colorful flowers were her favorite. They were bigger than bushes. She could use one as a bed if she wanted.

Amongst the foliage roamed the typical chara cats, insects, and featherless birds with two slick sets of wings, which helped them blend in with the bark. Lirah considered picking up a trealea to have a pet of her own. She spotted purple, orange, and pink ones trying to camouflage among flowers.

"I wasn't really that mad at Au." Lirah sighed. "He always needs time to think through things like this. He likes to be safe. But Riel and Riggul ... they aren't the most conscientious. They definitely could've wandered onto your territory without thinking. They didn't even leave us with any idea of when they'd return. They're already a burden. I would never abandon my group like that."

"Well, you just did," Suki said, kicking at a rock. It turned out to be an oversized snail shell.

"Hey, that was rude." Lirah picked up the muddy shell and made sure the snail wasn't harmed. "I'm planning on going back, of course."

"Why do you trust me? And think that I'll actually bring you back?" Suki asked coolly. "Your partner surely doesn't."

It was true that Lirah had no reason to trust her—or believe in this waterfall—but she did. She had an intense, positive feeling that she'd make it back to Au and Mala safely. It was hard for her to explain this instinct. Maybe she *was* overly trusting, like Au had said. Or maybe she had a skill for sensing others' intentions. Her mother had a special gift. So why couldn't these feelings mean anything?

"You have honest eyes," was all Lirah could think to say.

"*Ha*. Usually, I'm told the opposite. That my eyes are piercing like a snake's. But I suppose I'll take that as a compliment." Suki smirked.

Lirah smiled back, but she also started to hope she could remember the path they came from. Just in case Suki didn't guide her back.

The sound of flowing water became audible. "We're getting close," Suki said.

Lirah breathed a sigh of relief. She could make out the shapes of wooden cabins by a river. She couldn't see much water yet, but she could tell there was plenty of it. The waterfall roared louder with every step until she could see glistening creatures sunbathing on the rocks of the riverbank ahead of her. They had smooth, blue-grey skin with a complex scale-like pattern. Their bodies and big lips reminded Lirah of fish, but their heads were catlike with pointed ears and whiskers.

"Sumaras," said Suki, noticing Lirah's awestruck expression. "They're hard to catch. Don't be fooled by their laziness."

They approached the edge of the crystal-clear water, and Lirah looked to her right. A wide, roaring blanket of blue scaled far above her and the community. Endless amounts of sparkling water rushed down from a rocky cliff and crashed into the river below. It sprayed mist in all directions, creating a rainbow in mid-air. Cool mist brushed her face and she took a deep breath. The spray smelt faintly sweet, like orange blossom. She couldn't comprehend how the waterfall never stopped flowing. It was like a dream.

The cabins sat along the widest and deepest portion of the river, which was a safe distance away from the swirling water at the bottom of the falls. Two bridges crossed the river and connected the cabins on either side of the rushing water. One was built near the waterfall, and one was down where the river began to narrow. After that, rocks, fallen trees, and underbrush took over, and the cabins dwindled away.

Lirah had never seen a river this large in the jungle before, let alone a waterfall, cabins, and bridges. She felt a familiar stab of resentment for the Pride. Why did they never want to explore more? They wouldn't have needed to hunt as much or be as harsh about meal portions with a resource like this.

Lirah looked at the group of tanning sumaras again. They were funny things. Their heads turned back and forth in unison. She looked closer. The sumaras appeared mesmerized by creatures that Lirah had mistaken for lily-pads spinning on the surface of the river. They looked like plants, but they were not. They had flat green bodies with eyes bulging out of one side and lovely flower-like hats on their heads. She watched as more of the plant-like creatures crawled across the land, jumped into the river, glided across its surface, and spun around, spraying water up and out of their budded hats only to exit the water and do it again. The sumaras flapped their fins together in applause while Lirah laughed.

"Here we are! My home," Suki said, stopping before a wooden cabin. It practically touched the luscious river, giving it a wonderful view of the waterfall.

Lirah nearly stumbled into the door. She forgot that she was walking instead of floating aimlessly in a trance. The creatures here were so entertaining, and the waterfall so soothing.

Everyone here must be so relaxed all the time, she thought as she entered Suki's home.

"Careesa! I'm back. And I brought a Guzol," Suki called into the cabin, closing the door behind them.

Lirah could still hear the rushing water from inside.

"A Guzol?" a shorter version of Suki answered nervously, ambling out of a back room holding a cleaning rag. They had the same tanned skin, black hair, and curvy body. Careesa had green eyes in place of Suki's gold, though, and a flatter nose.

"No ... not really, just a wanderer. This is Lirah. Lirah, this is my older sister, Careesa." Suki added in a whisper, "She's not my actual sister, but everyone likes to call us that."

"Stop whispering about me." Careesa jokingly swung her rag at Suki. "Hello, beauty. What brings you here with my insane sister?" She smiled and wiped her hands dry.

They were standing in a room filled with bowls, baskets, and tools for cooking. A droopy cot had been pushed into a corner. Everything was the same shade of brown. In the center of the room, a sturdy table stood with a cut-up fish lying on it, the carcass vibrant red in comparison to its surroundings.

"Hello." Lirah waved. "I'm looking for two men I know. They went looking for food and water earlier. Suki found me out in the jungle and offered to show me your community. I thought they might be here too. But I *really* wasn't expecting all of this. I've never seen a river so abundant with life. And I've never,

ever seen a waterfall. It's lovely." Lirah grinned. She turned and curtsied to Suki. "Thank you for bringing me here."

Suki smiled and returned the gesture.

"Oh, wow!" Careesa said. "I heard a rumor today that two men were here. They were carrying a massive rutapuga. They offered some to our community leaders, Mori and Pecha, in exchange for water from the river." She smiled, looking pleased that she could be of service.

"That must have been the twins," Lirah said, thrilled that she had taken the chance and came here with Suki. She hoped they were still here. *And* they managed to hunt a rutapuga? So, they did have talent.

Rutapugas were fat, red, burrowing creatures. They had four stubby legs and two necks with big heads resting on each. Both heads had bright yellow eyes with vertical pupils. One head had a long snout with teeth protruding out of it, while the other had a smushed snout that looked like it got trampled over. Though Lirah hadn't seen many in her life, she assumed the different snouts helped in different burrowing conditions. The creatures preferred to eat root vegetables, and they travelled in herds. They weren't very fast, but they were sturdy and fought hard.

Lirah imagined the twins taking one down. Then more serious questions came to mind. "Were the twins allowed to take your water?" she asked Careesa. "Or were they told to leave? Were they locked up? Do you actually lock up men here?"

"Calm down." Suki laughed. "They're just *men*."

Careesa gave Lirah a strange look too. "Hmm, I'm not sure. We don't ... *lock* men up in Airis. But no stranger has ever offered us rutapuga before. It's a delicacy, so my bet is Pecha and Mori did *not* turn down that offer. Even if it came from men." She chuckled. "I can walk you over to where they would be if they're still here."

"That would be great." Lirah smiled, trying her best to ignore their obvious hatred towards men. She thought it best not to ask why. They were still helping her find the twins, after all.

"Right this way." Careesa threw her rag to the side and scurried to the door. Lirah and Suki followed her out to the riverbank.

Lirah breathed in the misty air and tried paying attention to the cabins as she walked. All of them seemed to be made of the same wood, but none looked exactly the same. Each had its own personality. Some had a triangular shape, others rectangular, and a few looked like hexagonal prisms. Some women had painted their homes with berry juice and clay, while others had planted colorful flowers and herbs out front. Several homes had bowls hanging from their porch roofs. They were filled with seeds to attract different flying creatures. Lirah already adored this place so much more than the hives in the sky, which had all been constructed identically and were therefore bland.

They stopped in front of an enormous, rectangular-shaped cabin. Spinning blue and purple flowers grew on either side of the door, and translucent moss dangled over the entryway, the sparkling kind that glowed in the dark.

Careesa knocked lightly on the door.

Almost immediately, a tall, slender woman with bright yellow hair answered. Lirah had never seen someone with yellow hair before.

"Oh, hello. You ladies picked a great time to stop by. Come in! We're eating *goood* tonight." The flaxen-haired woman waved them inside. Her beaming eyes cast over Lirah. "And who's this pretty thing?"

"Mori, this is Lirah. She's looking for the men who offered you and Pecha rutapuga earlier. She's friends with them," Careesa explained.

They walked through the door and crossed Mori's living room. It was much larger than Careesa and Suki's entire cabin. It reminded Lirah of the Pride leaders' hive. It was open and empty except for a long table covered in red cloth with over fifty black chairs placed around it. Unlit candles surrounded the perimeter of the room. At the sight of them, Lirah shivered. She kept her eyes forward and tried not to relive her last punishment as they proceeded into a friendlier room filled with cooking supplies.

Mori led Lirah, Suki, and Careesa to a table topped with delicious-smelling pieces of cooked rutapuga. Lirah realized how starving she was. She couldn't help staring at the delicacy; so much so that drool started dripping from her mouth.

"Usually," Mori began, as Lirah wiped her mouth and tried to focus, "I'd say *never* bother chasing after men. They'll only bring you harm. But those two know how to hunt and actually share their prize. And they were twins! Well, one had a black eye, so I could tell them apart. My, they were some funny fellows!"

Everyone seemed so happy here. Lirah wished men were allowed to visit so she could share this magical place with Au, but at least she could bring back Mala.

Mala. Lirah realized she had *completely* forgotten about what Mala might think of her absence. Hopefully, she wasn't too worried. *Ha*. Lirah knew she must be terrified, even though she had no idea what story Au had chosen to tell her mother. Maybe he was calming her imagination.

Suki looked around the room and sneered. "Aww, Lirah, it looks like your men aren't here. You better just forget about them."

"Suki, please. They're fine." Mori waved Suki's remark away like an annoying fly with her long, spider-like arms. "But they did leave quite a while ago. Fortunately, before they left, I had the chance to talk to them about the jungle and where they came from. They told me they fled from the Treetop Society a ways away. Is that where you came from too?" She raised her golden eyebrows.

"Yes." Lirah nodded. "I left with them and two others. We're just wandering the jungle right now."

"Oh dear, I've heard about that society. Some awful rules are in place there. I'm not surprised you left." Mori shook her golden curls around in disapproval. "*Is* that why you left? I don't mean to pry." She seemed genuinely concerned. Her raised eyebrows furrowed themselves down into worried yellow caterpillars.

"Well, yes ... the rules were terrible. But our situation is a little more complicated than that. When I was a baby, invaders unleashed chaos on our society. My group and I have reason to believe they're returning. We knew the Pride would refuse to take action, so we fled."

Mori stepped closer to Lirah and wrapped her arms around her. She smelt like cinnamon mixed with a hint of smoked rutapuga. "I'm *so* sorry. Who would do such a thing?" She retracted her long arms and looked straight into Lirah's eyes. "Do you think Airis might be at risk too?"

Lirah shrugged. She didn't want to mention Mala's vision. "All I know is that my mother said we were in danger. She remembers the last attack. Luckily, back then, the Pride was stronger. But now those brutes are definitely out for revenge. I can't imagine how much they've grown since." She shuddered. "But I don't know how they feel about this community. Or if they even know it exists."

"Airis is fairly new." Mori nodded. "We've always kept peace and I haven't seen any new strangers lurking around ... besides your man friends. Do you know what we should look out for? Have you seen them recently? Is that how you know they're back for revenge?"

Lirah opened her mouth to answer when Mori apologized. "Oh, I'm sorry. I ask so many questions. It must be difficult for you to cope with all of this, leaving your home and all. Anyway, I'm sure you don't know what to look for if this happened when you were just a baby. Silly me." She looked down disappointedly, her yellow curls swinging.

"It's all right," Lirah said. "It's really nice to meet a community leader who cares so much about her residents that she would take a stranger's word about these brutes. So, to answer your questions, I don't know what to look out for, except my mother said they wore masks. And, uh, are you familiar with ... er ... spirits?" she asked nervously. She didn't want to mention Mala's vision, of course, but she felt like Mori was open-minded enough to accept the idea of spirit communication. According to Mala, speaking with spirits used to be a common practice in the jungle (even if most attempts were unsuccessful), back before the Pride further isolated itself up in the treetops. It had been more of a hobby to try and contact them, rather than a rare and taboo ability that only a select few were born with. *Maybe some communities still attempt to communicate with spirits today.*

There was a long pause, then Mori clapped her hands to her mouth and turned to face Careesa and Suki. They hardly paid her any attention. Instead, they were leaning against the opposite end of the table, nibbling at pieces of the rutapuga.

Mori whipped her hair back around to face Lirah, her mouth hanging agape. "Maybe you've been sent here by spirits to warn us!" She clapped her spindly fingers together again and pulled Lirah in for a hug.

Lirah was glad Mori seemed more than accepting of spirit communication, but she could also feel her stomach caving in. All she really wanted to do was eat some rutapuga. She hovered over the table, getting closer and closer to the tray with every word she spoke. "My mother has made close connections with spirits too. Maybe you could speak with her about the attackers."

"Oh, yes! I have an entire room dedicated to contacting spirits. But lately, they don't seem to want to answer me. It's quite frustrating. Could you bring her here to discuss the matter with me? And with the spirits?" Mori batted her thick eyelashes.

Lirah took a bite of the tender, savory meat. *Yum.* It melted in her mouth. Her mind lit up. Maybe she could make up an excuse that would allow the men to come here too. After all, Mori basically said the twins were worth chasing after. Maybe she'd make an exception since they shared their "prize" with her. And Au *had* to see this place.

Lirah talked slowly, choosing her words carefully as she chewed on another piece of meat. "Well, yes … I could. But men aren't allowed here. I wouldn't want to break any rules, but … I know my mother wouldn't feel safe coming here—or *anywhere*—without them." This statement was partially true. Mala always had the protection of men around in the Treetop Society, so Lirah didn't know how Mala would react without them.

"Hmmm, a woman with traditional views." Mori paused to think, chewing on the inside of her cheek. "Well, I *am* a community leader around here … and those identical men were quite polite …"

"You're going to let her bring *men* into Airis?" Suki burst out, suddenly interested in their conversation. Careesa placed a hand on her sister's shoulder to calm her.

"Settle down. I'm just thinking," Mori said. "They would only meet with me to discuss a possible invasion. None of the other women would even notice."

Mori took another long pause, her eyes squinting with concentration. "I will allow your men to come," she said finally, smiling again. "I value your mother's talent, and I would love to meet her. If she can tell me whether or not Airis is at risk of destruction, then I see no reason to prevent that meeting. We will need time to plan an escape if we are in danger. So, I hope she accepts the invitation. Also, tell her and the others in your group that I'll have a meal laid out for them when they get here."

Suki scowled.

Mori threw her an awful glare. "That's enough treats for you, Suki. Now, bring Lirah back to wherever you found her … and why don't you stay with them for the night? You can lead them back tomorrow."

Suki stood, blubbering.

"And Suki," Mori's voice rang with warmth. "Thank you endlessly for bringing Lirah here. To think, you're our youngest member, and you might have saved our *entire* community by finding her. We're so lucky to have you." She embraced Suki in one of her gregarious hugs.

"Any time, Mori," Suki mumbled.

Mori and Careesa walked Suki and Lirah to the door. On their way, Mori caught Lirah gazing at the long, dark table in the front room again. "Isn't it beautifully made? We have all our community meetings there, and all our women take part in the decision-making. It's one of my favorite parts about Airis—everyone gets to have their voice heard."

"Except me," Suki said.

"Well, yes, except adolescents, which is only you at the moment. But we don't want to drag you into things that you don't need to worry about yet. You're young; go have fun exploring!" Mori gave Suki one last hug, then grinned at Lirah. "I'll see you again soon. I can't wait to meet your mother." She waved, her golden hair bouncing, and shut the door.

CHAPTER 9

The hike back to the curtain tree felt a lot quicker than the walk over to Airis did, maybe because Lirah was in a hurry now. Au told her that he would set out to look for her if she wasn't back after dark, and light was already fading fast.

Lirah remembered what the curtain tree looked like, but she couldn't fully recall the surrounding area. She was taking in as much stimulus as she possibly could now, forming a map in her mind. Before today, she only needed to memorize the territory of the Pride.

The jungle was limitless now. No more boundaries.

Meanwhile, Suki fumed over Lirah and Mori's conversation from earlier. "I can't *believe* Mori is bending the rules for you. I thought for *sure* she would convince you to leave those men and join us in Airis. You could've had access to all our resources! I never thought she would have let *them* come too."

"You thought that all you had to do was show me your community, and I'd forget about finding the twins?" Lirah snorted. "*And* abandon my partner, who I've known for as long as I can remember? Airis is astounding. But I wouldn't give up my partner for it. Or for anything."

"Do you think he would do the same for you?"

"Of course, he would. I'm the one who wanted to leave our Pride and all of its rules and boundaries. He was happy there, but he wouldn't have stayed without me," Lirah said, unable and unwilling to keep the satisfaction from her voice. "Oh, and then my Pride leaders gave me this ..." she pulled her bandage to the side so Suki could see the bubbling burn bracelet.

"That's disgusting." Suki turned her head away. "Why would they do that to you?"

"Because I was in Au's hive later than allowed," Lirah said, covering the blemish back up.

"No wonder you left," Suki said, then stuck up her nose to smell the air.

Lirah could smell smoking meat in the distance too. She knew it had to be coming from her group's campsite. Riel and Riggul must have found their way back all right.

It was dusk now. As they hiked closer, Lirah called out to the group so they would know she wasn't a predator.

"Lirah!" Au called back, his voice soaked in relief.

Lirah started running toward him. She couldn't wait to show him that she was right. She had created an ally with a community and its leaders were even bending the rules for them.

"Hey, wait up! Don't get too excited," Suki grumbled, taking off after Lirah.

They found the group sitting in a circle around a small fire under the giant curtain tree. Except for Au, who was standing with a bag and spear.

Au ran up and embraced Lirah, rubbing her nose with his own. "I'm so glad you're back."

"And you got here at the perfect time," Riggul said. "This rutapuga's almost fully cooked; Au was about to miss out by going looking for you."

A huge rutapuga was propped up by branches and rope above the center of the fire. Lirah peered at her mother's face across the crackling flame. She looked tired and angry.

"Who's that?" Riel asked, his wide eyes motioning at Suki. She stood in the shadows of the curtain tree with her furry pet trealea wrapped around her neck. It whipped its long body back and forth.

Lirah gave the introductions. "Everyone, this is Suki. She helped me look for the twins earlier. Suki, these are the twins, Riggul and Riel. And Mala, my mother. You already met Au."

Au and the twins waved.

Mala said nothing.

Lirah tried to ignore her mother's mood, but she knew she was the cause of it. Mala had every right to be upset that her daughter had left with a stranger. Then again, they were living in the open jungle now. Mala would have to get used to trusting others.

"This rutapuga looks amazing," Lirah said dramatically, maneuvering her way in to sit right between Mala and Riggul. She lightly rubbed her mother's back. She received no response; Mala only stared into the flames. Suki leaned against the curtain tree, and Au awkwardly sat down by the twins.

They stayed like this, listening to the crackling fire, silently waiting for the meat to finish cooking through. Finally, Riel broke the silence. "Lirah, guess what? Riggul and I found a whole *herd* of rutapugas today. There had to be at least fifty. And they were *massive*. We probably could've gotten two, but we thought that would've been overkill."

"Then we found a community by a huge waterfall," Riggul said. "With a river and cabins and some pretty women who came up to us. We offered them rutapuga meat, and they let us take some water. It was the best place ever."

"There were so many women. Like a lot. A lot," Riel said.

"I don't think I saw a single man," Riggul added.

"That's my home," Suki said, flatly.

"That's where I went looking for you both today. I thought you might've been killed," Lirah said.

"Yeah, we thought you might start to worry. We were gone a

long time. I'm sorry there was no way to let you know that we were okay," Riggul said. He sounded genuinely apologetic. "We thought the rutapuga meat would make up for it."

"How about we set guidelines for when we leave the group to find resources?" Au said, always the problem solver. "For instance, you have to set out right when light rises, so you'll have a full morning to hunt or collect resources. Then, you must be back as the light starts falling, right after midday. If you're in danger, we'll have time to look for you before the light is completely gone."

"That sounds perfect," Lirah said.

Riggul and Riel nodded in agreement.

Mala finally spoke, "I never want you leaving on your own again, Lirah."

"I won't, I promise." Lirah rubbed her mother's back.

The group went silent again.

Au stood and stabbed the meat with a spear, ripping out a chunk to check if it was thoroughly cooked. Clearly, it was, because he started lifting the rutapuga off the flame. Riel and Riggul stood to help carry it. It took the three of them to properly place it onto a leaf bigger than Au so it could be cut and served. After they evenly sliced it, Riggul gave thanks to the rutapuga for sacrificing its life for over eight others, including Mori and Careesa, and for giving them all the energy they needed to keep living healthy lives. Then, the group lined up to receive their portion.

Lirah took her slice and returned to her spot by the fire. She took one bite and instantly felt its nutrients rush throughout her body. It tasted even better than the way Mori prepared her portion. Lirah had only tried rutapuga twice in her life before today. Both times were at bonfire celebrations thrown by the Pride, who only cooked it for special occasions. Usually, the special occasion was that they were actually able to spot and catch a wild rutapuga or two. Rutapugas never wandered onto the Pride's territory, probably because they could smell all the hungry bodies there. And, of course, when the hunters did kill and cook one, every Pride member had to share, so they were only allowed a small taste.

Now, there was more meat on Lirah's plate than she had ever eaten at once. She was very pleased with Riel and Riggul's hunting abilities and obviously she wasn't the only one. Mori was so impressed that she was going to allow men into her woman-only community. Then Lirah remembered Mori's request. She cleared her throat to tell the group.

"So, while Suki and I were in her community, Airis, their leader told me that she'd like to speak with us about the invaders in the jungle—especially you, Mala," Lirah said. "She said she needs help contacting spirits to see if Airis is at risk of an invasion too. She also said she would have a meal prepared for us if we went." She looked to Mala, whose eyebrows were raised in curiosity at the phrase "contacting spirits."

"Wait, she wants us *all* to come?" Au asked, his face scrunched up like he had just eaten something sour.

"Yes. I told her that we fled our Pride as a group because we have reason to believe it will be attacked by brutes. She didn't understand how we knew that, so I asked if she was familiar with spirits. Then she got excited and asked for our help. She wouldn't have asked us to split up," Lirah said, leaving out the part where she told Mori that Mala would refuse to go anywhere without the men.

While Riel and Riggul added that they "would just love to go back," and "couldn't wait to hunt another rutapuga over there," Mala whispered softly to Lirah, "You asked her about spirits? Does she know about my vision?"

Lirah shook her head, then turned to respond to the twins when Suki perked up. "Did I hear you say *'vision'*? What's that supposed to mean?"

The group of runaways looked around at one another.

The fire snapped and popped.

They all knew about Mala's vision, but it was no one's place to talk about it except for Mala. And Lirah knew her mother wouldn't want a new community knowing about her ability.

What if they forced her to tell them their fortunes? (Which she couldn't do.) Or what if they felt threatened and wanted to hurt her? Only *her* group could know.

Mala sighed. "I have ties with spirits. Just like your leader does," she said. "I believe the signals they gave me were warnings that something terrible is coming back to our Pride. So, I guess it wouldn't hurt to go to Airis and see if I can help you all as well. We have nowhere else to go." She gave Suki a thin smile.

Lirah could tell her mother hadn't formed an opinion of Suki yet.

"But you just said *vision*, not spirits," retaliated Suki. "That's different, right?"

"You must have misheard a conversation that you weren't a part of. But I did tell you that I'd help your community, so we'll just have to see if I can," Mala said firmly, refusing to entertain the conversation anymore. Her face was obscured by a mixture of black shadows and orange ripples glowing from the fire.

"Okay, fine." Suki crossed her arms. "But who are these invaders? Do you know why this is all happening now?"

This, Mala answered, "From what I've been told by elders who passed away long ago, and from my own experiences when Lirah was a baby, there has always been a cult of brutes. It has been growing over time, organizing more members, and advancing its weaponry. Periodically, the brutes come out of hiding to try and tear communities apart. Nobody really knows if they want to take over the territories or if they simply want to destroy them. Their cult has never been large, but the last time they emerged, our Pride was shocked by their growth and their weapons. I can only imagine their strength now." She shuddered.

They all remained still, listening to the crackling fire and letting Mala's words sink in.

Lirah and Au had heard this explanation before. But hearing it in complete darkness—in the middle of the jungle with no protection—made it even more disturbing.

Lirah looked around the fire at everyone's reactions. Au and Riggul's eyes darted around the encompassing area. Suki kept her head tilted down at her lap. Mala gazed into the fire, the flames reflecting in her eyes. Riel had silent tears streaming down his hairy face. He started sniffling.

"Hey, it's all right. We'll be alright," Riggul said to his brother, patting him soothingly on the back. "Tomorrow we're going back to Airis, and Mala will talk to the spirits more about this."

Riel nodded and wiped at his hairy cheeks.

"Yeah, that sounds about right. Men are allowed to come in, *just this once*, because we're going to give them advice. They're just using us." Au snorted. "If the spirits warn Mala that the invaders are coming for them too, I bet their leader will beg us to stay. Then, when they're attacked, they'll force us to fight and be the first ones to die. They don't care about us."

Lirah gave him a nasty look. But Au wasn't looking at her; he was looking at the twins.

"Why does Airis hate men so much anyway?" Riel asked Suki. He blinked his sad eyes, and more tears rolled down his cheeks.

Suki glared right at Au. "Well, one reason is that they *think* they can do or say whatever they want, no matter how offensive." Then she squinted back and forth between Riel and Riggul. "Also, they're *very* selfish. They do things like leave their group with no idea of when they'll return, causing other *more thoughtful* group members to risk their own lives to go search for them."

Au scowled. More fat tears ran down Riel's face. Riggul looked like he was about to cry now too.

Suki's eyes widened, then softened at their emotional vulnerability. "Hey, don't cry about it. You're the ones who wanted to know," she said. "However, I found Airis when it was already established, so I'm not sure how the banning of men started. But the women in Airis are allowed to come and go as they please. Some spend time with men. They're just not allowed to bring them back."

"Where are the other men from?" Lirah asked.

"Wanderers, hunters, other small communities around." Suki shrugged. "It's a big jungle."

"What did you do before you lived there?" Au asked.

"I wandered on my own, digging up rare stones and bartering hem," Suki said. "Actually, when I stumbled into Airis, I was only trying to trade them stones for food. But they offered me a home. I took their offer, expecting not to stay long. I ended up loving it there, so I never left." She smiled. "I'm the youngest member besides a few toddlers that Mori doesn't consider conscious yet, so I feel like they all look out for me. Especially Careesa. She calls herself my older sister. And now that I think about it, we never seem to have problems. I think that's why Mori's taking this threat so seriously. She would have no idea how to handle this alone. So she's letting men in, for the first time in ... maybe forever."

CHAPTER 10

Fresh light slowly filled the jungle like water as the group of runaways awakened. Au was already awake, as he had been in the midst of his guarding shift. Lirah rubbed her eyes and stretched her arms up toward the canopy, dazedly piecing together everything that happened yesterday and deciding if it had been real or just a dream.

"I can't wait until I can change out of these dress cloths. I feel filthy. Can we go already?" Suki complained. She dangled from her mossy low-hanging branch, its leaves rustling back and forth against the jungle floor and persistently brushing against Riggul's face. His back was propped up against his brother's. They were having a difficult time keeping their eyes open.

"All right, all right. Make it stop. I'm coming," mumbled Riggul, positioning his feet to try and stand.

"Can someone hand me a water skin?" Riel asked. Au tossed one over, and Riel started chugging. "Wow, this is amazing," he said. Water coursed down his chin and dripped onto his fuzzy neck.

"What a mess." Suki groaned. She scooped up her sleeping trealea from the branch. It was coiled up, its ears drooping over its face and the 'leaves' on the end of its tail guarding its body.

It looked like the cutest little pile of leaves Lirah had ever seen. She stood up and petted its fuzzy back, confirming that yes, this was all was very real.

* * *

Lirah could tell they had travelled roughly halfway to Airis. She felt proud that this area already looked more familiar to her.

They passed the fallen tree with sticky pink fungi trailing down its bark like waves. And there was the giant spotted flower that would make a nice-sized bed for her. Further on, she recognized an open patch of grass shimmering in the light.

They walked through it. Lirah breathed in deeply and looked up. The light felt warm on her face. She could actually see a clump of clouds hanging in a creamy pink and peach sky from here.

But they passed the open sky all too soon, marching back into the usual humidity of the jungle, where the sky stayed hidden and limited light beams managed to seep through its dense canopy.

"We're getting close," Suki said as they passed a group of trees with translucent leaves, and the booming sound of the waterfall became audible. "You all should wait here. I'll get Mori to escort us to her cabin. I don't want to be the one questioned for breaking the rules and bringing men to Airis if anyone's watching."

Au didn't hesitate to start complaining the moment Suki walked out of ear's reach. "I still can't believe we're letting them use us. They only want us here for Mala's abilities. I bet this Mori leader doesn't even know how to communicate with spirits properly. It's not a simple interest to pick up, right

Mala?"

Mala let out an airy laugh. "It's still challenging for me sometimes."

"*See?*" Au shook his head.

"What else do we have to do, Au?" asked Riel. "It's not like we're busy. And maybe they'll like us, and we can stay."

"Why would you *ever* want to stay here?" Au raised his voice. "We just left our community. Why would we join another?"

"Okay, calm down," Lirah said. "Mori never said we could *stay* here. But Au, you know how much the Pride leaders hated spirit communication. Mori told me that she has her own room dedicated to speaking with them. Airis seems like an open-minded place. Give it a chance."

"Openminded?" Au threw his hands in the air. "They hate *all men.* We'd be better off sleeping against the roots of that curtain tree."

"You know," Mala said. "That may be why their leader has trouble communicating with spirits. You need *all* spirits, not just the ones who identified as women before they left their physical bodies. If she's only speaking with feminine spirits, that's a problem."

Suki marched back over with Mori. Their nearing presence silenced Mala and forced Au to quit complaining. Another woman trailed behind them, too. She had a plump body with plump red lips to match. She looked like a sumara. Lirah waved to them.

Mori gave her a huge smile. "Welcome back and welcome all! I'm Mori, and this is Pecha. We're the community leaders of Airis." Mori motioned to Pecha as she approached. "I'm just so grateful that you all decided to come and help us. As you might already know, I've been having some trouble communicating with spirits recently. My mother taught me a few techniques years ago, but it's a never-ending process of learning, really. But enough about me, how are you all doing today?"

Au opened his mouth to speak, but Lirah elbowed him in

the ribs before he could say anything rude.

Mala told Mori they were doing quite well considering their circumstances, then they all went around introducing themselves.

"Wonderful," Mori said. "Now, if you'll come with me." She turned and led them down the riverside and to her cabin. On their way, they passed some women standing in the river, glaring up at them, muttering back and forth.

"Ignore the stares," said Pecha, her voice deep and gruff. "We held a community meeting last night. We made sure to alert everyone about the situation. They know you're escorting a spirit expert assisting us in safety matters. They're just being rude now."

"I wouldn't say I'm a spirit *expert*." Mala's cheeks reddened.

"Oh, hush. You look like you are. With that long, beaded hair and those navy eyes." Pecha beamed at her.

Lirah kept eyeing Au in hopes that he would at least appreciate the scenery here as much as she did. The waterfall, rainbow mist, tanning sumaras, and performing plant creatures lifted her heart. But he didn't look impressed. He grimaced constantly.

When they entered Mori and Pecha's cabin, they found a lovely feast laid out for them on the long table in the front room. There was plenty of bright red fish, colorful vegetable arrangements, crispy bird wings, rolled-up dough smothered in pink sauce, and other foods Lirah had never seen before that wafted up a strange and appetizing assortment of smells.

After Mala tried a few bites of the crispy wings and vegetables, Pecha announced she would entertain the group while Mala and Mori went to her spirit room.

Mala nervously looked at Lirah. She didn't want to go alone.

"Could I come too?" Lirah asked Mori.

"Of course, dear!" Mori flipped her golden locks and motioned for them to follow.

Lirah looked at Au. He was visibly fuming. She shrugged and mouthed, *"sorry,"* then turned to leave the room.

* * *

Lirah and Mala followed Mori to the back corner of her cabin. They entered a small room about the size of a hive back in the Treetop Society.

Mori closed the door behind them.

Large drapes with mandala patterns covered the walls of the room. The fabric seemed to be stained using bright purple, blue, and red juices. There were no windows, but a few large candles lit up the tight space with a mellow light. There was just enough room for four chairs and a table. The table was covered with another painted drape and had a crystal orb in the center of it, held up by golden legs. There were smaller crystals in all colors and shapes lying on the table too, with colorful beads scattered around for good measure.

"Please take a seat," Mori said calmly.

Mala and Lirah sat and inspected all of the items on the table more closely.

Mori took the seat across from Mala, who looked very pleased by Mori's collection. "I've never seen so many different crystals in one place," said Mala. "Are you sure all of this is necessary?"

"I find the orb helps to balance the energy in the room. Having a focal point for the energy to enter and exit seems necessary to me." Mori smiled and shrugged. "Also, I like to hold one small stone in each hand while I close my eyes and connect with spirits. Sometimes, depending on which stones I'm holding, I get answers from different ones. Some spirits only seem to respond to the ribbon belly rhinestone, and others answer only to the vitreous sapphire."

Mala nodded along, but Lirah didn't see why any of this was necessary. Spirits didn't care about which nice gems you owned, did they?

"If we're curious to learn about potential destruction, I

think these would be best to use." Mori held up a battered indigo rock and a red stone that looked like solidified lava. She passed them to Mala to inspect.

"I've never used stones to communicate with spirits before," Mala explained. "I never wanted to use any mystical-looking items in my Pride. I was scared someone would find them and punish me."

"Well, now that you're free, I have duplicates of a few gems if you'd like to have them. Think of it as a thanks for coming here, even if we find no clarity now. Just know I'm grateful that you came."

Mala smiled wide, revealing her aging, jagged teeth.

"Are you ready to begin?" Mori asked.

"Yes." Mala took a deep breath and closed her eyes. So did Mori. Lirah kept hers open.

They stayed silent for some time, until Mori broke the silence and asked, "Are you getting any responses?"

Mala didn't answer. She kept her eyes sealed shut.

Lirah watched her mother's eyes. They were dodging rapidly back and forth beneath her eyelids, and her brows were furrowed. Lirah wondered what her mother was witnessing. Mala's chest heaved in deeply, and beads of sweat formed on her crinkled forehead. She didn't usually behave like this when she meditated and spoke with spirits.

This behavior is usually caused by a vision.

Mala's chest relaxed, and her eyelids ceased movement. Then, she opened her eyes.

Mori stared eagerly at her.

"I heard from spirits, but you're right ... the communication is limited here," Mala said, her voice quivering.

Mori shook her curls and threw down the stones in her hands. "This is so frustrating. But out of what you could see or hear, were there any clues about an invasion? Or a warning?"

"Well..." Mala wiped at her forehead. "Everything came through choppy... and honestly, it was all hardly comprehensible, like something was blocking my communication. Some spirits started to provide warnings, then quickly switched to peacefulness. Others sounded like they were screaming underwater before they randomly transitioned to the sound of playful bubbles. One spirit sounded like it dissolved the moment it tried to speak. Then, my mind went blank." She sighed dramatically. "This has never happened to me before."

"Hmm ... and when they spoke to you in the Treetop Society, what did they tell you then? What made you so sure to leave?" Mori asked.

Lirah watched as Mala closed her eyes again. She knew her mother must be reimagining her vision of burning treetops and hives falling from the sky, crashing to the ground with members still inside.

It surprised Lirah when her mother opened her eyes and said, "I only spoke to one. It was golden."

Mori gasped. "Golden? I've never seen a golden or even an orange. Only reds and blues, or no color at all ... only whispers."

"What's so special about the golden ones?" Lirah asked. Her mother had never shared this information with her before.

Mala frowned but obliged her daughter with the answer, "The only spirits that come in the form of golden orbs are assured spirits. It told me that there was only one outcome for the Pride. It whispered that if it didn't happen soon, it would come eventually. I interpreted this one outcome as destruction. If it wasn't destruction, then there would certainly be more possibilities of outcomes."

Mori vigorously nodded in agreement. "Did the golden spirit tell you anything else?" she asked, scooting to the edge of her seat.

"That was all. But I'm not receiving that same assuredness here. Your community has many options it can take."

"Oh, *please* tell me more," Mori begged. "Or teach me what you know about spirit communication so I can hear from them myself. I feel like I have a barrier up, and only lighter spirits can squeeze in. No deeper ones. Please, help me."

"It will take lots of practice to open up your mind," said Mala. "And I've never taught anyone before. But maybe the spirit world will open up to you and your cabin if you open up to it. You can't be scared of certain things, or they won't tell you. And you need both masculine and feminine spirit guidance."

"Well, why don't you stay here then? I can supply you shelter, water, and food in exchange for your guidance. Of course, you could leave whenever you want. It's just ... I know you don't have a home right now. This could be helpful for the both of us." Mori grinned eagerly, waiting for a response.

"But you don't allow men ..." said Mala.

"Oh, but this is an emergency! I understand that you like having men around for protection. If you're willing to help Airis, then I'm willing to make an exception. I would rather let a few men stay here than have the entire community face destruction," Mori said, her tone matter-of-fact. "If you built a cabin on the outskirts of Airis, nobody would even notice they're here. I'll even have food and water sent to your cabin so the men won't have to come inside our official boundaries."

It sounded like a decent offer to Lirah, but she knew Au would lose his head about this. Mala scratched at her hair, "We'll have to talk it over with our group first..."

"Please! Take your time. Pecha, Suki, and I can leave the cabin so you can discuss it here and eat more of the feast that we prepared for you. Here, I'll walk you over." Mori gave them a big, nervous smile. She stood and wiped her palms on her skirt.

* * *

They entered the front room, and every face turned towards them.

"So, are we all going to die?" Suki asked.

Mori laughed anxiously. "Well, things were a bit hazy for me. But Mala tells me there's lots of different outcomes for

Airis, depending on the choices we decide to make. So, I really don't know what that means for us or how to prepare for a possible invasion. I just hope that I get the chance to learn more from you, Mala." She paused to clear her throat. "Pecha, Suki, would you mind stepping out of the cabin with me so they can speak in private?"

Suki and Pecha followed Mori outside. Mala explained Mori's offer to the group—how she wanted them to stay on the outskirts of the community while Mala taught her the arts of spirit communication. How they were free to leave whenever. Mala explained how uncertain the spirits seemed to be in the back room and how her communication seemed blocked.

Lirah knew Mala had purposely left out information. Why? What would her mother want to hide? She pictured Mala in the back room with her eyelids dodging back and forth and her chest heaving like she was having a vision.

Unsurprisingly, Au voiced his feelings first. "It would be a huge mistake to stay here. Once Mori is fully confident in her abilities, we'll be kicked out anyway. We might as well find somewhere else to build a cabin."

Lirah was happy when Mala retorted, "It wouldn't hurt to stay here, take advantage of the free resources, and plan for our future. Airis would provide more safety in numbers, and we'd still be free to explore on our own. Yes, we will be kicked out eventually, but we'll be in the same position that we're in now. So, we have nothing to lose." Clearly, whatever information her mother was hiding didn't concern the safety here.

Riel and Riggul didn't seem to care much either way. They simply shrugged and said, "Where else would we go?"

Mala suggested they all take a vote.

Lirah, Mala, Riel, and Riggul voted to stay and help Mori and her community. Au voted against it. With the majority voting to stay, Mala walked out of the cabin to tell Mori the verdict.

Lirah dared to look over at Au. He was already staring back at her, jaw locked, eyes steady. It scared Lirah how emotionless he looked. She turned away and headed for the long table of food. She picked up a roll and tried to eat it, but suddenly she wasn't hungry. It felt like sand going down her throat.

Everyone else was elated by the verdict. Mori took no time finding the group of runaways a nice spot for a shelter on the outskirts of Airis. She gave them spare building wood, old furniture, and even made a teaching schedule with Mala.

For the rest of the day, Lirah and the twins assembled wood to build their new home by a beautiful old tree. Its branches sagged low due to the abundance of orange blossoms weighing it down. Lirah loved when the wind blew through it. The fragrant petals danced in the air and settled all over the ground around her. She could hear the melodious waterfall from here too. She couldn't see it, and their shelter hardly had a view of the river. But still, she loved it.

Au refused to help build the cabin. He kept himself busy by fuming instead, telling them all that it was a *"waste of time"* putting this much effort into building a temporary shelter. Lirah let him be. She figured he would grow out of this anger as time went on. How mad could he be about getting free food and water sent to his doorstep every day? They would be eating much better here than they had in the Pride, strict with its rationed portions.

That evening, Lirah and Mala left the men by their partially built shelter and took a stroll by the river. The waterfall glistened under falling light beams, which kept them warm against the misty air.

"Lirah, I know everything worked out this time, meaning the stranger you met happened to be telling the truth and took you to a beautiful place where we happen to be staying now. And because of this, I feel like I shouldn't be frustrated with you. But I am. You can't *ever* run off alone like that again. Next time we run into someone who wants to show us something or take us somewhere, we *all* go," Mala said sternly. Then she softened her tone, "I can't lose you, Lirah. You have no idea how worried I was when I woke up on those tree roots, and Au told me that you left with a random woman."

Lirah grasped her mother's hand as they walked, squeezing tightly. "I won't ever leave you again, Mala. I promise."

They walked until they reached the edge of the waterfall, where all sound besides the roaring water fell away. They stood, captured by its power and infinite capacity, until golden hour faded to dusk, and they turned back to where they came from. "Mala?"

"Yes, my light?"

"What did you see in Mori's cabin earlier when you were speaking with the spirits? I was watching your face and ... it looked much different than when you would talk with them in the Treetop Society. Did you have a vision?"

Mala swallowed. "I did."

"About what?"

"I have no idea, honestly."

Lirah shook her head. "Why would you keep secrets from me? I won't tell anyone else if you don't want me to."

"It's not about being secretive. I just don't want to worry you with a vision I don't understand."

"You *never* fully understand them, not right away. Just tell me what you saw. Come on, please?"

Mala sighed. She stopped walking, looked around, and sat down on the edge of the river. Lirah followed, dipping her toes in the cool water.

Mala closed her eyes in concentration. "Are you listening?"

"Yes."

"From what I can remember, after I witnessed that spirit dissolve when it tried to speak, my vision went dark. All the chaos went away. I felt calm. I was standing in an open field, and the sky looked as endless and full of color as the land. I watched as vivid orange and pink clouds fused together and floated off. I saw giant, surreal-looking creatures with eight legs grazing on the waving grass. They seemed peaceful. I thought I must be dreaming until I turned to my right and saw you, all too real. You were covered in filth, with tear marks streaking through the mud and blood splattered on your face like paint. Then, I turned to my left and saw Au. He was filthy too, and he had a lot of blood on his chest. I thought he was injured. I remember trying to reach out and touch the blood, but Au covered it up with his hand so I couldn't. Then, my vision ended." Mala opened her eyes.

"That was ... detailed," Lirah said. "I don't really know what to say."

Mala sighed. "Me neither."

"No one else was there?"

"Not that I could see, but visions never show you the full picture," Mala said, slowly standing. "Come on, let's get back. It's dark."

Lirah nodded. They walked the rest of the way in silence while Lirah's mind raced with ideas of what Mala's most recent vision could mean.

CHAPTER 11

Au hadn't budged over his frustration with their living situation. Several weeks had passed since the runaways first arrived in Airis, but he still wouldn't speak to Lirah. On the fleeting occasions that he did, he wouldn't look her in the eyes. He spent most of his time hunting and exploring other areas of the jungle with Riel and Riggul. They would leave early each morning and come back late with all sorts of animal meat. Au refused to eat the food the women provided.

Mala spent most of her time with Mori, who apparently wasn't improving much with her spirit communication. But luckily, there were no signs of invaders, and Mori had lookouts patrolling Airis throughout the day and night. Lirah wondered how her former Pride was doing. Sometimes, she even thought about checking up on them and scoping out their territory for invaders. But she knew if she was seen, she would be captured and killed for treason. So, with all of her other companions preoccupied or furious with her, Lirah spent most of her time with Suki. They played with Suki's pet trealea, tanned on the rocks, swam in the river, and caught fish with their bare hands.

Lirah even managed to catch a sumara, twice.

In no time, Suki introduced Lirah to the other sunbathing women in Airis. They all treated her like a sister right away.

When Lirah started getting frequent headaches, the women gave her plenty of natural medication to use along with massages, long hair-brushing sessions, and amazing facial treatments to ease her worries about Au. All the while they gossiped about their own male lovers and sons that they had abandoned, or who they still travelled away to see from time to time.

Lirah was grateful for the women's generosity and interesting conversation, but none of their remedies seemed to work for her. If anything, her symptoms only got progressively worse over the weeks. As her headaches worsened, so did her sight. Each day, the women's faces looked more and more like scrunched-up rutapuga heads. At first, Lirah discounted it as symptoms of the headaches. But over time, their skin turned pink, then red, then scarlet. Their teeth yellowed, their hair grew brittle, and their faces warped shape. Now, they all looked completely contorted.

Lirah didn't want to call any attention to their changes for fear that the women would get thoroughly insulted. Rutapugas were *not cute*. She did, however, mention a few times that she was having eyesight problems (without further elaboration). So, they gave her more medication. Which didn't help. But Mala and Suki never seemed to change. And Lirah didn't see the men enough to notice if they looked deformed. When she did see them, they were always covered in mud.

Lirah decided she had grown depressed from not speaking to Au. Headaches and eyesight problems must be symptoms that came along with her heartbreak. They had spoken every day for as long as she could remember, about *everything*, and now he was treating her like she had some kind of disease. Lirah couldn't help but think about leaving Airis just to make Au happy. Also, she knew it was ethically wrong that no men were accepted here. It was this community's only major flaw.

But if the twins could make the most of it and stay optimistic for a short time, why couldn't Au at least try?

✻ ✻ ✻

It was the middle of Spring, and though the jungle's atmosphere didn't change much, it had grown excessively hot outside to Lirah, and the women had somehow grown even redder. Her head wouldn't stop throbbing, and she was constantly sweating, even after cool swims in the river with Suki. Today, she decided to stay inside the cabin to rest. It had been completely finished for over a month, topped with a secure roof just big enough for the group of five. Inside, there were five cots provided by Mori, one table, and lots of baskets and buckets lying around and hanging from the low ceiling.

Lirah was sprawled out, lying on her cot with a cool rag resting across her forehead, when Mala came bursting through the door. She was scowling and muttering to herself. When she noticed Lirah, she immediately started pouring out her suppressed emotions.

"I don't know what else to do," Mala said. "Mori *still* isn't making any progress. I keep telling her we should try practicing in another room or go outside and speak to spirits by the river, but she always refuses. She told me that room is where her mother used to contact spirits when Airis was first built, so she wants to do the same. But there's something very wrong with that room; I know it. I'm always completely drained after our full days of lessons. I told her I had to leave early today."

"I'm sorry, Mala." Lirah attempted to sit up. "I'm not feeling well either. Maybe there's something wrong with our cabin too."

"Oh, my light! You look *horrible*. I'm sorry to phrase it that way, but you do not look well. This has been going on for too long. I'm worried that something more serious than basic headaches is causing your eyesight problems. None of the medication has been working?"

"No." Lirah frowned. "Have you had any visions lately? Or have the spirits hinted at anything regarding my health?"

"No … not really. Honestly, I haven't been speaking to spirits on my own; I've been too exhausted after helping Mori all day. And I can't seem to reach them in that horrible room she's obsessed with."

"That's really strange. I'm losing my physical sight, and you're losing your spiritual sight. What do you think it means?"

"Hmm, I'm not sure. I'll try speaking with the spirits again now." Mala sat down on the cot right next to Lirah's. She crossed her legs and closed her eyes.

Lirah dropped her neck back and dozed off into a light sleep.

* * *

"We need to leave." Mala's voice resonated in her sleep. She dismissed it.

"Lirah, wake up. We need to leave Airis, now. The invasion is occurring soon."

Lirah slowly blinked her eyes open. "The invasion? Here?"

Mala scooted closer to her daughter and looked straight into her eyes. Lirah was happy to be looking at a normal, familiar face. "I don't know if it'll be here exactly, but the spirits warned me to leave. Just now, they were restlessly flashing. I don't think we have much time. The brutes are coming."

"Wow—this is so sudden." Lirah rubbed her forehead, still in a haze. "Where would we go?"

"We have to leave the whole jungle. I don't know which communities are going to be attacked. It's only right to assume nowhere is safe," Mala said, searching for her sack and collecting small items to put into it.

The words were slow to connect with their meanings in Lirah's mind. To wake herself, she rubbed her cool rag all over her face. She stood, walked over to a water bucket, and splashed more water over herself. Energy crept up her body. "Au and the twins aren't back yet, and we need to warn the women, too. Do you think they'll be mad we're abandoning them? After they've been so welcoming?"

Mala looked shocked that Lirah would ever ask such a thing. "Mori said we could leave whenever we wanted," she said. "And even if she didn't, I would still be leaving now. We already abandoned the Pride, Lirah. I know I lived there much longer than you, but after leaving that place, it's safe to say we owe no one our company."

Lirah nodded.

She walked over to her scrambling mother and grabbed her hands. "We'll be all right." She pulled her in for a hug. "I'm going to find Suki and tell her about the invasion. Hopefully, Au and the twins are done hunting soon."

Lirah strolled out of the cabin, rocking side to side over a ground littered with fallen orange petals. She felt lightheaded and dizzy. She didn't want to walk far, so she was glad when she found Suki sitting by the edge of the river. But when Lirah got closer, she noticed Suki's eyes were filled with tears.

"What's wrong?" Lirah asked, sitting down beside her and dipping her toes in the river.

"I was about to knock on your cabin door, when—well, I didn't mean to—but I overheard you and Mala talking. Your window was wide open ... You're ... you're leaving?" Suki blubbered.

"Actually, that's what I came to talk to you about. Mala thinks the invasion is happening. We don't have much time. She said that doesn't mean the brutes are coming *here* exactly, but nowhere in the jungle is safe anymore."

"How ... how does she know for sure?" Suki whined. "If ... if the invaders are on the loose, what if ... you leave and ... and walk right into them? Shouldn't you stay here to hide?" Suki buried her face in between her knees.

"I don't know what to say. I'm so confused, and my head hurts *so* bad." Lirah pressed her fingers against her temples. "This decision isn't only up to me, Suki. It's up to my group, my Pride group."

"Hey, Lirah! Hey, Suki!" Riel called from a distance, pacing over with Riggul. They had spears over their shoulders, and dirt stuck on their bodies with sweat. It looked like they were finished hunting for the day, but when they reached the edge of the river, Lirah saw they were empty-handed. And they never came to the river.

Lirah waved at them. "Hey, where's Au?

"We were about to ask you that," Riggul said. "One second, we were all together searching for game in our usual spot. The next second, he was gone. We've been walking around trying to find him ever since."

Lirah's heart dropped. First, Mala told her the invasion was happening soon and that nowhere in the jungle was safe anymore. Now, Au was missing after wandering around the jungle.

"Don't worry, we'll find him," Riggul said, clearly trying to console Lirah after noticing her horrified facial expression. "He was acting funny today. He kept saying that he didn't have a good feeling about hunting. Maybe he turned back and left since we weren't listening to him."

That didn't seem like Au. He wouldn't leave his friends without telling them where he was going. She jumped to her feet.

"The invaders took Au! There's no other explanation. Mala just spoke with the spirits. They told her the brutes were coming. But it looks like they're already here! I need to tell Mala about this, and then we need to warn the rest of the community. The women can help us look for Au. Wait here!" Ignoring her aching head and body, Lirah ran to tell Mala the update.

"Mala! You were right!" she shouted into the small cabin.

"The invaders are here! They took Au! We need to find them and get him back. Then we can leave the jungle. I'm going to warn the rest of Airis!"

Before Mala could reply, Lirah ran out the door and back to the river's edge where she, Suki, and the twins planned to split up and alert the community. Suki said she'd go to Mori and Pecha's first, then she'd warn the women near the waterfall. Riel and Riggul would go to Careesa's and the other cabins on the right side of the river. Lirah volunteered to run across the bridge and warn the women on the left side of Airis.

The first cabin Lirah came to was covered in mold and algae. The wood was rotting, and there were some poorly patched-up holes in the roof.

Whoever lives here doesn't care about hygiene.

Actually, she couldn't recall ever seeing anyone come in or out of here, and it was the closest cabin to hers. For a moment, she thought it was abandoned, but they had no windows, so she couldn't be sure.

She knocked on the door.

There was no response, so she started banging on it, shouting that there were brutes coming to invade them and they needed to get out.

No response.

She started walking away, concluding it to be vacant, when she heard a loud, low groan. Then another one, in a higher octave, from a different mouth.

Lirah took a step back toward the rotting cabin, thinking that whoever was inside was probably sick. Maybe that was why they hadn't been coming or leaving lately; she could relate to that.

She went back and tried pushing the door open to help out the presumably sick women. But it was stuck like something was blocking it. She pressed her ear to the door and heard more whines and groans. Shivers jolted down her spine. She was torn. She wanted to leave but knew she couldn't.

She frantically ran around the perimeter of the cabin to find another entrance, her heartbeat picking up speed so fast it felt like it was coming up her throat.

She spotted a back door ... but why was there a back door? There was nothing behind the cabin except dense woods.

She leaned against the door and turned the handle.

It creaked open.

Instantly, the reeking smell of feces mixed with rotting fish seeped out and hit her in the face. She jumped back, coughing, and covered her nose with her dress cloth. She wasn't able to see a thing inside. It was pitch black without any windows.

The muffled groans grew louder.

Holding the fabric tightly against her nostrils, Lirah stretched her leg out and kicked the door completely open. Just when she thought the smell couldn't get any worse, she about fainted. Not just from the smell, but from what she saw.

Six bodies—naked male bodies—squirmed on the dirt floor, covered in mud, feces, and leftover fish carcasses. Fabric was wrapped around their mouths, and their arms were tied behind their backs with rope. Two of them looked at Lirah with wide eyes, their faces streaked with dried blood. The other four faced the darkness.

A shockwave ran through Lirah's spine. Her legs turned to jelly. Who were these men? Why were they tied up and thrown in here? Who put them here? Lirah's legs shook violently in protest to standing. Her head spun to the point where everything looked like a warped tunnel. As she began to fall, another one of the bodies flipped itself over to face her.

Au.

He looked like the freshest captive out of them all. He was less bloody and dirty, with the most energy. When he saw Lirah he started going wild, flailing around like a fish on a rock. He made the loudest grunts of all of them.

"Au?" Lirah murmured. "I found you."

She stared at him as she wobbled back and forth, propping herself against the doorframe with one hand and reaching out to him with her other. She wished she could grab him from here. She nearly forgot they weren't on speaking terms. She was so happy to see him that her legs stopped quivering, and her vision started returning to normal.

A hand grabbed Lirah's shoulder. "You were trying to warn my community about an invasion when you stumbled into this cabin, I presume?"

She turned around. Mori's tall frame loomed over her.

Lirah hadn't seen her in so long. She looked nothing like she had the day Lirah first met her. Her face was absolutely warped now. Her hair gleamed fiery red instead of bright yellow, her smiling teeth looked like golden daggers protruding from her mouth, and her eyes were nothing more than black holes. They looked just like Qualisiun's had right before Lirah received her burn bracelet.

"What is this ... how?" Lirah could hardly speak. The smell, Mori's face, and the fact that six men—including Au—were tied up and covered in filth right behind her petrified her.

"Suki came to warn me about Au's disappearance. She assumed the brute invaders must have found Airis. She went on to tell me that you and the twins were already warning other members. So, I decided to come searching for you before you could notify too many women." Mori flipped her fiery red curls.

"What ... are you doing? Who ... are all ... these men?" Lirah stuttered.

Mori didn't answer. She only smiled as she inched toward Lirah, directing her into the rotting cabin.

Lirah stepped off to the side, away from the open door. "Why would you want to take Au? You practically *begged* us all to stay here. *You* needed our help. And Mala has spent all of her time trying her hardest for you."

"Oh, please. I didn't need your hag of a mother's help with anything," Mori spat, her red face practically singing with flames. "I put a barrier around my cabin so Mala would never be able to speak with spirits there. All of those lessons were fake. I was stalling. But wearing down her mind was actually quite fun."

"Mala spoke with spirits today. In our cabin."

"Well, I guess I'll just have to make the barrier even larger next time. Thanks, dear." Mori stepped closer to Lirah.

Lirah backed away. "Then why did you ask her for help? Why did you beg us to stay? What did we have to do with your stalling?"

"Isn't it obvious now? You all knew too much. And you were *so* eager to help. I couldn't allow you to leave Airis and keep warning every little creature in the jungle about some masked brutes coming back for revenge. Not before the preparation was complete. But don't worry, I'm still planning to do something nice for you all. That Treetop Society will be the first to go." Mori's daggered teeth grinned wide.

Lirah's mind raced. Fake lessons? Spirit barrier? Before she could speak again, Mori grabbed her neck and pulled her close.

"This is what happens when you go meddling in affairs that don't concern you. You should've stayed home."

And right when Lirah thought she couldn't become any more revolted, Mori shoved her through the moldy back door and slammed it shut. Lirah stumbled to catch herself from falling and ran back to open the door. She rattled and pulled, but it was locked from the inside. She was about to shout when she heard Mori moving a log to block the door.

Lirah was trapped.

CHAPTER 12

Lirah turned around to face the bodies she could no longer see. It was completely black, and the smell was even more potent inside.

She crouched down and felt around for bodies to set free. She heard a loud grunt as she stepped on what felt like a leg and dropped to her knees, feeling for the body's face. They helped her by grunting louder and louder through the fabric covering their mouth. She found it and pulled it down.

Between heavy breaths, a raspy voice spoke, "There's a spear in ... left corner of room ... that Mori uses to threaten us. You can use ... cut our arms free."

Lirah sensed her way back to the wall she came from, side-stepping until she brushed against the spear. When she reached the man again, she felt for his arms and apologized if she cut his skin while tearing through the ropes.

Once he was free they felt around the mush and grime to find the other five bodies. Every man let out a deep sigh of relief when the fabric and ropes were removed, but none of them sounded like Au.

"Has everyone been cut free?" a deep voice called into the blackness. "Let's break down this door. I'm going to *kill* Mori!"

The other men shouted in agreement.

"Wait, there's one more!" yelled Lirah, crawling around with one arm in the mud and one arm stuck straight out, feeling around for Au. She could hear his moans.

She finally reached him, pulled off his fabric, and cut his arms free.

He embraced her.

"Au! I'm so sorry about everything. You were right about this place." Lirah panted. "Who put you in here?"

"Two women I've never seen before. Mori," he breathed in deeply, "put them up to it. We can talk more later. But we need to get out of here. I can ... hardly breathe."

"Mori is *evil!*" a voice screamed into the darkness.

"Let's bust down this door!" yelled another.

"Let's *kill* her!" shouted a third man from across the room.

The men stood back and counted to three. All at once, they launched themselves at the rotting door, collapsing it.

In the light, Lirah and the men all sighed with relief, breathing in the fresh air. They sprinted towards the woods and away from the horrid, rotting cabin.

Lirah could see the five other men clearly now. They looked even worse out here than they did when she first saw them tied up. Their bones were visible through their sunken grey skin, and the grime covering their bodies was more visible in the light. Their hair was long and smushed to their necks, and their teeth were brown.

"Airis imprisons men," one man said, his hollow eyes filled with tears.

"The women told me they invade territories ruled by men and take them down," another said. "That's what happened to us." He nodded at his frail friend. "They took us and killed the rest of the inhabitants there."

"They attack innocent wanderers too," another said. "One moment, I was out exploring the jungle. The next moment I woke up lying on my back in that nightmare of a room. It's like they do it just for *fun*."

"I'm so sorry you all had to go through that. I don't know what else to say." Lirah shook her head in disgust. "Except now, we need to get out of here. You're all welcome to come, but Au and I need to get back to our former Pride. Mori said they're the first to ... *go*." She turned to Au. "Let's find the other runaways."

The men thanked Lirah for freeing them before running straight for the river to rinse off. Au couldn't resist jumping in too. Lirah was about to argue that they didn't have time for baths but when she saw the feces plastered to her hands she decided to follow.

* * *

"Behind the waterfall is where they stored it all ..." Lirah murmured, staying low in the water. Terror and intrigue warred within her as she watched the brutes organize themselves for battle.

From this side of the river, Au and Lirah had a clear view of the organized chaos. Women emerged from their cabins and marched toward the waterfall, nodding as they passed by others parading out from behind it carrying bows, arrows, and spears. They handed them down the row until everyone had a weapon. They each had an intricate mask placed over their face, just like Mala described the brutes who attacked the Pride years ago.

Au pointed to a group lighting up torches together, pulling Lirah's attention away from two women chopping one another's hair off with knives. She shuddered at the sight of the flames meant for killing. "Let's go find Mala and the twins."

"I told you living here was a horrible idea," Au grumbled.

They climbed up the rocks and took off running.

"How did those women take you? How did it happen?" Lirah asked through short breaths.

Au lifted his hairline, revealing a bloody gash on his forehead. Lirah winced, nearly causing her to trip as she sprinted.

"Two women patrolling the area were following me and the twins on our hunt. Hiding behind trees, I guess. The twins walked off for a second. I heard a noise behind me. I turned around to see a rock coming at my head. Next thing I knew, I was tied up in the dark."

"But why *you*? Why would they randomly imprison some men and not others? None of this adds up."

"Not everything has to have a reason. Sometimes living beings do horrible things to others for no reason other than hate." He huffed deeply, annoyed. "That's what you don't get, Lirah."

"Well, I won't let their hate destroy the Treetop Society too. We may have abandoned them, but we still have time to save them."

On the outskirts of the unfolding madness, Lirah and Au threw open their small cabin door. They found Mala, Riel, Riggul, and Suki standing in the middle of the room, staring at them, wide-eyed and terrified.

Suki locked eyes with Lirah and started speaking frantically, "I swear I had *no* idea! That's what those community meetings must have been for—the ones I was never allowed into because of my age. I *promise* I never brought you here thinking they would hurt anyone. I care about you so much." Suki gasped for breath, which turned into hyperventilating. Tears streamed down her cheeks. "I want to stay with you. I'll help you all escape."

"It's alright, Suki. I believe you," Lirah tried to calm her. She stroked her hair.

Lirah surprised herself with how well she was able to react under pressure today, even with her sickness. "We need to warn the Treetop Society," she said to the whole group. "Mori told me, before throwing me into a rotting cabin, that she's planning to take down their territory *first*. As a favor to *us*."

Just then, arrows pinged and reverberated against the cabin walls. Some speared halfway through the wood before they stuck. Their shining tips poked through the boards, warning the inhabitants of their potential damage.

Lirah gulped. The masked women were done preparing. Now, they were targeting them. But they weren't close enough for her to hear their voices.

They must be aiming from a great distance.

"Let's go!" Au shouted. "Lirah, Mala, grab all the spears and weapons! And anything else you packed to come here. Riel, Riggul, hurry and help me bust down this wall!"

The men ran straight for the wall pointing away from the brutes and arrows, sending it crashing down easily. Lirah found four spears and quickly passed one to each of the men, keeping one for herself. Mala grabbed the dagger-looking rocks from the table, along with her bag of resources and two water skins. She handed Suki a couple of the daggers. Then they bolted.

Mala instantly fell behind, but Au knew the drill. He ran back and scooped her up. Suki took the lead.

"I know how to get to the outskirts of the Pride's territory! Follow me!" she shouted.

They followed, and so did the masked brutes. They marched maliciously behind the group of runaways, casting their arrows and small spears.

Before now, Lirah had no idea how many women actually lived in Airis. There had to be at least a hundred masked faces chasing her and her friends. She wondered how they all had managed to fit into Mori's living room for community meetings about destruction. And where did they all practice shooting arrows and aiming spears? She hoped their practice was limited. So far, no one in her group had been hit.

Riel called back to the brutes, "Watch out! Or you're going to run out of weapons before you've even begun your raid!"

Arrows whooshed past Lirah's arms, skidded through the dirt and fallen leaves, and pierced tree trunks only inches from her ears. Other than that, she could only hear the brutes chanting.

"We're free!"

"We'll never be silenced by men again!"

"Women will rule the jungle!"

"AYYYYAYYYAYYYYY!"

They hooted, cackled, and hollered. Their echoes rang throughout the jungle, sending creatures around them running for their lives.

Lirah caught the edge of a new sound coming from behind, mixed in with the piercing chants. It sounded like a deep yell. A man's yell.

She dared herself to look back.

The men she rescued were coming up in full force with weapons!

They must have waited in the river until the brutes left, then raided what was left of the weapons.

The women were forced to slow their march and handle their new obstacles. Lirah knew the men wouldn't last long. They would surely die. But their act of revenge allowed her group vital moments to create a gap between themselves and the women. She would be forever grateful for them. She gritted her teeth and tried not to listen to the sound of skulls punctured by spears or bodies lit on fire as Suki guided her group through narrow tree gaps, weaving in and out of spots that were trickier for an arrow to be aimed at.

"I'm doing my best to make it harder for them!" breathed Suki. "We're getting close!"

Lirah could feel they were growing near her old home too. She pushed through her pain, knowing it would be over soon. She felt like her body was filled with ice and fire at the same time. Her head was pounding harder than her heart, and her legs were shaking even as she ran. She tried her hardest to ignore the brutes' howls.

"Riel! Come take Mala from me! I need a break from the extra weight," Au called out desperately.

Lirah looked over her shoulder. Au was losing speed fast. Mala was slipping from his arms, gripping him with a face full of terror.

Riel slowed his pace for Au to catch up and hand Mala over, his arms reaching out to grab her.

Hurry up! Lirah thought. *And don't drop Mala!*

The high-pitched hollering behind them persisted while any trace of male's yelling had died away.

Lirah looked forward, then back again. Riel and Au were both holding Mala, jogging with her cradled in between their arms like a hammock.

"Come on, Riel, just *take* her! She's slipping!" Au yelled.

Lirah faced forward, barely dodging a tree trunk, then turned her neck back around. Time was moving slower than usual. Her eyes caught sight of a flash of silver hurtling for Riel, Au, and Mala. She opened her mouth to scream, but before the sound exited her mouth, Riel lurched forward. He groaned and fell to his knees, sending Au and Mala toppling to the ground with him.

Riel screamed in pain.

A gleaming arrow protruded from the back of his thigh. Lirah gasped, tripped over a root, and faceplanted in the dirt.

The brutes hooted with triumph.

"*No*!" Riggul shouted with rage.

As Lirah fumbled to stand, she heard him turning around on the fallen leaves to reach Riel. Besides Suki, they had all stopped making any forward progress.

"I'm sorry I couldn't take her, Au! Leave me here! Just keep going and warn the Pride!" Riel said. He had one arm around Riggul's neck and the other clutching his thigh, collecting the fresh blood trickling out.

Lirah didn't know what to do. She stood frozen in time.

This was the end.

She could see the masked brutes gaining on them, only a few yards away. They were so close that she could see their bright red faces and large snouts peeking out from beneath their masks. Everything else blurred from her surroundings.

CHAPTER 13

"Lirah, what are you *doing*?! Move!" Au shouted. He was lying on his stomach and gazing up at her.

Lirah shook herself back to reality. But instead of running forward, she ran back to help her vulnerable group. If they were all going to die, they would die together.

By the time she reached them, Au was nearly standing. Mala said she would attempt to run on her own. Riel was half jogging, half limping. And Riggul was trying to steady his brother while he jogged by his side. Lirah grabbed Riel's other arm to speed up the process. Au took a deep breath and grabbed onto Mala's waist, pulling her over his shoulders.

Luckily, Suki was far ahead, still sprinting in full force towards the hives in the sky.

Lirah could see them now. The dangling spheres where she had lived her entire childhood. She was equally relieved and terrified to see it again. She heard Suki's voice resonating up and throughout the jungle canopy, "*Invaders! Brutes!* Get your weapons! Assemble your guards! *Hurry*! *They're coming*!"

Meanwhile, Lirah, Au, Riel, Riggul, and Mala were only a

few feet in front of the brutes and a few feet away from the Treetop Society. Destined to reach it at the same moment the women shot them down. Lirah wondered if the women were purposefully holding back their deadly shots. After they hit Riel's thigh, their arrows had completely seized fire. Maybe they were collectively anticipating the perfect time to unleash: when they reached their main target—the Treetop Society.

Lirah saw images of her short life flash before her eyes. Memories of herself running through the jungle, climbing trees, laughing with Au, and lying on her cot with Mala.

Death was approaching.

They wouldn't make it.

No. No. *No.*

They didn't need to make it. Suki had just warned the Pride.

"Cut right!" Lirah shouted abruptly, making a sharp turn. She was still holding tightly onto Riel, who was gripping onto Riggul, who was being trailed by Au, who was carrying Mala.

She was leading them all away from the Treetop Society. *Again.*

"Suki! *Suki*!" Lirah screamed, sweat pouring down her forehead and into her mouth.

Pecha's gruff voice yelled, "You five, go after them! Make sure they don't come back! Use your ammunition wisely."

Dutifully, five masked women cut right and chased after the group of runaways.

Lirah turned to watch Suki, now only a small figure in the distance, as they ran further and further away. Suki was so close to the Treetop Society that she was standing beneath it, waving her arms around and continuously shouting up at the Pride to hurry and assemble their weapons. The brutes had spread out and formed a large oval around the perimeter of the Treetop Society.

"Suki! *Suki, hurry*! You're *surrounded*!" Lirah shouted, her eyesight blurring again, unable to pay attention to where she was running, momentarily oblivious to the fact that she was still being hunted. She could only think about how she had abandoned Suki. Her beautiful and determined friend, who was willing to die to help her and her Pride.

Suki had ultimately been the hero. In return, Lirah left her to fend for herself. "*Suki*!"

"Suki! *Suki*!" the twins started shouting along with Lirah.

Suki heard them at last. With her arms still waving frantically above her head, she spun around and faced the direction of their screams.

Then Lirah saw another flash of silver. An arrow. Not from the brutes. But hurling from above. It struck Suki, piercing her in the spine. Her small figure fell out of sight.

"*No*!" Lirah shrieked. She wanted to stop. She wanted to turn around. But her legs kept racing forwards. They just kept going, and the five brutes kept chasing.

Until all at once, she couldn't breathe anymore, she couldn't run anymore, she couldn't see anymore. Tripping over a root, she let go of Riel's shoulder and fell to the ground choking and sobbing.

Riggul let go of his injured brother. He stopped above Lirah and leaned down to help her. She reached up an arm, lifted her crying eyes, and saw the first weapon that the five brutes had released since parting from their marching brigade. A long spear.

It flew through Riggul's back and out his chest. His eyes went blank as he fell to the ground, blood sputtering onto Lirah as she rolled out of the way. He faceplanted where she had been laying only a moment ago, when he was still alive and reaching out to help her. Lirah was stunned by how fast someone could go from being alive ... to not.

Riel let out a horrendous scream as if a piece of him had died too. He ran in full force at the masked brute who killed his brother. But clearly, the brute was distracted by what she just did. She didn't see Riel coming. She was blankly staring at her only weapon jammed inside Riggul.

Delayed, the brute turned to run as Riel's spear entered her chest. She died instantly. Riel sped up as he positioned his spear further inside her limp body, using it as a shield against the other four brutes.

Arrows and spears sailed his way. Riel ran straight at them, ignoring the bloody arrow still deeply lodged into his thigh. Holding onto his limp shield, he knocked another brute coming at him in the stomach, bringing her down to the ground and kicking her face in. Riel's 'shield' fell to his left side, leaving an open shot for an arrow to hit his right shoulder. But he didn't notice. He fell to the ground, dropped his shield, and continued punching the dead body under him. Sobbing. Hyperventilating.

"I can't sit by and watch this anymore," Au spat. He stepped out from behind a tree and hurled his only spear.

As a brute prepared to launch her spear at Riel, Au's struck her in her side. She fell to the ground with a thud. Au motioned to Lirah—who was covered in Riggul's blood, traumatized, and lying on the ground next to Riggul's body—to pass her spear to him. She tossed it up. Au caught it and cast it swiftly through the side of another brutes's head. She toppled over, sending up a screen of dirt.

As the dust cleared, Lirah saw the last brute of the five sent to chase them carefully aiming an arrow at Riel.

Au noticed too. He started to move in her direction, but not fast enough. She let her bow go, sending an arrow into the back of Riggul's skull. His punching motions ceased at once, and he fell lifelessly on top of the bloody, very dead body below him.

For a moment, all was silent. The lone masked brute looked at her dead colleagues on the jungle floor. Then she peered up at Au. He was already watching her like a predator eyeing prey. She grunted, turned on her heel, and ran back in the direction of the Treetop Society.

Probably to report back to her leader and have more troops sent over, Lirah thought, still too stunned to move her body. Her mind had begun to function again, thankfully.

"She killed Riggul. She's not getting away." Au seethed through gritted teeth. He was weaponless. He started to chase the lone brute, stopping before one of the other dead women lying on the jungle floor. He pulled a bloody spear out of her skull and raised it back over his head. He took one step back, then ran forward until he released it.

Au and Lirah watched, unmoving, as the spear hunted down the brute running at full speed. It whizzed through the air. Closer ... *closer* ... but still looked like it would fall short.

The spear struck her calf. Lirah couldn't believe it.

The brute screamed and fell down, foolishly trying to remove it.

Au bolted after her.

"Here. Allow me," he said once he reached her. He pulled the spear out of her thigh, raising it to shove it down through her stomach. She screamed out, "Please! Don't! I'll do anything!"

"You killed my friend," Au replied. "Why would I let you live?"

She pulled off her mask, revealing a beautiful young woman, maybe a few years older than Au and Lirah. She had sad violet eyes and puffy lips.

"If you kill me ... what makes you any better? Please ... don't," she sputtered, blood pouring from her calf.

"Fine," he said. "I'll spare your life. *If* you promise me that you'll go back and tell your pathetic brute leaders that you killed us all. Tell them that you were the only survivor."

The woman nodded vigorously, biting her lip, fighting her pain.

"And *never* come over here again." Au helped her to her feet.

"Thank you," the woman said.

He watched as she limped back to her brute clan, as fresh smoke drifted over from the Treetop Society. Then, she was out of sight.

Au jogged over to Lirah and sat down next to her. He cradled her.

Mala came out from her hiding place shaking, her eyes taking in the scene. She joined Lirah and Au, and the three of them sat on the ground in a tight circle.

Lirah knew they were all thinking about the same thing —the deaths of Riggul, Riel, and Suki. They were all dead in a matter of minutes, and Lirah couldn't stop replaying the images of their bodies falling, one by one, over in her mind.

Lirah, Au, and Mala sat in silence and stared off in the distance towards the smoking Treetop Society. They leaned against one another, catching their breaths and sweating, with tears streaming down their muddy faces. They had no plans to move anytime soon. They had covered too much ground for the other brutes to see them from here, especially with smoke pouring through the jungle.

Lirah could still make out red flames in the trees from here. And she could hear the crashing of hives against the jungle floor through the shrill sounds of distant screams. Echoing screams that would haunt her forever.

Au wiped his eyes, blinked, and gazed around the area. He turned his neck. "Hey, look. It looks like we're near the edge of the jungle. Doesn't that look like somewhere different to you?" Au pointed to the west.

Lirah wiped the tears from her face and peered between the dense trees and vines. It looked like a flat oasis resting peacefully in the distance.

"I've only seen the edge of the jungle twice in my life. Bue took me." Mala sniffled. "It's the most breathtaking land I've ever seen. So stunning and vast. I always hoped I'd find it again. But there's nowhere to hide out there."

"Well, we're not safe in the jungle anymore. In case it's not obvious enough," Au said, coughing from the smoke blowing their way.

Mala nodded. "Absolutely; I told Lirah that earlier."

"I agree. We need to leave," Lirah choked out. "We need to keep going. What should we do with Riel and Riggul's bodies?"

"Bury them," said Mala.

So, they buried them under large fronds and leaves.

Mala closed her eyes and whispered mantras while she waved her open palms above the loose soil and foliage covering the twins' bodies.

Lirah wished they could have buried Suki. She couldn't believe the Pride shot her down after she tried helping them. Along with her grief, Lirah entered a state of shock. She couldn't wrap her head around everything that began unfolding mere hours ago. It all seemed unreal. This morning, she was lying peacefully on her cot on the outskirts of Airis, only to find out that the women there were the invaders she had been trying to run from all this time. They locked up Au in a rotting cabin, chased down her and her friends, and killed Riel and Riggul. Then they destroyed the Treetop Society, which ultimately destroyed Suki. It was too much.

Lirah could still hear sporadic shouting and crying in the distance, coming from the survivors of the deadly attack. Probably searching for, and finding, dead loved ones. She wanted out of this jungle, *now*. It had turned into a graveyard.

Lirah, Au, and Mala prepared for their departure. The trio collected two spears from their battle and filled up their water skins multiple times from a small stream nearby, each drinking an entire serving before filling them to carry along. Then they collected what edible plants and berries they could find around the stream, as they had no idea where they would find water or food outside of the jungle.

It was evening by the time they walked out and into the unknown, beyond the thick jungle wall. As they made their first steps into the soft and open grass, Lirah knew they would be okay. She felt it, and she saw it.

PART 2: UNDER SUBLIME SKIES

CHAPTER 14

Lirah, Au, and Mala walked only a few yards beyond the jungle border before coming to a halt again. Here, they stood side by side, jaws dropped, all too astounded with what lay ahead to continue.

Panoramic layers of tangerine, magenta, and lavender mist swirled around and through one another like swells over a soft peach and blush backdrop. At a certain elevation, they mixed into one long layer, creating a river of color across the center of the sky. Rose-gold light beams pierced through the mist at all angles, illuminating each vaporous color in such a surreal way that Lirah couldn't find words to fully describe this sensation. She felt like something was intentionally creating this scene before her eyes.

The rose-gold rays stretched down to the ground like long fingers, enhancing the shimmering waves of sweet-smelling grass. Mixtures of green, teal, aqua, and purple created ever-shifting patterns across the rolling hills, playing with the contrasting shadows and highlights of light. A warm breeze gently swayed the grass blades, consistently renewing their sweet smell and pattern arrangement.

Lirah shut her eyelids and tilted her face upwards, allowing the piercing light to kiss her cheeks. She took a deep breath and exhaled right as a fresh, strong breeze blew over her. She blinked her eyes open.

As she steadied herself, she watched the river in the sky move forward with the wind. Creatures that looked like giant white puffballs with bulging eyes and no mouths floated high above her. Carried on the strong breeze, they slowly bobbed up and down with no effort involved, entirely supported by the river of mist. Lirah wished she could float up and climb on one. She had never witnessed an open sky while living beneath the dense jungle canopy. It was like she had been unknowingly trapped beneath a bowl of steam for her whole life, and someone just lifted it from the table for the first time. Her senses were nearly overwhelmed. Her heart felt like it was filled up with light and risked bursting.

Au took hold of her hand. She smiled, and using her other hand, she grabbed hold of Mala's. Together, the trio walked hand in hand through the most beautiful, sweet-smelling place they had ever encountered.

As they progressed, a large herd of furry beasts, calmly grazing on grass, came into view. In the distance, the beasts would have been nearly impossible to see were it not for their ridiculously enormous size and constant movements. Their patches of woolly fur matched the shades of greens, purples, and blues of the grassy hills, and their horns were dark brown like the few scattered trees.

Aside from their colossal, nerve-racking bodies, they looked quite cute. Each grazing beast had two tails on its bottom and two horns curving in odd directions on its head. Some of the beasts' horns curved so far to the right or left that they swayed in that direction with every step. Their lack of balance wasn't helped by their eight legs that were so long that Lirah could have comfortably walked between them like they were tree trunks. Their colorful fur draped over their eyes, giving them a hair style that made Lirah laugh.

Very clumsy designs for such large creatures, she thought.

The trio giggled while they watched eight-legged calves chase each other around, get tangled up in their own legs, and fall over from the extra weight on their heads. The furry parents strolled over to rescue their young, pulled them up with their snouts, and shook their many legs free.

Lirah's heart melted a little. She had never seen creatures this intimate and untroubled before. She'd never witnessed creatures this *large* before, either. But she had no fear. The creatures seemed to be herbivores, and tiny travelers would pose no threat to them. They could all live harmoniously together.

Au looked down at the grass and let out a peculiar snort. "This grass is blinking at me."

Lirah and Mala dropped their eyes to the ground.

"Is it glittering? Flashing?" Lirah asked, confused.

"No, look closer," said Au. "I can see it *blinking* … like we do. They have *eyes*."

"No way!" Lirah giggled with delight. She let go of Mala and Au's hands and stooped down to get a closer look.

Every piece of grass had an eyeball. Or two. Or three. And each individual eye had the ability to look in every direction. Some blades made direct eye contact with her before casually looking away, blinking every so often, unphased by the giants lurking before them.

"This is miraculous." Mala stepped forward and looked out into the distance, her hands pressed firmly against her heart.

Lirah observed the grass for another moment then looked up at her mother's silhouette, beautifully positioned in front of the sublime sky. She wished she could capture this moment forever. She stood and walked to her mother. Au came to Mala's other side.

"This was my *vision*," Mala whispered. "The one I had when I met Mori for the first time."

Lirah nodded. She remembered the depiction Mala had laid

out for her when they were by the riverside in Airis. She watched with curiosity as Mala turned to face Au and reached out to touch the blood on his chest.

Au protectively covered the smear with his hand before Mala reached it, just like in her vision.

Mala's hand fell.

"The twins' blood." He sighed. "I don't want to wipe it off yet. I want to imagine they're still with us, somehow..." He paused and shook his tousled hair. "Why did they have to die before witnessing this?"

"And Suki ..." Lirah murmured.

"It certainly feels like they're all here, almost as if they formed this scene for us to enjoy." Mala smiled softly.

Au nodded. Tears bubbled up and streaked down his cheeks. "Lirah?"

"Yeah?"

"It doesn't matter anymore, but ... just know, I'll never stop speaking to you again, *ever*. No matter what. No matter how many sexist, brute-filled communities you drag me to." He choked on his tears, then exhaled. "I don't know what I would've done if you died back there ... before we had the chance to really make up."

Lirah embraced him and rubbed her nose against his. "When I rescued you from that cabin and you first turned over and looked up at me, I knew we made up." She smiled.

Tears started falling from her eyes too.

* * *

Originally, the trio expected more trees to reveal themselves. A sign of more life. But as they trekked over more and more hills, it became clear that only a sparse number of trees occupied the entire grassland, and the trees that were present had no leaves.

Although lacking foliage, they did have the most intricate

branches the group had ever seen. The trees twisted themselves into shapes, mimicking the scarce number of muses they had around them. An array of branches twined itself together to form a lone bird, while other branches took on loopy shapes like clouds in the sky. Some trees literally waved at the trio, arching their branches like they had elbows, when they passed by.

The trio decided to rest against a tree that ecstatically waved them over before twisting into a large heart shape. They settled into the soft, teal grass that rose up higher around the tree's trunk, and pulled it over their legs like a blanket, nestling in for the night.

With tired, dark-ringed eyes, they watched as the orange ball in the sky sank lower and lower, unable to look away as the sky continuously changed forms before them. It was as if a painter was mixing water and ink right there above the ether, blotting out the scene.

The vibrant, flowing river was the first to disperse, along with the bobbing puffballs it supported. The tangerine, magenta, and lavender mist faded into shades of mauve and deep red, then into a dull, grey blue. The artist even smeared away the peach and blush backdrop, darkening it through hues of purple and blue before settling on indigo.

Eventually, after the orange ball had taken away all its light and completely vanished beneath the ground, all of the dull mist dissipated, and new small lights started filling up the emptiness. The backdrop got blacker and blacker as more and more lights popped up against it.

Lirah imagined little silver shards lining up on the other side of the atmosphere, counting down and flinging themselves through the barrier in groups to see who could carve the biggest hole and have the best viewing spot of the world below.

While she had seen light shards like these before, through small gaps between tree branches in the jungle, she'd never had the slightest clue what their purpose was. She'd only known that the orange ball of light's purpose was to determine the time of day by its placement in the sky.

Out here, with a clear view, Lirah *still* didn't know what the light shards were for. But whatever they were, there was an infinite amount of them. Shining from so far away... and *so small*. If they looked this small to her, she wondered how small she looked to them.

They probably don't notice me at all, she thought as she smiled to herself.

For the first time, Lirah felt like her problems were insignificant. Laying in this open field, gazing at a sky filled with unknown gleaming lights, she realized this was an experience she had unknowingly been waiting for. Somehow, her instincts knew this phenomenon existed before her conscious mind had. This moment proved her right, that she never belonged living in the Treetop Society her whole life, even when it was still intact.

She shifted her sleepy gaze.

Maybe most peculiar of all, out among the millions of small lights, three enormous glowing spheres dangled. They hung much closer to the ground and were much larger than any of the lights beyond. She wondered just how huge these spheres must look up close. She wanted to reach out, grab one, and pull it down to her chest to inspect it.

Each sphere looked different. The largest one was dark gold, positioned the furthest away, and slightly concealed on its bottom right by the second largest sphere—a predominantly dark outline with a shining white crescent glowing on its right side. It was only slightly smaller than the biggest one.

But the smallest sphere was Lirah's favorite. It stood out, all alone, hanging off to the side and below the other two, and was multiple times smaller. And while it may have been the tiniest, it was by far the brightest. It had an aura around it, lighting up its surface so much that Lirah could make out every crack and marking across it. It looked bumpy, like there were hills covering it, along with large holes filled with some kind of liquid substance. Lirah wondered if anything lived there.

"What is all of this?" she brought herself out of her thoughts to ask.

"Who could possibly know?" Au said. "It's all too far away."

"I can feel the spirits," Mala said. "We're very safe with them."

Lirah sighed happily, breathing in the balmy, fragrant air.

"I can't believe I've never been out here before," Au said.

Mala smiled and opened their sack of resources. She pulled out a water skin and berries. They snacked while they gazed at the grand night sky until they drifted off into sleep, along with the furry beasts snuggled in a tight group a few hills over. Even the grass blades finally closed their dimly glowing eyes.

* * *

Light rose the following morning, waking Lirah from her dreams of destruction and death. She had seen Suki brutally die over and over again until finally, after nine times, Suki's spirit lifted from her body and up into a satin pink sky. Above wavering grass and gentle beasts, she drifted too far up for Lirah to see anymore. Lirah wanted to rise with her. She wanted to see just how big the spheres beyond the ether looked up close. She wanted to meet the creatures who lived on the small sphere's rolling hills and ask them questions.

But they were nowhere to be seen now. The glowing spheres and every last silver shard had disappeared in the morning's light. The peach and blush sky had returned, though nowhere near as vibrant as last night. The painter was just beginning their process again. Way up, the river ran through the center of the sky, its bobbing, bulging-eyed puffballs calmly passing through.

Lirah sat up and rubbed her eyes, recalling her dream. Au woke with a start beside her. He looked around as if searching for a predator hiding nearby or unsure of where he was. Then his shoulders slumped down in realization. Lirah watched his facial muscles unclench as yesterday's memories flowed through his mind.

"I can't believe we're out of the jungle," he said with a smirk. "And no one kept guard *all night.* Look what you got me into. More trouble." He shook his dark hair.

"Well, leaving the jungle wasn't really a choice." Lirah yawned. "But I can't believe it either. I feel like I'm still asleep."

Au reached over and pinched her.

"*Hey*!"

"Oops, did that hurt? In your *dream*?" He teased, tickling her stomach.

She rolled over, trying to block her stomach from his reach. She squealed, "Stop, Au; you'll wake Mala."

But Mala was already awake. She rolled over to face the young partners and smiled. "I'm still alive," she murmured. It sounded more like she was asking a question than making a statement. She sat up and meticulously stroked her tiny arms, shoulders, and thighs before pulling her knees in for a hug. "I don't know how I made it through yesterday." Mala scooted her hips against the tree trunk and leaned her head back. "I never want to move *again*."

"Well, if you don't want to move, you don't have to," Au said, standing and stretching. "But I need to figure out how we can find food and water out here. I would hate to kill one of those eight-legged beasts. They seem like they have such close bonds with one another. If I even *could* hunt one. They're bigger than trees. Well, the babies aren't." He shrugged. "If we can't find anything else ..."

"I'll join you on your search. I don't want to kill any of them either," Lirah said, standing up beside him. She shook one of the water skins to check its supply. Nearly empty. Luckily their other one was still full.

"I wonder if we could eat this grass. It smells super sweet." Au squinted down at the millions of blinking and goggling grass blades.

He ripped one out and smelled it. "*Yuck*. This smells rotten inside, like that cabin from yesterday. I do *not* need any more reminders of *that*." He cringed and threw the blade into the warm morning breeze.

"I fear those women are going to invade every community in the jungle," Mala said, her voice hollow. "Maybe a society will stop them in their tracks. One with more weapons. But we'll never know ... we can only hope."

Au shuddered. "We stayed with them for weeks and weeks. How did we not know they were the brutes?"

"Suki lived there much longer than us, and she never knew," Lirah said, her words bringing back her nightmare. "But let's not talk about that now. Let's save our energy for finding food." She gazed around at the barren, sloping hills. "It doesn't look like we'll have many options."

CHAPTER 15

Lirah and Au strolled through the colorful grass, glancing back every now and then, keeping an eye on the tree they had slept by. They could tell it apart from the others by its twirly heart shape. They hoped it wouldn't morph into something else while they were away, as Mala chose to stay there alone and rest. Lirah never would've left her mother alone in the jungle, but the grasslands seemed safe. The day was beautiful and clear, and not much was out here besides short grass. There were no signs of predators, but if one showed itself, Lirah and Au would be able to spot it from miles away and bolt back to Mala. They also left her a spear, just in case.

In her mind, Lirah ran through these precautions, but in her heart she felt no fear. These grasslands were a tranquil dream, though she knew she couldn't stay here forever. She didn't mind drifting, but she knew her group would keep searching for others of their kind. A community to join. At least that's what she assumed they would look for since not much lived here, and definitely no one like them.

"I know we just escaped the jungle yesterday, but what do

you think we should do now that we're free?" Lirah asked, spreading her arms out to catch the sweet breeze between her fingers while they walked. "No rules, no others around. Do you think we'll keep moving until we run into others like us?"

"I haven't put much thought into our future yet. It's all really uncertain, isn't it? No matter what we choose to do," Au said. "Is that what you want to do?"

"Well, you know I'd love to keep going as far as we possibly can." She grinned. "But I'm worried about Mala travelling so much ... and you. You'll be the one who has to carry her when her little legs can't take it anymore." She laughed.

"Now *that* I've been thinking about," Au said. "I think she'll be fine if we move slow and steady. She just can't run."

Lirah nodded as another sound came from the back of Au's throat. He awkwardly opened and closed his mouth, flexing his jawline.

She stopped and stared into his rich, honey-brown eyes. They gleamed as he looked off into the distance, hints of gold flecks revealing themselves within his irises like treasures in the open light.

He made eye contact with her and sighed. "It's going to be difficult. But we should keep moving like you said. We can't stay out here forever, and we do need a community. I would *like* to be a part of one ... others to care about me, and you, and—" He broke eye contact and started blushing uncontrollably.

"What?" Lirah smiled. "Just say it. You were already going to twice now."

"And I want a family one day. You knew that, right? It's no big deal." His cheeks burned crimson. "I'd like that baby to have others around. So, let's keep moving forward. After talking with Mala, of course. But she seems to do anything that you want." He smirked as his cheeks faded to rose.

"See, that wasn't so hard to say, was it?" Lirah playfully rolled her eyes and leaned in to hug him, trying to keep from blushing about his baby comment herself. "And maybe Mala's already had visions of the future beyond this point ... ones that she hasn't told us about. She doesn't seem too worried right now."

"*Hey*!" Au abruptly pulled away from their embrace, stooping down to peer at a small flowering plant. "This looks like food to me."

He came back up with a plump, red, juice-drippling fruit. It filled the majority of his palm. Compared to the small shrub he ripped it from, it was absolutely overpowering in size.

When Au pressed it to his nose and smelled it, Lirah could hear his stomach growling. Hers decided to join in.

"It smells *amazing*," he said. He lifted a finger, swiped off a drop of its overflowing juice, and transferred it onto his tongue. His eyes lit up.

Lirah looked at him with wide, worried eyes, questioning his sanity. She pictured him seizing up and foaming at the mouth.

"Look, I know it's edible," Au said. "Riel and Riggul taught me a lot about plants during our time hunting together. They told me every warning sign you could possibly look for when analyzing fruits and leaves. Looking back, I don't know why everyone in the Pride always called them dumb. They knew more about plants and animals than anyone else I've known. Maybe guarding just wasn't their strength ... or most social interactions." He shrugged and lifted the dripping, palm-sized fruit. "*This* is hydrating *and* full of sugar. It'll sustain us for hours, even though it's pretty small."

"Okay, but we still need to find more to eat besides this," Lirah said.

"Of course. But now we know we'll be able to find food out here." He held the fruit up higher in the air, as if toasting a celebration, then he took a big bite.

Lirah watched the bright red juice drip down his chin as he extended the fruit out for her.

She grabbed the small stem with her fingernails and smelled it. She shrugged and took a small bite.

Her mouth danced with the lush flavors of sweet and tangy.

It was the best thing she had ever tasted. She took another bite, then another.

"Alright, *alright*, save some for me!" Au laughed, quickly taking it back from her.

"It's ... s'good," Lirah attempted to say between bites, causing Au to laugh even harder while he chewed.

He swallowed the rest of it. "Okay. Let's find more ... hmmm ... or more of *anything*."

* * *

The sun had nearly risen to its peak. Lirah and Au continued their search for signs of food or water, making sure to stay somewhat close to the heart shaped tree. Unfortunately, they weren't finding anything edible in this area.

They did, however, come across a curious boulder.

Lirah and Au sprawled across its flat surface, as it was an ideal spot for taking a short rest, when suddenly they were lifted up and shaken around. In confusion, they jumped off the rock. As it inched away, they noticed tons of stubby legs beneath it.

"That rock does *not* mess around. It wanted us to get off!" Au laughed.

His laughing made Lirah start laughing. Then they couldn't stop. It just kept getting funnier that a rock had shaken them off.

After their long laughing fit, Lirah wiped tears of amusement from her eyes, blinked, and realized the rock was in the exact same spot.

It hadn't moved at all, or had it?

She inspected and poked the boulder. She even attempted lifting it to try and aggravate it again, without luck. "This *did* move, right?"

"Lirah, we both saw it," Au said, wiping his tears of laughter away.

"Well, it looked like it did. And we felt it lift us. But now ... I'm not sure."

"It's alright. Relax." Au laid down on the soft grass, planted his arms behind his head, and closed his eyes.

Lirah stopped tempering with the rock and sat down beside it. She wiped the sweat from her forehead and squinted off into the distant grassy hills. They looked different than they had yesterday, when they were sturdy and upright. Now, the peaks were bending themselves in and out, curving down into troughs and arching back into crests before her eyes. Back and forth they waved. Lirah started to feel nauseous and wondered how she wasn't toppling over.

She looked up to distract herself.

The sky was still painted in soft shades of peach and pink with waves of thin mist and puffy clouds drifting by. It seemed normal enough, until the clouds and mist started building and disassembling themselves into intricate designs. Lirah watched in amazement as the mist morphed into various floral shapes and sizes that spanned all directions of the sky. The mistflowers danced around and came together. They stacked themselves precisely on top of one another, largest to smallest, until a dense trealea-shaped cloud slithered through the flowers, dispersing them. Lirah didn't even have time to gasp before the cloud shrunk into a baby trealea, turned into a long-snouted rutapuga face, twisted into a skittering lily pad creature, and dissolved. All in a matter of seconds.

Shaking her head clear of what she just witnessed, Lirah turned to Au, curious if he had watched any of the show. But he was still lying with his eyes closed, calm as ever. Except, his face did not look like *his* face. It hadn't morphed into a red, smushed rutapuga face like the women's faces had. It was downright dilapidated. One of his eyes appeared much larger than the other, and his lips were sliding down his chin and right back up into place. Which reminded her; she still hadn't told him or Mala about the women's gradual transformation.

Now that Lirah thought about it ... since the women turned out to be evil brutes, it made sense that she had been witnessing their true identities slowly seeping out from beneath their friendly facades over time. Until finally, they fully became what they looked like on the inside ... maybe?

Okay, I need to tell Mala about that theory, but what is this?

What she was experiencing now felt different. More dissociative. Her thoughts were wandering in ways they hadn't before, and it was hard for her to differentiate between what was real and what wasn't. Was this all happening inside of her mind or outside of her mind? Or *both*?

Au had felt the rock shaking them around too, and he had seen its little feet when they jumped off it. Still, Lirah wasn't sure if that really happened, multiple witnesses or not.

Ugh. She needed to stop thinking so much. She sent her focus outward again, looking down.

The blinking grass was covered in designs and textures, its colors pulsing and dripping down into the ground. The wind smelled sweeter, and she could feel the light being absorbed by her skin. Maybe focusing on her surroundings was a bad idea too. This new environment overwhelmed her.

She looked down at her own familiar hands and arms. Even they were pulsating like the sky and grass, and she swore she could see *through* her skin. She watched her blood flowing while her vision involuntarily zoomed in and out, closing in on her veins before panning out for a view of her whole arm.

"Er ... uh ... Au?" Lirah asked, trying not to sound like she was freaking out. "Are you seeing all of this?"

"Oh yeah, and I feel *great.*"

"Do you know what I'm talking about? The patterns, the movement, the smells, the—"

"Yeah. If you close your eyes, you can still see different designs projecting on your eyelids," Au said.

"I think there was something weird in that fruit," Lirah muttered, scooching closer to him. She laid down next to him, supporting her head with crossed arms on the warm, wavering grass.

"There was *definitely* something weird in that fruit. But nothing toxic," Au said matter-of-factly.

His lopsided eyes fluttered open, and he gazed at the misty patterns above. His black pupils took up the entirety of his eyes. "This experience is changing my entire perception of this place. Maybe we should stay here forever. I haven't been able to think this clearly in ... maybe my entire life." He beamed. "I feel full of energy. Like light is flowing into me. But I'm also not anxious to do anything. Why do we always worry so much when everything is pointless besides just ... being together? And *existing,* you know? I'm already doing what I was made to do."

Lirah had no idea what he was going on about. "Um. I don't know. I kind of feel like I'm going crazy."

"It's alright. Just go with it, Lirah. There's nothing you can do but hang out and wait for the fruit to run its course through your body. Then the feelings will pass." Au sat up, propped himself on his elbows, and looked around at their multi-colored, panoramic view.

"You know," he said. "I blamed myself for the twins' deaths. After it all happened, when you, Mala, and I were sitting together on the jungle floor, I thought if ... if I would have just turned around and attacked those five brutes that followed us ... *right* when the rest of their army was out of sight, I *know* the twins would've turned and started attacking them too. And you could've helped. We could have beaten them. Instead of blindly running. Waiting until it was too late."

Au shook his head with disgust. "We could've scared them off or come to some kind of agreement with them like I did with that last brute. *'Leave us alone, and nobody gets hurt.'* I should've said, *'Lie and tell your leader that you killed us.'* Then the twins would still be alive. I just waited too long ... because I didn't know what to do when it mattered. I didn't *want* to attack anyone. And then the brutes started killing first ... and I ended up having to kill *two* of them."

Tears started to form in his dark eyes, but he sucked them up, and leveled out his voice. "I guess that's what I've learned from this fruit ... that you can't blindly run and wait until someone kills the ones you love before you retaliate. You must act *first*. You can't assume life is going to miraculously grant you a different outcome if you're not doing anything to change it. But that's all in hindsight." He sighed. "There's nothing I can do about it now. I just have to go with it because all we're made to do is live ... live and protect the ones we love so that they can live too. That's what I meant when I said that everything else is pointless. Because now I know if someone is threatening the only job that I have, to protect the ones I love, then I have to turn around and attack. We need to survive, Lirah. Together. That's all. It doesn't matter where, or how, or in what conditions ... we just have to keep on living." He exhaled.

A gentle wind began as he finished speaking. Lirah let his words sink in as she stared at the transforming mist in the sky. He was worrying her a bit. He never rambled like that.

"Wow, Au ..." She sighed. "That's all very profound of you to say. I agree ... we need to stay alive and protect one another. And I'm really sorry about the twins. I miss them too. But their deaths were *not* your fault. Don't blame yourself. You didn't want to kill anyone if you didn't have to. And you showed mercy to that last brute. You let her go, and that says a lot about you. I wouldn't want to be with a mindless killer. I think you're the absolute best. I'm lucky to have you."

Au nodded. A few tears silently streamed down his cheeks.

Lirah rubbed her nose against his. "Let's find Mala and make sure she's doing her job of staying alive," she said. "Maybe she'll know what we ate too."

"Don't worry, I've been keeping an eye on that tree," he said.

"But you're looking at the sky."

"I am *now*."

Lirah rolled her eyes and sat up, leaning back on her arms and positioning herself to stand, when she started feeling lightheaded. Then, all at once, her senses shut off.

* * *

Lirah's empty mind filled with color in the way water slowly fills a cup, taking away the hollowness. Beneath her eyelids, intricate mandala patterns swirled like she'd never seen before. The patterns progressed into short scenes—flashbacks of swimming in the river with Suki; arrows flying at her in the jungle; Mala shaking and scared.

Lirah swore she could hear Au's voice coming from somewhere, but it sounded muffled and distant, and she couldn't respond. She was paralyzed. Under her sealed eyelids, she was forced to passively watch random patterns and blurry clips of her past as they emerged and melted away in her mind, seamlessly blending from one image to the next.

Then, a clear scene bubbled up to the surface, taking over her brain and pushing the other nonsense to the corners. Somehow, she had felt this coming up from the depths within her. It looked different from the flashbacks. The image was so clear that she felt like she was actually there instead of watching from afar.

She could see her arms cradling her mother's head. She could feel her mother's tangled, thick hair lying in her hands. Her tears fell onto Mala's forehead. She even felt a sharp, grieving pain inside her heart.

"I love you," she heard herself say.

Her muddled, tear-filled view panned up to an open sky. She heard herself begging to it, "Why today? Why now?" She dropped her head back down in defeat. "Mala—*Mala* ... I love you, don't ... don't die."

Her mother's navy eyes parted slightly. "I won't be gone completely," she whispered. "I'll simply take on a new form ... It'll be alright, my light. It's my time to go."

Mala's eyes fell shut, and the image melted away from Lirah's mind.

CHAPTER 16

Lirah jumped up, gripping her chest like she had been trapped underwater and finally reached the surface to breathe.

"Lirah!" Au shouted. His voice quavered.

Lirah could hear him loud and clear now. He stood directly over her, his shadow blocking the angled, lowering orange ball of light. "I've been calling your name! You just lay there mumbling to yourself with your eyes closed."

"I ... I think I just had a *vision*," she said, stumbling to find the right words to describe what just happened. "It was like ... something outside of my mind ... was happening *inside* of my mind."

She clutched onto her head with both hands in an effort to stop its harsh pounding. "I felt like I was there, but it wasn't a memory ... but it felt so *real*. But—maybe—it was just the fruit. Yeah ... I've never had a vision before ... why would I have one now? And you said you could see images when you closed your eyes too."

"What did you see?" Au asked her slowly, seriously, crouching down before her, his hand on her shoulder. His enormous pupils stared down at her with concern like she was a deranged animal he needed to tread around carefully.

"Mala died."

Lirah didn't know if Au responded, because after speaking those words, everything fell silent around her again. Mala was going to die, and she had no idea where or when it would happen, and she didn't know how to prevent it.

She reconnected with her surroundings when it started to rain hard and all at once. The sky was still light, but it was pouring. The giant grazing beasts had lain down to rest. Au held his mouth wide open, catching the rain in his mouth. Lirah joined him until she wasn't thirsty anymore.

"Let's go back to Mala," she said flatly.

Au shut his mouth and began walking beside her. "Lirah, are you alright?"

"Everyone's dying. How could I be alright? Suki, Riel, Riggul, the Pride," tears welled up in her eyes, "and now Mala." The tears fell, mixing with the rain.

"Hey now, she's still here. We'll just ask her if what you experienced was a vision or not."

"No. *No way* am I telling Mala about that ... *vision* ... or whatever it was. She doesn't need to know. I'm asking her about that bizarre fruit and that's *all*."

* * *

At the heart shaped tree, Lirah and Au found Mala safe and fast asleep, oblivious to the rain splashing down on her.

Something must be in this air, something that makes you careless about everything.

"Mala, wake up!" Lirah shouted over the loud rain.

No response.

Lirah shook her.

"*Lirah*, my light. What is it?" Mala asked, only partially awake.

"You didn't wake up from the rain?" Lirah asked her, concerned.

"Oh, I did, and then I fell right back asleep. I haven't felt this relaxed in weeks." Mala yawned and stretched her arms up toward the sky. "Did you find any food? I saw you both lying on that rock earlier. I wasn't sure if you were resting because you were having trouble finding food, or if you stuffed yourselves after finding too much."

Lirah was almost embarrassed to say that, after sharing the fruit, they didn't try very hard to find food at all.

"Well…" Lirah said. "We didn't have much luck. But we found one thing. I wanted to ask you about it. Have you ever tried a juicy red fruit, about this size?" She held up her hand to represent it. "One that makes you see designs in the sky and causes everything around you to move, and even when you close your eyes you can still see images?"

Mala's face turned hard and stern. She remained silent, contemplating Lirah's words in the raucous of the rain.

Then all at once, she busted out in a fit of laughter. She laughed, and laughed, and laughed so much that when she tried to answer Lirah, she couldn't.

Lirah and Au looked at each other, dumbfounded, while Mala collected herself.

"A wabelloo fruit," Mala said simply, wiping at her eyes.

Lirah and Au had no idea what a wabelloo fruit was. They stared at Mala, waiting for more explanation.

Mala cleared her throat. "I'm sorry I laughed," she said, with sincere apology. "It's only because I can't imagine how bizarre it must have been to eat one without knowing what would happen afterwards."

"It *was* bizarre," said Lirah, growing annoyed with Mala's withholding of information. "Can you tell us a little more about what a wabelloo fruit is, *please*?"

"Lirah, you are absolutely fine, so calm down. If anything, you're lucky that you found one. They're small fruits, but they're powerful and rare," Mala said. "I once knew a woman who grew her own wabelloo fruits, back before the Pride rebuilt up in the treetops. One day, I saw her trading a small handful of them for three fat rutapugas. When I asked her how she was able to trade a few measly fruits for all that meat so easily, she explained to me why they were special. She told me that after you eat one, they make you see your surroundings in a whole new, beautiful way. They help your mind see things that you normally can't, and they heighten your consciousness and other senses too. She said she wouldn't advise eating more than a couple at a time, and I've never had one myself because of their cost, but I'm positive that eating *one* wabelloo fruit, *one* time, is completely fine. Actually, quite beneficial. You tried it too Au?" she asked.

"Yes. We shared one."

"Well, that explains why there's no food then. Wabelloo fruits take away your appetite and your urge to do much labor, if any." She giggled.

* * *

The rain began to lighten, coming down as mist now. At the same time, the remaining effects of the wabelloo fruit wore away in Lirah's mind. Hunger set in as the rain let up completely.

To make her hunger even more pressing, the rain left a new sweet smell in its wake. Pungent and edible. A different sweetness than that of the breeze. But Lirah was too exhausted to search for its source. She knelt, turning to rest against the tree beside Mala, when the smell became stronger, like it was protruding from the tree itself.

The bare trunk looked like it was slowing melting. Lirah pressed her nose up against its moist bark. Above her, a lone green bird swooped down, nibbled on the bark, and flew away. Lirah shrugged and copied the bird. She easily stripped a piece of bark from the tree. It felt muddy in her hands and the sweet smell was stronger than ever. Her mouth salivated. She took a small bite. Then another. It tasted so sweet while also slightly bitter, and very rich.

"You *have* to try this," she said, eagerly tearing off pieces for Mala and Au, who had been watching her skeptically. They accepted the muddy-looking bark and took in its sweet aroma. Au inspected it, poked at it.

Probably making sure it would've been up to Riel and Riggul's standards.

Au finally took a bite. His eyes lit up. He nodded at Mala. She took a minuscule nibble. Then she devoured the rest and held out her hands for more.

Lirah grinned and started shredding the bark from the tree in larger chunks. She handed Mala and Au a pile each before settling down to dig into her own small feast. She could feel the nutrients rushing throughout her body and veins, replenishing her.

Once the trio completely stuffed themselves with bark, they rested side by side against the stripped tree trunk. Calm and satisfied, they settled in for the night. Soon, the vibrant colors of the evening would be back, followed by the silver shards and glowing spheres.

Lirah closed her eyes, resting them before the show. Her body felt exhausted, but her mind was wide awake. She thought about what Mala said regarding the wabelloo fruit, and what that could mean regarding her horrible vision ... or whatever she had experienced.

Mala said the fruit was powerful and heightened your senses, that it made everything beautiful. Well, her vision of Mala had *not* been beautiful. It had been quite the opposite—completely tragic. Still, Lirah held onto hope that it had just been the fruit tricking her into seeing things.

But it had felt so *real.*

But it *couldn't* be.

No. No. *No.*

She had to pull herself away from the image of her mother

dying. What good would it do to relive it?

Think about anything else, she told herself.

Squished, bright red, rutapuga faces came to her mind. *Great.*

But then she remembered she actually wanted to ask Mala why her eyes had made the women's faces change overtime when she got sick.

She cleared her throat. "Mala, there's something I need to ask you."

"What is it, my light?" Mala replied, her tone soothing.

Au, who was sitting on the other side of Mala, leaned forward and gazed at Lirah with wide eyes. He let out a small cough to grab her attention.

He must think I'm bringing up the vision after I said I wouldn't.

She glanced at him and gave him the slightest shake of her head before looking into Mala's calm navy eyes. She knew she had never mentioned what she was about to say to anyone before now.

"My headaches have completely stopped since we left the jungle," Lirah said. "I've been thinking about what might have caused them and my eyesight problems—"

"Oh, that's great!" Mala interjected. "I've been meaning to ask how you've been feeling. You don't feel sick at all, anywhere?"

"No, but mother, listen."

Lirah dropped her eyes down to her lap, watching her fingers twist themselves nervously through one another. She was scared they would think she was delusional. She knew that what she was about to say *would* sound delusional, but then again ... so was the idea of having visions.

"When I was having eyesight problems, it wasn't just my vision blurring and making me dizzy. It was actually more than that. All of the women in the community ... their faces started to look like ... rutapuga faces," Lirah said, embarrassed. It sounded so much sillier when she said it out loud. "First, their skin turned pink, and overtime they became red, then scarlet. They formed snouts and had slanted eyes and yellow teeth."

She looked up, noticing Au's bewildered facial expression and Mala's attentive one.

"But!" Lirah said, speaking faster, rushing to get to her point. "But you stayed the same, and you did too, Au. So did Riel, Riggul, and Suki. Now I realize that it was only the brutes who started to *look like brutes*. Does that make sense? It got worse and worse and now that we're not around them anymore, I'm fine." She exhaled.

Au was looking at Lirah like she was dying, probably without knowing how loud his expression was speaking. But Mala looked as calm as the grasslands around them when she answered her daughter.

"I only wish you would've told me this sooner, so I wouldn't have been worried to death about your headaches. I actually know someone who experienced symptoms like the ones you've just described. They could sense others in a way that no one else could. In other words, they could see other beings' true colors ... that's how they phrased it." Mala's smile was somber as she grabbed hold of Lirah's hands. "That someone was your father."

At the sound of those words, Lirah's heart gave an excited leap.

Au let out a soft gasp.

Mala's smile grew and her eyes wrinkled into happy slits as she continued, "He could see every Pride member's true intentions. He would know instantly if a member was a true friend or someone to avoid whenever possible. As you can imagine, this ability helped him a great deal. You know, he told me that every time he saw me, I looked *iridescent* ... that I sparkled like running water when golden light hits it. That's what he said."

Lirah started to tear up, and from the sniffle coming from Mala's other side, it seemed like Au was too.

"Much later in our relationship, your father told me that the moment I smiled at him for the first time, he knew he wanted to be my Always and Forever mate. I will always remember that as the highest compliment I've ever received. He fell in love with my true colors. And it seems to me, my light, that you have this ability now too." Mala's voice cracked with emotion.

Lirah's heart fluttered. Her father was still with her. His abilities had been passed down to her. But then her heart deflated … she could only see evil. Mala didn't look iridescent to her, and Au looked the same as he always had. Her smile dropped.

Mala clearly sensed why. She squeezed onto Lirah's hands tighter and looked deep into her eyes. "My light, it's quite normal for abilities to develop overtime. You're at the age where, if you possess a special ability at all, it's just beginning to emerge and bloom inside your spirit. I started having visions when I was about your age. They were brief and not very detailed, infrequent. But the older I got and the more I realized what the visions were—actual glimpses of the future—the more I practiced and perfected my ability. I did this through speaking with spirits, because they're connected to the past, present, and future. My visions were the very reason I got involved with that practice. Only the spirits could help me plan for these flashes of images in my mind or help me to decipher what had happened in a vision after I had one." Mala smiled. "This is all so exciting, Lirah. You'll continue developing along with this ability, and who knows what else it might bring about? So don't be upset that it's not perfected yet, or that you didn't know it was time to leave Airis after the women had started to turn red. You had no idea what it meant. It's partially my fault; I never told you about your father's ability before."

"Yeah, why didn't you ever tell me about his ability before?"

"I didn't want you knowing that both of your parents had abilities and then feeling less about yourself if you didn't develop any." Mala shrugged. "I'd still think you're extraordinary either way."

"Ugh ... why can't I have powers?" Au groaned.

They all laughed.

"It's not fair," he said. "But in all seriousness, I'm really happy that you can tell if others are evil, Lirah. That's really going to help us while we're travelling. We'll know if we can trust someone, or some creature, or not."

"Very helpful indeed. So ... what *is* the plan for our travels?" Mala asked, reclining herself further back against the trunk. "I'm just here to follow while you both lead the way."

"The plan is to keep walking that way." Lirah pointed towards the sloping hills in the west. "Starting tomorrow."

* * *

The open sky burned with vibrant colors that faded just as quickly as it had ignited, making way for the silver lights to appear in groups. Lirah watched the three spheres in wonder as they brightened into exquisitely detailed worlds while she rested peacefully between Mala and Au.

Each night, the spheres were suspended in different spots and the light covering their surfaces looked slightly different, moving across them at different rates. Sometimes one was just an outline, while another looked like a sphere chopped in half. Lirah loved pondering what these phases could mean. She felt like she had entered a new phase in life herself.

She already felt profoundly different from who she used to be while living in the Treetop Society. She felt older now, permanently branded by her recent encounters with violence, deception, loss, and uncertainty of the future. She had more questions about the world now that she had been exposed to more of it. But she was gratified, nonetheless. She had made it this far with the ones she loved most, and she knew it was entirely up to them to keep pushing forward. Life was not required to provide her with any outcome in particular. It held no promises, except death. It was like what Au had said earlier:

"All we're made to do is live ... live and protect the ones that we love so that they can live too." ... "It doesn't matter where, or how, or in what conditions... We just have to keep on living together."

Lirah knew there must be more to life than *that*, even if she didn't know how it all fit together. How could that depiction of life's meaning, or lack thereof, even begin to explain love and relationships, mysterious events that seem too extraordinary to be accidents, signs that appear at just the right moment, connections between the endless assortment of plants and creatures, golden spheres in the sky, spirits, and plenty more.

But Au's view was simple. She liked that. She could put aside all of her fanciful expectations about what would be over the next hill and just breathe, knowing that she had not only accomplished 'living,' she was on a grand adventure.

CHAPTER 17

Was this all there was outside of the jungle? Grass?

The trio had travelled relentlessly, stopping only to sleep, for sixteen days now. Lirah wondered if it would ever end. She expected some sort of distinct border to suddenly reveal itself —like when they stumbled into the edge of the jungle and a completely new terrain opened up on the other side. But here, every rolling hill they hiked up only greeted them with a view of more hills sprawling far into the unforeseeable distance. The sweet smell that wafted up from the grass, which used to provide Lirah with comfort, made her nauseous every time a breeze blew by now. And she was absolutely sick of eating nothing but tree bark and relying on rain for water.

The only elements that had changed over the past several days were the lack of new sneglow herds—the name Lirah had given to the eight-legged beasts—and the colors of the grass. Bright shades of teal, aqua, green, and purple had gradually transitioned into dull hues of sapphire, steel blue, grey-green, and faded plum. At first this wasn't obvious, but over the days Lirah noticed how gloomy and dark her surroundings had grown, even though the amount of rainfall and light remained the same.

Maybe the changing grass is why the sneglows never graze over here, she thought to herself more than once. *Or maybe we'll see another herd right over the next slope and I'm just overly aware of their absence because I have too much time to think and not enough variety of life to look at.*

Thankfully, around their seventeenth day of nonstop travel, the trio was lucky enough to find and capture a small group of worm-like rodents. They had long furry bodies, similar to a trealea's, except they also had four stubby legs to help them burrow.

Mala had spotted the first one. Its squirming body was digging frantically, trying to hide itself beneath a bare tree. The group followed the burrowing rodent and Mala grabbed it by its tail and peeked inside the hole, where she found six more huddled together.

The trio celebrated, killing the rodents easily, making death as painless as possible for the little creatures. But cooking them proved harder than expected. Building a fire with the edible tree bark, the only kindling source around, was nearly impossible. The fire refused to light, and when it did it constantly dwindled away. Au tried tossing in handfuls of grass to keep it going, but violent screams issued from the blades like they were being tortured, so he quickly stopped using that tactic. After several hours of roasting the rodents over dying flames, they were finally edible, but tasted terrible.

After that, the trio never saw another squirming creature again. With their malnutrition and apparent lack of progress, they had all grown more tense and high strung by the day. Lirah constantly found herself annoyed at anything Au and Mala said or did. Every time one of them simply coughed, hummed, or mentioned the weather, Lirah cringed. Even the way they chewed on the tree bark drove her insane.

She could *not* go on like this forever. She knew she wanted more from life than living for the sake of it. *Living for the sake of it* translated to there was *no other point.*

Life is about seeking, learning, and pushing through obstacles until a better way of living is attained, Lirah believed.

That's why she hadn't been content living in the Treetop Society, and that's why she was growing restless here. She knew Au couldn't argue with this perspective either. His actions proved it. He was just as eager to keep exhaustedly pushing up and over every hill. He had even said, before eating the wabelloo fruit, that he wanted to find a community and have a family.

Thinking about the meaning of life, Lirah decided, was like entering a constantly changing maze with an endless number of routes, none of which seemed completely right or wrong, making it inescapable. And it was driving her crazy. She blamed Au for bringing up the topic of life's meaning in the first place after he had eaten the fruit and said that all they were made to do was stay alive.

Or maybe her short temper stemmed from something else, something more subconscious. New fears she didn't want to speak of.

Every morning for the past five days or so, Lirah woke up with the same odd feeling that they were being watched, and it wasn't because of the blinking grass. Each time, she jumped up from her sleep and frantically looked around, only to find nothing abnormal. She'd tell herself that she was only being paranoid, push her fears to the back of her mind, and think about more sophisticated things. Throughout the day, her innate fears would return, periodically nagging her. She'd push them away again and again.

Currently, the sky was fading to indigo, right on schedule, as the trio stopped at another barren tree for the night. Tonight, it was Au's turn to guard first.

Lirah requested that they start taking guard shifts again, right after her feelings of paranoia set in. Nobody argued.

"Au, I can guard for a while," Mala said. "You look exhausted."

"It's alright. I prepared myself for this." Au yawned. "I've had a pit in my stomach for days. I didn't want to worry either of you ... but I think something's stalking us. I can feel it."

"I know," said Mala, unemotionally. "And if it finally shows itself, I'll wake you up right away. You both are the ones who should be well rested if we need to fight it."

Au blinked. He looked at Lirah. She nodded.

They all knew.

"I wonder what it is. It could be ... no. It's not a brute still stalking us ... couldn't be ..." Au trailed off.

"No. This doesn't feel personal. Hunger is most likely its motive." Mala motioned for Au to hand over his spear. "It's behaving so patiently, whatever it is. It's waiting for just the right moment to attack so that it won't have to work as hard to get us, which means it must be weak too."

Au passed his spear uneasily to Mala and lay down beside Lirah, who had closed her eyes but couldn't sleep. Her nagging mind escalated into full on tormenting her now that she knew she wasn't just paranoid or going crazy from this atmosphere. Something really was stalking them. But these grasslands had a way about relaxing you, and against her own will, she fell asleep before her mind could draw up any more chilling ideas about what this 'something' could be.

* * *

Light. Again. Day eighteen of wandering.

Lirah woke up tense and almost wished their stalker had revealed itself last night. At this point, she figured her anxiety about the looming attack probably felt worse than the attack *itself* would. Of course, she didn't *want* her and her loved ones to be ambushed, have to fight, and possibly die, but she knew their stalker would reveal itself eventually. How big could it be anyway? If it was able to hide in this short grass and needed to wait until they looked weak enough to attack? She wanted to get it over with.

Not to mention her current anxiety brought other horrible images back into her mind too.

Suki falling in the distance. An arrow buried in her back.

Riggul's face hovering over her own. The life leaving his eyes.

Qualisiun's black hooded eyeholes. The pain of her burn bracelet.

Why did these horrible things have to happen? There couldn't possibly be a higher purpose for why her faithful friends had to die young, but evil Qualisiun got to live and torture Pride members well after his skin had formed wrinkles.

He's probably dead now, Lirah told herself. On the account of even *more* evil. The brutes. *Life is not required to provide any outcome in particular, it holds no promises, except death.*

When she thought of this statement she tumbled back down into the maze inside her mind. *Ugh. Then why can I see other's true colors? And why does Mala have visions that help save us? And why is Au the most naturally gifted problem solver I know? Are we special? Or are talents dispersed to babies at random?*

Lirah pulled down on the skin under her eyes. *Stop thinking about this.*

"Come out stalker!" Lirah shouted abruptly. "COME OUT!"

Au, freshly awoken, climbed the bare tree branches and searched the area. Nothing.

"Let's keep moving," he said, rubbing his eyes and sighing deeply. He climbed down the tree and plopped onto the soft grass.

Halfway through a typical day of silent irritation for Lirah, it began to rain. A lot. Usually, it was pretty hard to tell when it was going to rain in the grasslands because there were always clouds in the sky. Somedays, the clouds gave in and let go their entire water supply. Other days, they sprinkled just enough to make you want more. And sometimes they greedily held onto all of it.

Lirah wanted to feel grateful for this rain, but it was coming down hard and loud, clouding her vision and her hearing. If something wanted to attack them in secret, now would be the time.

That's when she saw it. Something lying in the grass ahead. A large, looming body blurred by the rain.

She ran towards it, leaving Au and Mala shouting at her back.

"Where are you going?"

"What do you see?"

"Lirah come back!"

She ignored them. They were annoying her. How did they not see this body? She had to kill this thing. It was killing her mind.

Lirah sprinted at the massive creature, spear overhead, and stabbed its back with as much force as she could muster before it could notice her and retaliate.

She stood over the motionless body, tired and woozy from running, when a shock ran up her arm. Another pained her shoulder, and another her leg. Viscous shocks ravaged her whole body. Was something biting her? In this hard of rain? She brushed at her skin and jumped around. The sensations didn't stop. If anything, they grew more intense. But she couldn't see anything on her skin. From Mala and Au's perspective, it must have looked like she broke out in a strange dance to celebrate her kill.

Her mind screamed at her to run away, but her body felt so, *so* unbelievably tired. She walked sleepily back towards Au and Mala, being bitten all the way. Small red lumps formed all over her body. She had given up on brushing them off, whatever they were. She didn't have extra energy to expend. Then, right as she slumped before Mala and Au, the biting and electrifying sensations stopped.

"Stop ..." Lirah moaned. "They ... stopped?"

"You left your spear in the body!" Au scolded her. "What are you doing? What's wrong with you today?" He jogged away, towards the body to retrieve the spear.

"No. Don't. *Bites*," Lirah warned. But he couldn't hear her tired mumbles over the rain.

Au ripped the spear out of the creature and circled around it, assessing its face and limbs. That's when he started jumping. He swiped at his legs, his arms, his hair, and his crotch. He started to run but instantly fell. He stumbled to get up, yawned, stood, then fell again. He scratched at his body as he crawled back to Lirah and Mala, dragging his spear along the wet ground beside him.

He yawned at Lirah's feet. "Sneglows. A baby and a mother."

"What?" Lirah asked.

"You speared ... a mama." He heaved, spitting out wet grass and slowly regaining his footing. "Laying by her baby."

"That body does *not* have the same coloring as the coat of a sneglow," said Mala. "That body is grey."

"Well, it is one," Au said. "Looks like they've been dead for a while."

"Wait. What happened to your *skin*?" Mala petted Au's arm, then Lirah's face.

Lirah shrugged. "Shocks. Or bites." She felt so sleepy, she just wanted Mala to keep petting her face.

Au nodded wearily, his shoulders sagging, knees wobbling.

They yawned in unison.

Mala looked at them in horror. She looked down and gasped. Lirah and Au slowly followed her gaze.

There was the border Lirah had been longing for. *Sort of*.

A distinct, thin line of navy grass separated the area where Lirah and Au had been shocked from the area they were standing in now. They looked down at the faded plum grass, smushed and wet with rain under their feet. The grass that the dead sneglows were laying on was somehow even duller, coming in waves of grey and brown.

Lirah gazed up and down the navy line. It went on endlessly, running from north to south. She carelessly stepped over it, partially out of curiosity and partially because her mind was still disoriented from the shocks. She felt like she had been given a large dose of chomomull sedatives.

"Stop, Lirah!" Mala tried pulling her daughter back over the line.

"I'm just seeing," Lirah groggily shook her mother's arm away, "what happens."

At first, nothing occurred. Then, all at once, the shocks returned. It was like tiny warriors had detected her, made their way up her limbs, and were stabbing at her to defend their territory.

This must have been how the sneglows died.

But even though she was in a lot of pain, she didn't try to fight the tiny warriors. She rocked woozily on her toes, yawned, and faceplanted in the grass. The top half of her body fell over the line and back on the safe side, while her bottom half remained on the deadly side. Her face and shoulders no longer felt like they were under attack, but her bottom half was on *fire*.

Au and Mala dragged her entirely over to the safe side, turning her over so that she was laying on her back. Lirah opened her eyes. Her mother and partner looked fuzzy, slanted, and shifted around in wonky circular patterns. They called out to her, asked if she was okay, told her that she was crazy. But she was too tired to answer. She simply opened her mouth and let the rain fall in. Her enflamed body throbbed like it was filling up with poison, but the cool rain helped. She felt Au shake her body. She saw Mala reaching down to slap her face. It looked like she had three hands. She felt the impact of a hand hitting her cheek.

"Leave me alone." Lirah groaned. "You're *annoying*." She closed her eyes and fell asleep.

CHAPTER 18

Murderous screams came from behind Lirah. She sat up and shifted around. Her brain, which felt like mush slopping around in her skull, tried to recenter itself.

What is going on? When did I fall asleep? How much time has passed? She asked herself as she rubbed her eyes and flickered them open.

Through the rain she could see Mala. High up in the air. Screaming.

Neon green ooze was dripping down onto Mala's petrified face. Fanged jaws were opened wide, salivating above her forehead.

The jaws were that of a translucent snake. It was massive and had reared up in the air, wrapping Mala in its dense body.

Their stalker.

It had to be thirty feet long, with dense clear scales covering its entire body like invisible armor. The colors of the dull grass showed through its scales effortlessly. No wonder they couldn't spot this predator before.

The snake's emerald-green pupils grew, the color matching

the ooze salivating from its mouth. It widened its jaws further, lowered its head, and hovered closer to the face of its long sought-after meal. Mala.

Lirah couldn't believe this was actually happening. She thought she must be dreaming. Her mother was fine, surely.

Lirah panned her eyes away from the beast's towering face and down to the ground.

There was Au, standing directly below it, continuously jamming a spear into its scales. He looked like a puny speck compared to the serpent.

The beast's scales were too thick to crack. Still, Au's efforts were helping keep Mala alive. Each time Au jabbed at the beast, it lifted its head and hissed, momentarily backing off from its mission—ripping Mala's head off.

"*Argg! Argg!*" Au grunted with rage each time he stabbed at the snake

Mala's deafening screams progressed. They had turned into "Lirahhhhh! *Liraahhh*!"

Maybe, she thought, *this is real.*

She stood, foggy headed, and ran over to Au. Her body was sore and heavy, like her skin was filled with poison.

"Lirah! *Argg!* Finally! I'm trying— *Argg!*—to lead it—*Argg!*—over the navy line!" Au said between jabs. "Help me! Jab it! *Hurry*!"

Lirah found the other spear and joined him.

They thrusted and stabbed at the serpent's lower half over and over and over. Each time, it moved slightly closer to the navy line. Finally, the tip of its tail crossed over to the dark side.

"Keep stabbing! Don't stop!" Au commanded.

"We can't pass over the line too!"

"Just keep stabbing!"

The snake did not want to budge any further. It clearly knew what crossing over the navy line entailed.

Maybe it doesn't realize the tip of its tail passed over already. Are its scales really too thick to feel the shocks?

Apparently not. Just then, the beast let out a deafening hiss.

It turned its head around to assess its tail and away from Mala's slime-covered face.

Lirah kept stabbing, harder and harder, squinting through the heavy rain, pushing the beast further back over the line, trying her best not to cross over it herself.

The massive snake, still reared up off solid ground, loosened its grip on Mala and sent her falling from twenty feet in the air. It caught her again around ten feet up, smushing her face inside its coiled lower half.

Lirah's toes burned. She had crossed over the threshold.

She grew sleepy, but she kept stabbing at the impenetrable scales before her. "You won't kill my mother! Not today!"

The serpent let out a piercing shriek.

The tiny shocks must have found a way beneath its scales and attacked its sensitive flesh directly, Lirah thought. *Nice.*

The snake tried to squirm its tail away from the microscopic predators and back towards the spears. But snakes weren't built to move quickly while they were reared up. Lirah knew it would have to drop Mala before it could successfully slither away from the painful grass. She could see Mala's face buried down inside the snake's translucent coiled body, suffocating.

Lirah panicked, provoking the beast with a new fury. It was all she knew how to do in order to save Mala. Even when the snake dipped its head low and snapped at her spear, her face, or Au's face, Lirah kept stabbing. Green ooze splattered her face. It burned. Her muscles burned. Her skin burned. *Everything burned.*

Lirah started to circle the beast while she stabbed at it so it couldn't snap at her as easily, without realizing her whole body had crossed over to the deadly side.

She felt a tingle on her toe. The sensation moved up her limbs and quickly advanced into attacking, shocking, and intensely biting her entire body. She felt her eyes involuntarily closing again. No. *No*. Not now. She dropped her spear and fell to the ground, managing to part her eyes open slightly.

"*Arrrgggg*!" She saw Au stab at the beast so hard that he sent it back a whole yard. It was well over the line now. He backed away from it, looking down, making sure that he was still planted on the safe side.

The snake shrieked and dropped Mala, sending her tumbling down. She rolled limply over to the safe side. Lirah sighed a breath of relief and dragged herself over the barrier like a wounded creature, legs immobile.

The serpent slanted its angry emerald eyes at Au, lowered its head down to the grass, and slithered to Mala's limp body.

It was nearly invisible now, with its entire body resting against a single background and blending with the grass. Lirah could hardly make out its fluid movements. All she could see were its eyes. Then it opened its mouth, and she could see its oozing fangs. They were heading straight for Au.

"Au! *Watch out*! *Move*!" Lirah screamed, though she wasn't sure if any sound had actually come out of her mouth.

Au didn't step aside. Instead, he sprinted at the beast slithering towards him. He held his spear over his shoulder, pointing it at the snake's open mouth. A tender, unarmored spot.

But the snake appeared to have caught on to Au's tactic. It closed its wide jaws right before its throat was about to collide with Au's spear. Lirah watched powerlessly as the snake swiveled its head to the side and swung its tail forward to sweep Au from his feet.

It was too slow. The snake's head swayed drunkenly and collapsed on the ground with a reverberating thud.

Au's spear pierced the snake's nostril, and blue blood poured from its eye sockets. Au stepped forward, digging his spear as deep as it would go through the snake's nostril and down into its mouth.

Lirah sighed an exhausted breath of relief. She turned to look for Mala and tell her that the snake was dead. But she wasn't where Lirah had watched her land after the snake dropped her.

Lirah crawled around and looked for her.

She discovered her mother's limp legs hanging over the line, getting bitten on the dark side while she remained unconscious.

Lirah stood through her pain, gasping as she pulled her mother's small body over to the safe side. How did she not notice this sooner? *When the snake trampled over Mala it must have moved her again*, she thought, pressing her head against Mala's chest. She couldn't tell if it was still rising and falling. Mala's breathing was very light.

Lirah crawled to her mother's head and pressed her hands against Mala's faded cheeks. "Mala don't die. You can't ..."

Au limped over, splattered head-to-toe in goopy blue blood. He tossed his equally bloody spear aside and felt for a pulse in Mala's neck.

The rain began lightening up. The clouds remained dark.

"Au, I think this is what I saw ... after eating the wabelloo fruit ..."

"Lirah—"

"What are we going to do?"

"Lirah, she's breathing. It's alright."

The serpent shook abruptly behind them.

They turned around. Au reached for his spear.

The snake fell once more and became very still, as if the motion had been a release of the last bit of life it had left inside, and now it was fully at peace.

Lirah and Au turned and faced Mala's body again. Her wrinkly, torn up body. Her *live* body. Lirah cried, slouching over her mother. She frantically brushed Mala's tangled hair with her fingertips and whispered her favorite mantras to her.

They sat like that for a while, regaining their energy.

"Mala's lucky she passed out," Au said, breaking the silence. "I think that's what saved her from dying during her fall or when she got trampled. Back in the Pride, I was told that when you're passed out your body is more malleable, less rigid. It can handle more strain when it's not resisting."

"Well, that's good," Lirah sniffled. "But what do we do now? How do we wake her up?"

"We can only wait," Au said, elevating Mala's head up on their sack of dwindling resources like it was a pillow. "Let's collect water before the rain completely stops. Then stock up on bark."

Lirah definitely had *not* been thinking about collecting resources. They just killed their thirty-foot-long stalker, Mala was lying unconscious, *and* they were sitting next to a border that held death on the other side if they wandered over it for too long. If those microscopic warriors could kill an obscenely massive sneglow and the giant serpent, they would easily be able to kill Au, Mala, and her.

Lirah stood and paced from north to south, eyeing the sinister, dark grass that spanned in all directions besides to the east. The way they had come. "Where are we going to go?" she asked, more to herself than to Au. "We can't cross that line. And there's no other way to pass."

Au wasn't paying her any attention. He held open a water skin, collecting what little rain was left falling with diligence, his tongue sticking out with concentration.

Lirah rolled her eyes. Who was Au kidding? This was the end of the line. They were left for dead ... life's only promise. They may as well have been killed by the snake.

The snake. Its scales.

Scales that were impenetrable to our spears. The snake hadn't been fazed by the microscopic creatures in the same way that we had ... because of its *scales.* Scales that provided an extra line of defense before the tiny warriors could manage to burrow their way onto the tender skin that held them in place.

Could Mala, Au, and herself cut the scales off the serpent and use them to cross the dark grass? Yes! How long would that journey take? Lirah didn't know. But what she did know was that sneglows travelled in herds. A herd must have ventured through that grass recently, and most of them had passed through quickly enough to live. So, this deadly stretch of land couldn't go on for *too long*.

Lirah hypothesized that the dead baby sneglow Au saw was the only one in the herd that didn't have the strength to go on, and its mother refused to leave its side. That kind of behavior happened all the time in the jungle.

Or maybe that scenario didn't happen at all. Maybe the baby ignorantly ran past the border on its own, without its herd, and the mother followed it over.

Lirah liked the sound of the first scenario better. If the latter had occurred, the mother would have been strong enough to save her baby.

"Au!" She called out, pacing over to him. He had moved on from collecting water to stripping bark from the closest barren tree. Its branches were twisted up in a fancy braid. "I know how we can cross the dark side. We can use the snake's scales as steppingstones."

Au stopped stripping the bark, turned, and gave her a peculiar look, "Can you read my mind?"

"What?" She laughed. "No. You're joking right?"

"Well, I know you have other powers." He winked. "And I was about to come over and tell you the same idea."

Lirah let out an amused snort. "We think alike, huh?"

"Yeah. We make a good team."

The partners rubbed noses and went to work. They used two knives from their sack of resources to cut the snake's thin flesh and meticulously pull up its dense scales. Luckily, the scales weren't exactly sharp. Just heavy and very invisible.

Mala regained consciousness somewhere in between Lirah sawing off her third scale and losing sight of it, and Au deciding to paint over the invisible scales in the snake's own, bright blue blood.

As the partners sat there smearing the scales in blue, Mala sat up and said, "I wondered when you were going to think to paint those."

"Mala!" Lirah dropped her dripping scale and dove into her mother's arms. "We knew you would wake up! We knew you just needed your rest. Don't worry, we weren't ignoring you."

"I know, my light," Mala stroked her daughter's hair. "So, we're crossing this death trap, I presume?"

Lirah nodded.

"There better be someplace good for us out there ..." Mala whispered, though she said it like she already knew the answer.

CHAPTER 19

Lirah, Au, and Mala decided to wait until they were absolutely prepared before crossing over the border and into the deadly, eyeless side of the grass.

Something in that grass not only had the power to kill with painful force, but whatever exuded from it (pheromones or toxins of some sort) caused extreme drowsiness too.

A deadly duo.

Using the scales as steppingstones would help the trio cross without pain. But they needed durable coverings for their mouths and noses to prevent them from breathing in ... whatever the fumes were.

It didn't seem like the fumes could sink through skin, but they could travel by air. Sweet wind lifted the invisible sedatives and pushed them around, far beyond the border where the dark grass ended.

That would explain why we all feel so relaxed in the grasslands. Even miles away from this spot, Lirah thought.

Mala peeled long strips of skin from the serpent's body and hung them over the bare tree branches, letting them dry out like wet dress cloths. "We'll tie these strips around our faces," she said. "Gross? Yes. But thick, stretchy, and better than death."

Au and Lirah cut chunks of meat from the beast, which luckily turned from clear to white once it detached from its source. But the trio had just as much trouble starting a fire here as they had back with the burrowing rodent-worms.

They sat patiently and tried again and again until eventually they were able to start a fire, cook the meat, and fill themselves with the surprisingly delicious roasted snake. They hung thin, leftover strips of it along tree branches to dehydrate and store it for more consistent meals over the next few days.

* * *

By the third day of doing nothing but eating and sleeping, and with the relief of knowing their stalker was dead, the trio was much happier and looked much healthier. The serpent had provided their first hardy food option since leaving the jungle, and they were stuffed with it. Even though only a few days had passed, the difference was tremendous. The dark circles around Mala's eyes were gone and the bruises on her arms from where the snake had coiled itself around her were healing properly. Lirah felt less irritable, and she could tell her ribs were filling out already. And Au looked … gorgeous. Lirah couldn't help but stare at him. The meat had filled his body with all the right nutrients. He had bulked up and his skin was glowing under the midday light.

Now that they were all full of energy, they decided it was time to test out the durability of the scales against the dark side of the grass. Au volunteered to take on the painful work while Lirah tracked how long he could stand the discomfort.

"Okay, let's review one more time," Lirah said to Au as the trio approached the edge of the dark border. "You stand on a scale and call out when you feel a tingle, or even just the slightest feeling of the little warriors on you. Then, call out again when the bites travel up your feet and get too painful to stand still."

Au nodded.

"Ready?" Lirah asked.

"Ready." Au placed a blue dyed scale over the line and stepped on it.

Lirah counted, "1 … 2 … 3 … 4 … 5 … 6 … 7 … 8—"

"*Tingle!*"

"10 … 11 … 12 … 13 … 14 … 15 … 16 … 17 … 18—"

"Okay, okay, it's starting to *hurt*." He stepped off the scale, picked it up, and walked back over the border.

"I wonder what will happen when you lift the scale and place it in a different spot before stepping on it again, rather than staying still for a full twenty seconds," Mala suggested. "I wonder if it will always take the same amount of time for the shocking creatures to detect the scale, or if they'll detect it faster because you're already close by."

"We'll see." Au picked up another scale in their pile. He laid it on the dark side and stepped on. He called out when he felt a tingle, placed a second scale down in front of him, hopped on, and picked up the scale behind him.

"*Ouch*! My hands." He instinctually shook the scale out in front of him before placing it down and stepping on. "Hm, that worked. I think I shook the creatures off."

He turned, picked up the scale behind him, shook it, and placed it down again. He continued on like this for a few more paces before turning around and crossing back over to the safe side. He was completely unharmed, except for a throbbing pain in his hands from grabbing the contaminated stepping-scales.

The trio tested the different shaking and standing methods a few more times with Lirah and Mala also taking turns on the scales. They concluded that they could all stand on a scale comfortably for an average of ten seconds with minimal tingling, but once they hit twenty seconds it would get painful. Longer than thirty seconds and the pain would become unbearable.

For lifting and shaking the scales in between steps, the trio determined that the microscopic creatures would continue to shock their hands until they shook the scale twice. That got most of the tiny warriors off, but three shakes really did the trick. Then, when they laid the freshly shaken scale down, the creatures always had to redetect it. But Mala said she didn't want to waste so much energy lifting *and* shaking the scales after every step she took. She dried out more snakeskin for them to tie around their palms to protect against the leftover warriors when they scooped up the scales.

That evening, they celebrated. They danced and swayed beneath a colorful sky and light rain, relishing in their intelligence and determination to overcome their obstacles. Their experiments ensured that they would be able to trek across the dark grass with minimal harm if they had the willpower to refrain from stopping for no more than thirty seconds at a time. For the *entire* journey. Despite her rejoicing, nervousness crept inside Lirah's stomach, especially concerning her mother's endurance.

But that night, as the clear sky faded to indigo and the silver shards came out to play as they always did, they seemed to shine extra brilliantly to Lirah. Maybe the spirits were trying to assure her that the end of this tiresome excursion was near. That beyond the dark grass there would be an oasis. She told herself that she just needed to hold on a little longer.

Lirah wanted to believe these lights in the sky carried signs for her, like her mother so entirely believed in spirits. She wanted to believe something *Out There* really did care about her life's outcome. So, she did. Even if this confidence only lasted for a moment. Lirah looked up and thanked the lights above her. Then she requested that there be no more massive serpents in their future, please.

* * *

From an outsider's perspective, maybe a bird flying overhead, it probably looked like Lirah, Au, and Mala were playing a game. They were all standing in a line, amusing themselves with two blue-smothered scales each. Balancing on one scale while placing down the other, stepping forward, turning around to grab the one behind, and repeating. All with dried snakeskin wrapped around their mouths, noses, and palms. They looked like bandits.

At first, this progression really did feel like a game to Lirah. Several hours in the appeal had disappeared.

Her arms had grown weak from lifting and dropping the heavy scales over and over again. She couldn't imagine how her petite mother must feel, even with the extra energy from their days of bulking and rest. At least they had two filled waterskins, thanks to the light rainfall last night, but they didn't know how long they would need this supply to last.

Lirah requested a break. She reached for the sack slung across Au's back. He carefully removed it and passed it to her. She grabbed a water skin and pulled her snakeskin bandana down to her neck so she could drink, trying not to breathe as she did so. She swallowed and quickly lifted her bandana back up, passing the water to the others. She picked up her scale and moved it forward once, restarting her silent countdown to track how long she had until the invisible warriors shocked her again. She waited for the others to finish drinking, wiped at her forehead under the intense light, and gazed ahead at their upcoming path.

It was still fairly early in the day. They had a long time before light would inevitably disappear. She had no idea how they would travel through the night in this manner. Well, she had *some* idea. They would have to keep moving. They couldn't touch the ground to rest, and the three spheres were bright enough to guide them. Though, in the dark, picking up the scales, placing them down, and safely stepping on them would be much more difficult.

Luckily, they wouldn't have to do that. The sign that the sky had given to Lirah last night—the beaming lights, the spirits' delight, whatever it had been—had proven true. Soon, Lirah spotted an area, new and bright.

More grass, yes, but this didn't surprise her. And the barren trees that took on intriguing, twirling forms were still sporadically spread out. But instead of green, blue, or purple varieties of grass, light yellow patches spanned far off in the distance, covering a predominantly flat orange land. The patches of grass ahead reminded Lirah of the speckles covering a chara cat. And she swore she could make out flowers from here too. She hadn't seen any since her days in the jungle. Spikey green stalks acted like thrones for large blue flowers resting majestically on top, and many bushes with orange leaves and yellow flowers were scattered around.

"Look!" Mala pointed at the pleasant sight ahead.

Lirah cheered, ignoring the tingling that had started to travel up her toes and feet. A sweet breeze rushed over her. She hoped she would never have to smell that sickening sweetness again.

"We'll make it there within a couple of hours if we hurry," Au said.

They hooted and howled, but not at all how the brutes howled at them back in the jungle. These howls were the calls of discovery, not terror. The trio picked up their scales and started moving forward with a newborn sense of enthusiasm that none of them had felt in a long time.

* * *

Lirah's final step across the border and onto hard land (that wouldn't shock her) felt like her first step into a new life. Au and Mala joined her, then they tossed the heavy scales that had served their purpose aside and stretched their free arms into the fresh warm air.

They had most of the afternoon left to explore this new terrain before the evening lightshow began. They trekked on, exuberant with having overcome the deadly dark grasslands and high on newfound hope.

This new land was predominantly orange dirt, and without much grass covering the ground there were minimal places for insects to hide. Au discovered that they could walk up to any of the withering bushes, shake them, and insects of all sizes would come crawling out. Some larger bushes even had small rodent-worms resting in them like the ones from the grasslands, except lighter in color.

The group snacked on the insects they found in silence, sucking their juices slowly to keep themselves preoccupied and hydrated. They stabbed whatever rodent-worms they could find and stored them in the sack for a future meal. They hardly spoke in order to save their diminishing water supply, and they didn't eat any of the neon flowering plants in fear that they were poisonous. Au pointed at the plants and shook his head violently, dramatically gesturing with his hands around his neck that they could kill you.

Riel and Riggul probably educated him that those colors are fatal.

Some elements of this new terrain reminded Lirah of the grasslands, though thankfully not its smell. This dry region didn't smell like much of anything, and it was completely flat, not hilly. But the colored mist in the sky remained the same—peach, creamy pink, and a touch of yellow.

Lirah grew excited when they passed a herd of larger creatures. They looked like sneglows grazing on seldom tufts of dull grass and flicking their tails back and forth. They were colored orange and yellow, like the land around, and were significantly shorter than the sneglows in the grasslands. They had six legs each, instead of eight, but were just as cute and clumsy with their curved horns and funny hairstyles. After that sight, Lirah hoped other creatures would reveal themselves, mainly creatures like *her*. But there were still no signs of proper shelters or communities out here.

Probably because this area is just as exposed as the grasslands.

She wouldn't want to settle here either. It was hot. Very hot. And she was thirsty. She didn't know if it was best to conserve the water or to hydrate herself now before it was too late. She didn't know when it would rain again. Her anxiety surrounding their water supply was building when she happened upon another small rodent-worm. It had its head buried in the spikey base of a neon flowering plant, one that Au had assumed was deadly. The rodent-worm was tearing out tiny mouthfuls of the soft, dribbling pulp inside.

Lirah bent down to look more closely at the jellylike substance. She tried to clear her dry throat. It felt like sandpaper. "Hey Au. These rodents are eating the flowering plants. Couldn't we try them?"

Au stopped and assessed the plant, sending the rodent dashing off. He touched the gooey, milky pulp, then dabbed some on his tongue. "You're right. The base seems fine." He coughed. "Just don't eat the flower."

Mala leaned over him and pulled the plant from the ground, keeping her fingers away from its randomly dispersed, protruding spikes. Its tiny roots dripped with the cool milky liquid.

Then, using the small, sharpened rocks from their sack, the trio broke open the plant's thick exterior and ate the hydrating, slightly bitter jelly inside, just as the creature had done. The sandpaper feeling in Lirah's throat was momentarily quenched. Relief rushed through her.

"Let's stock up," she said.

They gathered up as many of the plants as they could, shaving off their spikes and buds before storing them in the sack. The farther they looked into the flat distance, the less striking neon bulbs they saw. Even the dried tangled bushes seemed to diminish in quantity.

* * *

The next three days blended together. Lirah's surroundings, and her thoughts, seemed to cycle, looping around like the ball of light above her. She didn't care to ponder the all-consuming maze that was the *Meaning of Life*. She constantly daydreamed about the different kinds of communities she may stumble into. She imagined all the ways they could look, dress, and the rules and customs they might follow. She smiled when her favorite imaginary community came up in the rotation. Every member had draping colorful clothes, and warm eyes surrounded with laugh lines. In truth, all their faces looked like Mala's. The smiling leader always welcomed them with open arms, handed them towers of food and water, and provided them with cool baths and stable shelters.

Lirah remembered, back in the jungle, when she would daydream about a society with luxuries that she couldn't even fathom, one that allowed free thinking and had helpful rules, not commands. Now, she primarily wanted *any* sane community to feed and bathe her, and she wanted proof that the jungle wasn't the only place where societies could thrive.

The lack of life that Mala, Au, and she had found in the grasslands still shocked her. At first, it seemed like the most glorious and promising place in the world. Its colors, mild breeze, sweet smells, and herds of sneglows all seemed like good signs that there would be more life there. So, what was she expecting to come of this orange, dwindling, *already* uninviting terrain? Would they ever find an ideal place to settle?

Not that these questions mattered much. They had to keep going through the dirt and brush. They had nowhere else to go but forward.

On their fourth day in this unpromising environment,

Lirah noticed they were no longer occasionally passing herds of six-legged sneglows, or bushes full of insects and rat-worms. And the neon flowering plants had fully disappeared yesterday. Her feet were numb, and she wanted to collapse just like her surroundings had. Cracked orange clay and broken rocks spanned in every direction.

All morning and afternoon, like each day prior, Lirah, Mala, and Au trudged wordlessly through the endless dust and dirt, leaving a wake of billowing orange dust behind them. They sucked on the last of the hydrating roots and plant guts they had. Both of their water skins were empty. Their bodies sweated out the small amounts of liquid they had left faster than they could refill themselves. It was worse as light approached its zenith for the day; it grew to be the time they dreaded most.

They desperately needed rain. They hadn't received any since the evening before they crossed over the dark side of the grass. But the cloudless sky didn't seem to care.

Life didn't care.

Lirah's feet were numb and blistered. Her dress cloths were soaked in sweat and coated in a layer of orange grime. She had never felt so weak. Her body ached and her arms hung limp. Her head felt light. Ideas floated around but couldn't stick together. Walking had become automatic.

She wanted to rest. Yes—that's what she wanted to do.

This was a nice spot.

Lirah sat down in the orange dirt.

Au and Mala stopped above her, their shadows covering her in a nice shade. Mala let out a helpless sigh.

"What are ... you doing?" Au asked with great effort.

Lirah looked up at him.

Through her muddled vision she noticed that his eyes had sunken deep into his face, which was completely coated in orange dirt. The pieces of skin showing through looked blistered and red. His cheek bones were defined, and his ribs were protruding while his stomach had concaved. She turned her gaze to Mala, who somehow looked even worse than Au. Her beaded, straggly black hair was covered in dirt and matted down over her hollow eyes, making her look more like a hairy creature than a mother. Her skin was blistered and very wrinkled, aging quickly out in the desert heat. Her lips were cracked open and bloody. Her petite, frail body swayed where she stood, like something was holding her up and threatened to send her toppling over at any moment.

Lirah didn't want to look at them anymore. It was too sad. How consistently needy their bodies were, demanding more and more resources on this unpredictable journey. Not even a week ago they were filled with meat and rainwater, their bodies glowing and minds sharp. Now, they were dying. The weight they had put on from the snake meat had melted away just as fast as they had gained it.

"I'm going to sleep," Lirah said.

"You can't. We need," Au coughed, "find shelter."

"There's none," Lirah said, laying on her back and closing her eyes.

"My light. You can't … give up.," Mala wheezed.

"Let's turn … back," Lirah mumbled sleepily.

"And cross … dark grass? We threw … scales. *Can't*," Au said angerly, exerting so much effort that he dropped down next to Lirah.

"I want … jungle …" Lirah smiled to the sky. "I feel mist. The river. Yes. Let's go there …"

Mala knelt on wobbly knees and sat on the other side Lirah. "If we stayed there," she gulped, grabbing hold of Lirah's knee, "we would … be dead … already."

Lirah wasn't listening. She was busy floating in the river, bobbing up and down. She had already made it back somehow. She had her eyes closed and her arms sprawled out, letting the crystal-clear water sink into her blistered skin and heal her body.

"Lirah … Lirah," she could hear her name coming from the sky.

Leave me alone, she thought.

She wanted to go underwater and get away from the nagging. She tried dunking her head farther under. It wouldn't budge. A hard blow stung her cheek.

"Hey!" She sat up, opening her eyes to the searing light above, clutching her face. "Why'd you ... *ouch* ... hit me... so *hard*?" She glared at Au as she slouched back down into the dirt.

But it was Mala who answered, "I had to. You can't ... fall asleep."

"Why?"

"You'll die. We're ... overheated."

"And have ... nowhere ... to go." Au sighed. "Trapped ..." He squinted into the distance.

All directions held the same flat, orange nothingness. Wind didn't even come here.

The group sat in silence, taking in their defeat, growing used to the idea of a deep sleep. They were going to die, and they felt strangely at peace about it.

CHAPTER 20

"We should … list … all … we're grateful for." Mala wheezed. "Think happy thoughts … before we …"

So, they did. Laying side by side, Lirah, Au, and Mala took turns listing things they appreciated in their lives.

Mala said she was grateful for her own courage, which she had passed down to her daughter, as that was what had gotten them this far. Au said he was thankful that he got to see what was beyond the jungle with his loved ones, and that he was sure they were some of the only beings to ever see this land. Lirah said she was grateful that Au had chosen her to be his partner all those years ago, and that after everything she had put him through, he had still chosen to run away with her.

Mala started the cycle again, saying that she was grateful for her ability to see the future, even if her powers had subsided recently due to exhaustion. Lirah remembered her vision, or whatever it had been, of her mother dying. That meant it was about time for her to cradle her mother's head in her arms. Except she didn't feel the same way she had felt during the vision. In the vision, she was bubbling over with a mixture of grief and love, but right now she felt nothing but overheated. She concluded that she never had a vision at all. She was right before. It had just been the effects of the wabelloo fruit.

"Lirah, it's your turn." Au coughed.

"Oh ... I'm thankful for ... Mala. The best ... mother."

"Good one." Lirah barely heard Au whisper.

They let the quietness around them take over. Absolute peace.

No birds chirped. No insects buzzed. No trees rustled. No wind blew.

Mala began mumbling her final mantras and connecting with spirits. Lirah went back to her cool river, and Au sat up to look around him one last time.

Au's crackling voice broke her peace. "What is ... that?" he asked, squinting at something, his arm shading his eyes. He pushed himself up to stand, falling back down a few times before succeeding. "What the ..." he whispered, wobbling around on his feet.

Mala sat up.

Lirah huffed and managed to prop herself up on her elbows, her head spinning in nauseating protest. Once her head had balanced itself out, she squinted in the direction that Au was pointing towards. She saw nothing. He moved his arm again.

"That!" he exclaimed hoarsely.

That's when Lirah saw a twinkling flash of light.

"And *that*!" He whipped his arm towards another flash so hard that he toppled back down to the ground. Slowly, he managed to stand again.

All at once, beneath the shifting angle of light above, many, *many* twinkling lights revealed themselves. It looked like a performance carried out by oversized fireflies, except they were in the middle of the desert during the day.

"I've never ... seen ... anything like them." Au's hoarse voice carried notes of hope.

Strengthened by this discovery, Lirah sat up straight, finally giving up her peaceful river. "Is it ... a community?"

Au shrugged. "Who knows. Could ... have water. If we ... can make it." He swallowed, coughed. "Don't know ... how far ..."

"I hope ... we're not ... imagining. Possibly ... our minds ... tricking us." Mala heaved, her eyes dodging back and forth between the blinking lights. "But ... it's worth it. To go."

They had nothing to lose. With their arms wrapped around each other's necks to steady themselves, they limped on. A breeze of hope survived in the burning air of a merciless desert.

* * *

The closer the trio stepped to the glimmering specks, the more perplexed Lirah became as to what the twinkling objects could be. She thought about how settled she had been with dying just moments ago. Now, she was determined to walk until her body physically gave out and her heart burst. Where this surge of energy came from ... she had no idea.

A cloud of orange dust billowed up in the air, growing larger as it rose higher and closer in the harsh, slanted light. A small brown dot exposed itself, leading the orange, hazy trail in its wake, growing into a bigger brown dot with every passing second.

"What is ... *that*?" Lirah nodded her head weakly toward the speeding dot.

"It's moving ... so fast," Mala said, awestruck.

"Predator?" Au asked. He heaved a nervous sigh.

If he was right, which he most likely was, they wouldn't stand a chance against it. They still had both spears, strapped across Au's back, but they had no energy to use them.

Over the course of minutes, the brown dot sprouted legs and a snout. Then, before their eyes, it transformed into a sneglow-like creature. Except it was angry, agile, and fast. It was coming straight for them at full force. Only a few miles away now.

Four, six-foot-tall legs were attached to a dense, ten-foot-long body. And an even longer tail swished wildly behind it, pulling up massive amounts of dust that surrounded the creature like a large orb as it ran. To make matters worse, a random hot breeze picked up, pulling the beast-made dust storm towards the frail group.

They froze, gripping one another even tighter.

The beast hurdled closer and closer, causing the ground below the trio's feet to vibrate. The kicked-up dust pelted against their skin. It felt like dry rain. The experience felt so overpowering that they had no choice but to let go of one another, close their eyes, and crouch down to brace themselves for the worst. Blinded and doomed with nowhere to hide, all they could do was listen to the huffing and galloping of the beast.

Then, all at once, the vibrating stopped. The dust swirled and settled down around them. The powerful huffing was the only sound that remained. After a few moments of uncertainty, Lirah dared to straighten her crouched legs and open her eyes.

She jumped.

She was face to face with the beast, its black pupils staring down into her own. Its gaping nostrils rose and fell, sending warm air that smelled of fish into her face, blowing back her dirty hair. Its sharp, straight horns bobbed up and down over its head. She wanted to scream at the top of her lungs, but she didn't dare move. She flicked her eyes back and forth. Mala and Au were standing beside her.

"Well, well," a mighty voice called out from above. "I wasn't expectin' kin! I was expectin' a meal! Well … surprises never hurt I guess." The voice chuckled deeply, and a dusty rope ladder came unravelling down the side of the giant beast.

Lirah, Au, and Mala backed up, glancing at one another in search of some form of guidance. But none of them spoke. Mala's cracked lips quivered. Lirah swore she could hear Au's stomach rumbling. Her heart thumped so fast that her pulse had travelled up to her ears.

In the glare of the light, a silhouette of a man swung his legs over the beast and slowly made his way down the ladder, one step at a time. Once the man climbed halfway down, Lirah could make out his features. He was short, stocky, and covered head to toe in orange dirt. He wore tattered boots, blue pants, and had puffy brown tufts of hair on top of his round head. When he reached the end of the ladder, he was still swaying two feet above the ground. He looked back, grunted, and jumped down, hitting the ground with a thud. Lirah noticed an odd device placed over his nose that wrapped behind his ears. It had clear circles incased by wire that covered his eyes and seemed to magnify them, because his eyes took up almost half of his face. Besides that, he looked similar to them in most ways, except his skin was orange. Lirah didn't know if he appeared orange to her because of her ability to see true colors, the dirt covering him, or if that was his actual skin tone. But at least he didn't look like a malicious red rutapuga.

"Well, well. Ya gonna say somethin'?!" the man boomed up at them. "Or ya just gonna keep on starin' all wide mouthed? Ya know … yer gonna catch flies like that!" He sounded like he was attempting to be funny, but when nobody answered him, he tucked his hands into his pant pockets and shifted uncomfortably up on his toes and back down again.

"Well, what are ya doin' out here? I don't recognize any of ya from the settlement," he said, followed by another chuckle.

He's really trying to come across as friendly, Lirah thought.

He seemed absolutely amused by them, and not much of a threat. But the giant beast with its fish breath was still hovering so close to her face that she didn't dare open her mouth.

"We have … travelled … a long way," Au spoke up for the group, trying to sound confident despite his hoarse, shaking voice. "We're searching … for water. Food. Not looking … for a fight."

The man laughed harder than ever. "A fight? Josie here is a bulla," he said, patting the fuming, brown, sneglow-like creature. "Bullas can kill ya in less than a second flat … if they sense yer tryna fight." He waddled up beside Lirah, who quickly glanced back and forth between the bulla's dark eyes and its approaching owner. "Look, see? She knows yer alright." He reached up and stroked its huffing snout.

The bulla stepped backwards, dipping its head and thick horns down to receive better pats. Lirah sighed with relief that it had given her more space.

"I could help get ya some water, and food too. Sure does look like ya need it. If ya don't mind a bulla ride." The man smirked.

The group looked at one another. How could they know if they could trust this man? Or his colossal pet bulla? Which he seemed to have domesticated and trained to kill his enemies in less than a second flat.

"Uh … could you … give us time … to talk?" Au swallowed.

"Well, sure I can! But it seems like yer gonna die out here if ya don't come with me."

Au nodded at the small man, then he turned to Mala and Lirah. They slowly inched away from the bulla and huddled close.

"How does … he look … Lirah?" Au asked. "Red? Contorted?"

"He's orange … to me. But maybe it's … just … the dust." Lirah whispered hoarsely. She was thinking about water.

"He's orange … to me … too. Does he look … trustworthy?" Au coughed.

"He looks … normal," Lirah said. "And … we have to go … with him. We have … no other choice. Right … Mala?" She looked towards her mother.

Mala was staring at Josie with a hazy, yet terrified look swept over her eyes.

"Mala?"

Mala turned to face Lirah, attempting to clear her throat. "Yes. We need to go … with them."

"I wonder … if he's … from the lights," Lirah whispered.

"I guess ... we'll see," Au said.

Lirah and Au inched their way back over to the man with Mala trailing behind, a glazed look in her eyes.

"I'll talk," Lirah said. She wanted to make a good first impression, show that they were all worthy of being kept alive, and that Au was not the only one in their group capable of speaking.

She smiled down at the cheerful man. "This offer ... is very kind of ... you," she coughed, "we ... would love ... water. Can you show us ... how to get on... *er* ... Josie?"

PART 3: THE SCOPE SETTLEMENT

CHAPTER 21

Lirah was in love with the powerful feeling of being ten feet above the harsh land beneath her, flying above the dust with Au and Mala, a clear view of society resting just miles away.

Maybe something *Out There* really did care about their life outcomes. They just cheated death after all. And water, shelter, and sustenance finally lay dead ahead on their adventure into the unknown. Even with her exhaustion, hunger, and quenching thirst weighing down on her, Lirah felt better than ever before. The breeze created from Josie's pace cooled down her burnt skin and blew through her long auburn hair.

The orange man sat and steered at the front of Josie, heading straight for the flashing lights. The closer they galloped, the more confused Lirah became as to what the lights were. They looked less sparkly now, though still hauntingly beautiful. Whatever they were, she would find out soon enough. Lirah was enjoying this joyride too much to worry. She trusted this man. She figured if he wanted to kill them, he would've done it already. She closed her eyes and took in the moment. She felt wild and free, while safe at the same time with her arms wrapped firmly around Au's waist.

"We're gettin' close," the orange man shouted. "Up here's the Scope Settlement!"

He pointed towards a collection of about thirty identical metal domes. They looked like massive silver mushrooms reaching for the sky. Lirah had to squint to see them well. It was like they only wanted to be admired from afar. Up close they were painful to look at. Too bright. The angle of the dropping light in the sky bounced off every point of each structure. She couldn't figure out if the blinding mushrooms were homes or contraptions, but the fact that she was witnessing a group of structures at all made her eyes well up with happiness.

Lirah had hoped for a moment just like this so many times while trudging through the grasslands. Of course, she hadn't imagined riding up on a bulla, or for the structures to look like these did. But in her past, reality had always turned out differently from her expectations, and this outcome saved her from dying of heat exhaustion. So, she felt nothing but gratitude.

When they came to the first structure, just on the outskirts of the Scope Settlement, Josie slowed to a trot.

Lirah's breath rushed out of her.

A brilliant, crystal-blue river laced through the flat-orange land and the cluster of silver mushroom estates, supplying the only shock of color to the community. It wound through the gaps between the structures like an endless pulsating snake and had short silver bridges built sporadically over it to unite the community.

As Josie crossed over a bridge, the man commanded her to slow her pace even further. "Look there!" He nodded down at the river.

The trio gazed into the flawless water on either side of Josie. The neon scales of large schools of fish gleamed. Shimmers of blue, purple, pink, yellow, and green maneuvered their way through blossoming water flowers, tentacled plants, and algae, flowing like the river itself, seemingly unaware of Josie's massive footsteps jostling them back and forth.

They passed over the short bridge all too quickly. Lirah wanted a taste of that water more than anything, but Josie moved like an expert on a mission, her large body weaving acutely around every mushroom-shaped structure they passed. Lirah noticed only two metal structures that weren't shaped this way. Instead, they were massive rectangular prisms reaching high into the boundless sky. One was placed in the center of the settlement, the other far off on the outskirts.

Lirah couldn't help but be reminded of Airis despite the obvious differences. The women's unique wooden homes had surrounded a river too. Lots of the women had sat outside and swam in the river, which made them appear friendlier. Of course, that had been a very wrong impression. But Lirah didn't see a soul outside here, and she couldn't tell any of the mushroom structures apart. They were all the same shade of rusting silver metal. There was nothing aesthetic like the women's blooming flowers, sumaras, welcome signs, or wind chimes here either. Some homes had small, steamy, glass prisms filled with vegetables out front, cages filled with small squawking creatures, or piles of rusting tools. Josie came to a final halt in front of a structure with a large metal hut beside it.

"Well, well! Here's my home! And that's Josie's right beside it," the man said excitedly.

"'Scuse me." He turned around and reached beside Mala. She leaned back as he untied a rope ladder hitched to the saddle. It fell down Josie's side and they each took turns climbing down.

As Lirah's feet hit solid ground, her legs felt simultaneously weighted down and numb. She saw Au and Mala wobbling too.

"Take yer time gettin' back yer balance. 'Specially after the first ride," the man said. "Wait here. I'll just be a second gettin' Josie's meal ready, and some cups for ya to drink from. Here, let me store all yer belongings too. Ya won't need 'em here."

Au hesitantly passed over their spears and empty sack for

resources.

They watched the man shuffle over to the gated hut and safely store their things as he had promised.

Lirah dizzily leaned back against Josie and used the bulla's dense body as a support to make her way to the front of her. Then she pushed back onto her feet and looked deep into Josie's sweet, black eyes. Appreciation flooded through her. Josie saved her life ... all of their lives.

Josie swung her snout up and down, as if she recognized Lirah's thankfulness and wanted to respond. Then, as if on cue, her black mane started to sparkle and her eyes lightened to a blue-grey. They glittered like rare gems. Now, Lirah could make out her wide pupils and saw that her eyes were welling up. Lirah was amazed by Josie's emotional intelligence. Did other creatures understand gratitude too?

Lirah turned around to see if Au and Mala had noticed Josie's change in appearance too.

She jumped and nearly bumped noses with Au, given how close he was to her. She had been too entranced by Josie to notice him approach.

Mala seemed to be having a similar experience. She was staring absentmindedly at Josie with her eyes glossed over, her facial expression caught between a mix of wonder and distress. But Au wasn't watching Josie. When Lirah met his eyes, he was already smiling right back at her. A look of deep compassion spread across his face. Now his eyes were welling up too.

"Josie is *sparkling*. Can you see it?" Lirah whispered, her throat still dry as ever, leaning in to rub Au's nose with her own.

"It must be ... your powers. You can see ... her true beauty. Since, she saved us," Au replied hoarsely, rubbing her back and pulling her into his warm chest.

"We lived," Lirah squeaked in his ear.

"I couldn't ... be happier," Au said.

Meanwhile, Mala continued to gape at Josie, who had

evidently noticed the obsessive staring too. Josie had shifted her gaze away from Lirah and over to Mala, nodding her snout up and down as if trying to get Mala to move or smile.

The man appeared from the depths of Josie's hut. He held a large bucket filled to the brim with dead fish in one hand, and three cups balancing in his other.

"I'm mighty glad yer all gettin' along with Josie! Here," he said, stopping inches in front of them and handing out the cups. "Scoop up some water from the river and drink up. It's mighty clean, so don't be scared."

Lirah and Au took their cups and thanked him. Mala absentmindedly reached out for hers, her focus still firmly locked onto Josie.

Lirah nudged her mother. "Are you coming?"

She got no response.

Au shrugged and nudged Lirah along to the river edge.

Lirah glanced back at her motionless mother, shook her head, then crouched down to fill her cup. She dunked it down into the cool water and watched the masses of small fish flowing by — they quickly separated and changed their groupings so they wouldn't run into her submerged arm. She pulled her cup back up and gulped down the icy liquid. It coursed down her throat and into her empty stomach. It almost tasted *too* good. She filled her cup again and sloppily drank it dry. She repeated this several more times, slurping and gulping until she soaked her chest with as much water as filled her mouth.

Beside her, Au looked the exact same. In between slurps they locked eyes and giggled at each other's full cheeks and dribbling chins, which only caused more of the water to escape from their lips. Their giggles escalated into hard laughter, and Lirah hardly noticed when Mala joined them at the edge of the river.

Lirah looked over her shoulder to check on the orange man's whereabouts. He was handfeeding Josie dead rainbow fish from his bucket and patting her head in between scoops.

Just then, he started to sparkle too. He looked like a gleaming orange fish with massive goggling eyes. This made Lirah smile. She knew she liked him.

She turned to Mala, whose hands were shaking as she filled her cup, water splashing over its edges. "Are you alright?" Lirah asked her.

"Yes," Mala panted. She took a large gulp of water before speaking again, more evenly. "That ride was exhilarating, huh? Marvelous creature, that Josie. I can't keep my eyes off her."

I noticed, Lirah thought. *Everyone noticed.* But instead, she asked, "Did any spirits contact you while you were staring into her eyes?"

Mala didn't answer. She loudly sipped her water. It dribbled down her chin.

Lirah went on, "I wasn't sure what you were doing back there. You looked very distracted considering we haven't had actual water in days."

There was another uneasy pause.

Lirah scooped up what was probably her fifteenth cup of water and took a sip to fill the silence. Au appeared to be on his twentieth cup. He slurped noisily beside her. She knew it was to cover up his obvious eavesdropping. His eyes were dodging back and forth between her, Mala, and his cup. But Lirah wanted him to hear this conversation. They were all on this journey together. If Mala knew something important that they didn't, he needed to know too.

"No, my light," Mala finally answered. She sounded calm, but she wouldn't make eye contact with Lirah. "I'm still too malnourished to tune into my abilities or speak with spirits. I'm just ... in complete awe with our new company ... and where we are. We *survived.*"

"I know right?" Lirah said, though she wanted to call her mother out for hiding something. "I can't believe we're alive either."

Lirah had never seen Mala look at anything the way she just looked at Josie. Something about it made her uneasy. Had her mother been looking at Josie in … terror? No. Mala's facial expression looked very different when the massive serpent had her twisted up and twenty feet off the ground. Now *that* was terror. So, could she have been looking at Josie in awe? According to Lirah's new *powers*, as Au had called them, Josie and her owner were sparkling and sweet. Maybe if she told this to Mala, she would tell Lirah whatever it was that she knew too.

"I think I saw Josie's true colors when I looked into her eyes," Lirah said. "You know, when I was leaning against her back there? Her entire mane started sparkling. It still is." Lirah smiled and looked back at the sparkling bulla, who just finished slurping up the last of her fish. "She looks like the open night sky. So do her eyes. And her owner is sparkling too. I like them."

Mala looked into Lirah's eyes and grinned. "That's wonderful."

But before Mala could say anything else, if she was even going to, the stocky man sidled up to the river's edge. This time, he was holding a large bucket in each hand. He dropped one down beside them. "That one's fer ya to rinse off with," he said, then continued past them. He leaned over the edge of the river and filled Josie's empty fish bucket with water. He dumped it out, filled it again, then dropped it on the dirt.

"I'll be back with some old clothes of mine for ya!" He grinned.

The trio stood by the river and watched the man make his way back over to Josie's little home, dragging the sloshing bucket of water beside him. He placed it on the far back wall of her hut, returned to guide her inside, then closed the creaking gate behind her. Her tail swished happily back and forth.

Their eyes continued to follow the man. He disappeared through the door of his metal mushroom home, but not before he said, "Better hurry and clean off! Light's 'bout set and gone. Everyone else has been inside fer ages!"

Lirah looked around and really absorbed this strange

miracle of a community for the first time since they climbed off Josie. The man was right; the sky was lit up in an effervescent pink, but it was fading fast, along with the heat. And it was dead quiet. Nobody was anywhere to be seen, which Lirah was grateful for. She didn't want to be gawked at by settlers walking by or questioned about who she was right now.

The trio took turns dumping the bucket of water over one another and refilling it. They let all the dust and sweat fall down their bodies, cleansing their faces and skin from the desert grime for the first time in days. They looked significantly better after a rinse, but still had burns and blisters all over their arms and legs.

The man reappeared through the door as the group was assessing each other's burnt skin. He tossed them each a clean white dress cloth with arm holes, which he called "shirts." He pointed to a small area in between Josie's hut and his home. He said they could change there while he rinsed himself.

They followed his directions, changing out of their stained, soaking garments and into his dry, oversized ones. The white cloth came down to Au's knees, Lirah's calves, and all the way to Mala's ankles. Lirah giggled, gripping onto the hem of her new shirt and twirling around like a dancer. She didn't know what to expect next. They were waiting on the man to finish bathing and changing, but then what would they do?

Mala hung their wet dress cloths on Josie's fence to dry, then tugged on Josie's tail, persuading her to turn around. Josie snorted and maneuvered awkwardly. Once she was facing out of her hut and blinking expectantly at Mala, Mala didn't pet her, or say hello, or anything. She just stared, unmoving, like earlier. Lirah couldn't figure out if her mother was transfixed by Josie herself, or by other thoughts the sight of Josie brought to mind. But whatever the reason, it was extremely creepy, and she was definitely keeping something from Lirah.

Lirah heaved a breath of relief when the freshly-cleaned man came over. He waved, forcing Mala to shift her eyes away from the bulla. He slicked back his tuft of brown hair and pulled down on the white shirt he wore. It clung to his large belly just right, like peeling skin. Now they were all matching, except for their skin tones. Lirah noticed the man's skin still glowed bright orange, even without the dirt covering his body. "Come on in now!" He grinned.

The man opened the door to his strange estate and leaned his back against it, swinging his arm across his chest and motioning for his guests to walk through the opening.

Lirah, Au, and Mala obeyed, though hesitantly, undoubtedly stunned by his hospitality. They had hardly spoken a word to him. He didn't know their names and they didn't know his. He didn't have a clue where they had come from or where they were heading, and yet, he trusted them enough to give them water, dress cloths, and allow them inside his home.

Well, trust goes both ways, Lirah thought.

What else were they expecting to happen after he rescued them anyway? To be given water and tossed back into the dust? Maybe. Or maybe this strange place was the fanciful, ever-accepting society that Lirah had dreamt up over the years of her life. The home she had been waiting for. Would they live here? In their own silver mushroom contraption? She pictured herself poking her head out of a window, waving at a giant bulla nodding by, shaking out dirt from a rug with Au. The orange dust would become a permanent fixture in their hair.

But Lirah knew she was getting ahead of herself. She cleared her thoughts and stepped inside behind Mala and Au.

The man shouted, "G'night Josie; good work today!" and closed the door behind them.

CHAPTER 22

The temperature inside was surprisingly cool. Even though the natural light was dying outside, it wouldn't usually feel *this* cool, this quickly. Especially in the desert.

The man turned a knob on the wall and dim lights switched on overhead. He turned the knob three more times, and each time the lights grew a bit brighter. Lirah stared. She had no idea how this was possible. It was like the man had created his own daylight. The lights shining above them now, on turn three, looked about how the light shined outdoors at midday.

Lirah was about to ask the man about his celling lights, but became speechless, mesmerized by the rest of the room around her. She had never been in an enclosed space as massive as this before. This room was larger than the Pride leaders' hive had been, or Mori and Pecha's entire cabin, by far. But at the same time, it felt snug in here. It was decorated rather homey instead, in contrast to its slick and bolted exterior.

The walls were painted a light blue over its silver base, the latter which shone through in some spots that weren't painted thick enough. Long rectangular windows were placed on either side of the door and spanned across the left wall, with thin cream curtains covering them. In the middle of the room, a circle of four plush, terracotta-colored cushions sat around a round table with a vase planted in the middle. Beautiful abstract paintings adorned the walls around the table, adding whisps and splatters of color that mimicked an evening desert sky to the room.

To the right of the living area, pressed against a wall near the door, an L-shaped counter extended out into the room with cups, bowls, and strange devices resting on it. It seemed to separate the areas meant for lounging and for cooking. Au hovered over a metal contraption embedded in the counter itself, with knobs placed on either side of it and an empty pot resting on top. Beside the counter, a bulky, silver box that stretched up halfway to the roof and had handles on the front rested.

Lirah stared at the smaller devices resting on top of the counter. They all looked very breakable and strange. She wondered what they all did. But she didn't feel capable of asking any questions. She knew they would come out of her mouth like a jumble of mush. Anyway, she didn't want to break the silence. No one else had spoken a word since they walked inside. The man simply stood, grinning proudly in the center of the room, watching them all gawk over his possessions. Clearly, he took their bewildered expressions for curious compliments, and didn't care to explain what anything was.

Maybe he doesn't want to insult our intelligence, or maybe he's just enjoying himself and doesn't want to break the silence either.

She gazed past Au and noticed Mala inching up to a flight of steps, her white dress cloth dragging on the floor behind her. Lirah could see the first few steps, narrow and metal, then they curved up in a spiral and disappeared behind the wall. Lirah wondered where they led to. She took her first step away from the entrance and followed her mother for a closer look.

A surge of energy filled her chest, similar to nervousness, except she felt like the energy was coming *to* her, not *from* her.

Her heartbeat grew stronger the closer she stepped to the staircase, which only intrigued her further. But when she approached her mother's side and lifted her foot to climb the first step, her surroundings vanished. The swell of energy vigorously emptied out of her, and she felt embodied by pitch-blackness, like she was stuck floating in a dead silent night where not even insects chirped.

She stayed very still, her leading leg locked in a hovering position, her fingers nearly tracing the handrail but just falling short.

The color indigo bubbled into her mind's eye.

Then, slowly, numerous sparkling bits of orange, blue, red, and white floated down from somewhere above the frame like falling flower petals. They settled one by one in the center of her view before sinking down into the indigo backdrop like it was a thick liquid. Wispy clouds of reds, blues, and purples swelled like smoke as they drifted down into the scene next, plopping on top of the glimmering muck and melting down into it.

Lirah had no idea what she was witnessing, but it was magical. The energy that had emptied from her was quickly replenishing itself. She wanted to lay down on the gleaming indigo liquid, sink into it like a warm hug, and have it run over her fingers like honey.

Then the indigo muck began to gurgle, pulling down the remaining sparkles and clouds resting on top and swallowing up their colors. The indigo didn't stay long either. Different shades of blue gradually shifted and lightened beneath Lirah's eyelids, then solid blackness came gliding up from beneath the frame and down from the top, meeting in the center, closing up her view and stealing away the energy again.

A deep feeling of emptiness dragged on for what felt like years to Lirah.

Then, all at once, she could open her eyes again. The spiraled stairs refocused in front of her, her foot still hovering over the first step.

Only mere moments had passed.

Lirah quickly dropped her numb toes down to the floor and stepped back. Her heart started racing again, except she lost all desire to find out what dwelt at the top of the spiraled stairs. She turned to face her mother.

Had Mala just seen the same images of indigo and melting colors behind her eyes? Followed by the same dragging feeling of emptiness? Lirah felt both comforted and alarmed to find Mala wearing the same expression on her face that Lirah was feeling.

Lirah shivered.

This experience felt all too similar to the one she had in the grasslands ... after she ate the wabelloo fruit ... then got trapped watching Mala pass away beneath her locked eyelids.

That must have been a vision after all, and not just side effects the fruit.

This meant that Mala really *would* die in her arms, sooner rather than later, right? Mala never had visions that didn't come true within a span of a year. But Mala had also been experiencing visions long before Lirah was born, and Mala said they still confused her, that they were still unstable. Lirah just had her second vision *ever*. How could she trust this young power? Couldn't the future change?

Lirah's head spun like she had just fallen from a tall tree and landed on her head. A breakdown bubbled within her, and she hadn't even started to think about the strange vision she just now had.

Well, *now* she was.

How could abstract patterns of colors and dragging emptiness even *be* a vision? How could that become a reality?

Lirah really hoped Mala wasn't looking at her.

She knew she must look sick.

She couldn't handle being questioned now.

She sighed with relief when the man finally broke the silence, pulling Lirah out from the depths of her thoughts. It was like being pulled out of a rushing, ice cold river.

"Well, well. Enough standin' 'round like dallyin' dodos. There's plenty of chairs for ya." The man chuckled. "And I'd say it's 'bout time fer introductions. Don't worry now; you'll all see my room upstairs soon enough."

Lirah grimaced and turned away from the stairs, shaking. Mala wasn't standing next to her anymore. She and Au were already making their way over to the plush cots where the man was sitting and eagerly motioning for them all to join him.

Lirah made her way over to the last open cushion at the low table, taking deep breaths to calm herself.

Right when she sunk down into the plush seat, the man jumped up like he had forgotten something. Lirah spun around, thinking he was heading for the stairs, but he, instead, pulled out a handful of crumby yellow lumps from a cabinet beneath his counter. He handed them one each, sunk back down into his cushion, and started munching away at his own yellow lump.

"Biscuits," he said, noticing their unsure facial expressions. As if a name would help them recall a food they'd never seen before.

Lirah, Mala, and Au politely bit into their 'biscuits,' which turned into devouring them.

Lirah didn't realize how hungry she was before now. She had been so distracted by everything else that had happened this evening. She couldn't believe this was *still* the same day as when they were quite literally dying in the desert heat.

"Don't worry, that's just to hold ya over 'til I make my favorite recipe. I cook it fer my friends when I'm trying ta impress 'em, ya know? So, I have ta get to know ya first." The man let out a deep chuckle then stridently propped his chubby bare feet on the table in front of them. He cleared his throat with a grunt.

The trio directed their attention to his clear-covered, magnified eyes.

"The name's Axal McAdoo," the man announced, looking from one face to the next. "But everyone here calls me Axoo. I guess it's a blend of the two ... and that rhymes ...which I didn't even mean ta do!" His large stomach shook up and down as he laughed.

His audience politely watched in silence.

Now that Lirah had no other distractions, she stared at nothing but Axoo for the first time. She was completely enthralled by his form—from his skin tone to his magnified eyes and protruding stomach. She wasn't used to seeing someone this well fed with so many strange, technologically-advanced items, and a pet bulla. He was quite a character. Would everyone here have the same deep orange skin tone? And wear contraptions over their eyes? Were there beings in other places that looked even more unique? Green skin maybe? With three arms instead of two?

"I've been livin' here my whole life," Axoo said. "Livin' a simple life as a scientist, collectin' data. Lucky to have everything I could possibly need and more to cover my basic needs while I work in peace. Though not much ever changes 'round here, so I do like travelin' from time to time with Josie. Discoverin' new creatures or findin' new ingredients to spice up a meal. I like to cook, ya see?" He motioned behind him over to his fancy kitchen. "You all might be the first newcomers to come to this settlement in 'bout ... well ... maybe fer'ever. Which makes me wonder ... what brought ya over to this part of the world? I've been waitin' to hear 'bout ya the whole evening. Just thought it'd be more polite to wait and ask inside where it's cozy. And after gettin' the chance to drink an' eat a snack," He smiled, then looked at Mala expectantly, waiting for a response.

Axoo probably wants to hear from Mala because she's the wisest of us, Lirah though, *and he looks around the same age as her. Or maybe it's because she's the only one who hasn't spoken to him yet.*

She watched as Mala shriveled back into her seat. She wasn't surprised after her mother had personally dedicated so much time to helping Mori with her 'spirit communication lessons' only to discover that the lessons had not only been a sham, but a way to keep Mala and her loved ones held hostage while Mori organized her brute soldiers. Oh, and then to be chased, attacked, and driven out of the jungle? Of course Mala didn't want to open up to another stranger. And Axoo's mysterious staircase probably wasn't helping either.

But Lirah knew things were different this time. She had seen Axoo's true colors. He had good intentions. He was still vaguely sparkling in her eyes even now. She recognized instinctually that he wouldn't always look this way. She still wasn't able to decipher how her new ability worked, but since she had seen that Axoo was good, she knew her ability would ease off now. It would be a waste of brainpower for him to look this way forever. Anyway, it was quite odd to witness a plump orange man with magnified eyes who *also* sparkled.

Mala still hadn't answered Axoo, so Lirah reached over and squeezed her hand for reassurance.

Axoo waited patiently.

Finally, Mala looked into his magnified eyes and asked, "Do you promise that your intentions for us are pure? Before I tell you our story."

Ouch. Lirah was offended that Mala didn't trust in her ability, even if it was still in its early stages.

Maybe this means my visions can't be fully trusted either, Lirah thought hopefully. *Or maybe Mala's only questioning Axoo about his intentions so that he won't take this conversation lightly.*

Everything did seem rather like a joke to him, given the amount he chuckled. Choosing to share their past with him while being this vulnerable was a *big deal*. If they disappeared, no one would ever find out, and he would know that once he heard their story.

Axoo nodded. "Of course! My only intention is to make new friends. It gets kinda lonely livin' here on my own, and when I go out, I'm seein' the same folks I've seen every day of my life. Like I said, yer the first newcomers I've ever seen."

Mala straightened her spine and tilted up her chin. "Then, may I send generosity spirits into your soul? They should bring you good fortune in exchange for viewing your soul, after they see your selflessness. This process only works under conditions such as these—the fact that you saved us and took us in."

"Why sure," said Axoo. "How do ya do it?"

Mala shifted her gaze from Axoo's enlarged eyes and pointed down at his right hand, which he in turn extended. She scooted forward in her seat and placed it lightly in her right hand, flipping his palm so it faced upward. Then, with her left index finger, Mala began drawing invisible circles over and over again on his palm.

Lirah and Au watched in confused admiration as Mala drew her circles. They had never seen her do this before. She had her eyes closed and her lips were citing a mantra under her breath.

Axoo laughed lightly at Mala's finger tickling his palm. She ignored him.

After ten more circling motions, Mala opened her eyes and released his hand. "You have a good soul," she said. "The spirits have accepted my request of them to watch over you and help ensure you possess good fortune." She smiled lightly at him.

"Thank ya very much." Axoo pulled his hand back into his lap.

"So, would you like to hear our story now?"

Axoo nodded, rubbing his palm where Mala had drawn the circles.

Mala slumped back into her cot, appearing much more relaxed now, and began. "I am Mala, and this is my daughter Lirah, and her partner Au. We have lived the majority of our lives up in the canopy of a jungle, called the Treetop Society, where we were part of a Pride. But recently," she paused, then sighed, "it was invaded by brutes. They launched arrows and fire into the air, targeting the Treetop Society and ending many innocent lives. A group of their brute fighters chased us to the edge of the jungle. Since then, we have been drifting forward, beyond the jungle wall. We spent many, many days making our way through grasslands. They were beautiful at first, then a huge serpent stalked us and tried to kill me right beside a strange, dark, deadly stretch of grass. The snake proved to be a necessary evil. We eventually crossed over the deadly grass by using its scales as steppingstones after we killed it."

Axoo's eyes had somehow grown even wider under his eye contraptions.

"We assumed that after we passed that evil strip of grass, we would be safe. A new land was glowing on the other side—an orange and yellow land with prickly vegetation. We had never seen anything like it. But the terrain only became more desolate with every step we took. Eventually, we were completely out in the middle of nothingness. No plants or animals were anywhere to be found. We were ready to drop dead. But we saw sparkling lights in the distance and kept moving, determined. That's when you found us, and the lights ended up being your settlement." Mala smiled and fanned her arms out, referencing the room around her. She had tears dewing at the corners of her navy eyes. Axoo was tearing up at her story too, blubbering quietly.

"We lost brave friends along the way. Their names are Suki, Riel, and Riggul. Also, we were betrayed by a community that we *thought* was originally helping us, since we were helping them. Clearly that wasn't the case." Mala winced. "But we're here now, safe and lucky to have found solace once again, even if it's only for a short time."

Lirah's heart swelled. She was so proud of how eloquently her mother recounted their story. It wasn't easy for Lirah to think about their past, and it was treacherous to dream about, so she was glad that she didn't have to *speak* about it. She could've never left out the most gruesome details like Mala had, which bubbled to Lirah's mind the most readily.

Axoo sniffled. "I'm s'sorry to hear 'bout what ya had to go through ... that's more horrific than I ever imagined. And yer both so young to go through all that." Axoo shook his head and looked solemnly from Lirah to Au. "I'm sure happy Josie spotted ya when she did. Yer all welcome to stay here as long as ya like."

"Thank you," Mala smiled somberly.

Axoo lifted his facial contraption and wiped his wet eyes, then he clapped his hands together and stood up. Just like that, he shifted back into a cheerful mood. "I'd say it's time fer my favorite meal then. Axoo's spicy stew!"

He toddled over to the counter and turned a knob next to the silver appliance with the pot resting on top. It clicked a few times, then a flame began to burn steadily beneath the pot on the metal appliance.

Lirah's eyes bulged. She looked over and saw Au's mouth had dropped open in absolute captivation.

She had seen Au assemble and light countless fires in his lifetime, some more difficult to make than others, but all of them had involved a long process. He had many burn marks on his arms from attempting to revive dying flames. Not to mention the scars he received from cutting down and transporting the wood to the dining hall. This instant flame was a technology the trio had never seen before, much like the lights above their heads now.

They all goggled at Axoo like curious infants as he pulled materials out from different compartments below and above his L-shaped counter—perfectly crafted measuring cups, mixing tools, knives, and spices in see-through jars. He walked over to the tall, silver box and pulled its handle open. It lit up inside. It was filled with fresh produce, fish, containers of white liquid, and Lirah couldn't make out what else because Axoo shut it too quickly. He dumped an assortment of the white liquid, fish, vegetables, and spices into the warming pot.

Axoo looked up at his wonder-struck audience and offered his signature chuckle. "Well, well. If ya like my stove and fridge this much, I can't *wait* to show ya somethin' even better after dinner. When it's completely dark out." He smirked. "*Ooooo*, yer in fer a treat."

Lirah caught a twinkle in his eye before he turned back to his current cooking mission. She didn't say anything, but she wanted to know more about the surprise. Why did they have to wait until it was completely dark?

CHAPTER 23

Lirah's stomach rumbled so hard it felt like it was turning itself inside out by the time Axoo's recipe was complete. He poured the steaming, chunky stew from the pot into four small bowls and passed them around.

Peering down into her steaming bowl, Lirah was hit with the pungent aroma of fish tails and spicy herbs, which were bobbing on the surface of a creamy broth. She ignored the dainty, curved tools that Axoo placed on the table and lifted the bowl straight to her mouth, vigorously slurping down her first actual meal in days. It tasted salty, spicy, warm, and had an interesting new aftertaste. She loved it. She licked her lips and waited for a second helping. Au and Mala had slurped their bowls clean too. Axoo looked around at their eager eyes with glee. He was only halfway finished with his bowl, having chosen to use the tool that could only scoop up small quantities of the stew at a time. He swigged little amounts into his mouth, which seemed like a waste of time to Lirah.

"Yer welcome to get more stew!" Axoo told them. "I'm happy ya like it. Just keep scoopin' til' the pot is empty." He chuckled and raised the dainty tool up to his wide, smirking mouth.

Once they were full and the pot was emptied, the trio thanked Axoo and laid back on their cushions, nearly asleep. They hardly noticed when Axoo magically dimmed the lights on the ceiling down to a late evening glow.

"Well, well. Now seems like the perfect time fer the real treat," Axoo said, pulling back the cream curtains and peering through the window into the clear blackness of the night.

Ignoring the fact that his guests were exhausted, he stomped to the opposite end of the shelter and stood in front of the spiraled staircase. "Yer not gonna *believe* yer eyes! Follow me!" he shouted at them, like a child with a voice too deep for his age. He couldn't contain his excitement. He continued his stomping all the way up the stairs.

Mala and Lirah slowly pushed themselves up, yawning. Apparently, Au had been completely asleep. He was so startled by Axoo's stomping that he fell completely out of his cushion.

It took Lirah a few moments to realize what was going on.

Axoo had gone ... upstairs. *Uh oh.*

Why couldn't this have waited until the morning at least? She had no desire to go up those eerie stairs, especially this late at night.

Axoo clomped back downstairs. "Come on! Come on!"

"Coming," Mala mumbled for the group.

Lirah linked arms with Mala and they unwillingly trudged to the stairs, Au yawning right behind them.

Lirah's whole body ached, but she knew she didn't really have a choice in climbing these stairs with the way Axoo was behaving.

She had climbed halfway up the stairs when they curved enough to give her a peak into the room they led to. Her heart started thumping wildly, penetrating her grogginess like the harsh light that pierced through jungle fog in early mornings. She unlinked arms with Mala and gripped onto the railing with both hands to steady herself.

"Are you alright?" Au asked.

Lirah felt his hand touch the small of her back, steadying her. She didn't want to tell him that she was terrified to feel the emptiness, or the *lack* of feeling, that she had endured during her vision.

"I don't think I can do this," she moaned. She turned herself around, passing Au and heading back down the stairs.

"Come on, Lirah, yer almost up! This'll make ya feel better, I promise," Axoo called to the back of her head, not realizing it was the surprise itself that was worrying her.

She groaned and reluctantly turned around again, repeating in her head over and over, "Axoo has a good soul. Axoo has a good soul."

She took the final step and joined Au, Mala, and Axoo up in the snug, dome shaped room. She looked around the dim, artificially lit space. On one side of the room, she saw a large cot propped on a frame, a small desk covered in papers, and a chair with lots of fancy knobs and levers lining the wall behind it. Positioned across from the furniture, there was only one other thing in the room: a thin, curved piece of transparent crystal.

The crystal looked quite similar to the material and shape of the contraption on Axoo's face, except that it was *huge*. It easily covered over half of the wall and wrapped over their heads. A thick metal tube was suctioned against the back-center of the transparent crystal, extending up to the roof of the highest part of the shelter—the top of the mushroom head.

Axoo eagerly looked back and forth between his audience and the plain crystal.

Lirah felt strangely relieved. This was it?

Au let out a loud yawn.

Mala shuffled over to the bed and sat down, also yawning.

Axoo looked like he was about to cry. "Not impressed yet, huh? Well, watch this."

He walked over to one of the many knobs planted in the wall facing the giant sheet of crystal and turned it several times.

Nothing happened.

"Shoot." He stamped his foot, sending an echo throughout the room. "Let me go adjust some wires downstairs." He shimmied straight past the group, his face bright red, and down the stairs.

Knocking and banging sounds vibrated from underneath the top floor.

The trio exchanged nervous looks. Mala patted the spaces beside her on the bed and Lirah and Au joined her.

"I'm sure everything will be fine," Mala whispered.

They sat side by side in silence.

Lirah felt both exhausted and anxious, a peculiar combination of emotions. She knew if she wasn't so drained from their long journey of drifting through the desert, she wouldn't have been able to bear this anticipation. Her mind was trying to sharpen itself, to get her body to go downstairs, but her legs wouldn't budge.

After a few long minutes of loud banging, Axoo bounded back upstairs.

"Sorry 'bout that," he said. He turned the same knob that hadn't worked before, except this time Lirah heard a switching sound.

"Finally," Axoo muttered. He walked back across the room and closed the door. He turned a knob next to it, cutting off the dim lights on the ceiling.

Lirah panicked. It was too dark.

She was about to tell Axoo to turn the lights back on when the whole floor beneath them started moving upwards. Rumbling noises and more vibrations emitted from the floor. Lirah's heart raced. She couldn't speak.

She looked up at the ceiling right as a thin slice of the dome started pulling itself back, groaning as it moved automatically, revealing a portion of the night sky. The tube that was connected to the back of the giant piece of crystal was pointed at the open air now, instead of the dome ceiling.

Lirah started to sweat, her mind sharpening, the light clearing up the fog in her head more quickly now. They were rising faster. She knew that she looked terrified. But no one could see her. The room was completely black and even the open roof wasn't letting in much light from the three spheres in the sky.

What was this contraption? Did all scientists do this? Was Axoo going to try and shove them each through this tube? It looked small, but Lirah bet that if he tried hard enough, he could shove them through one at a time.

"Axoo has a good soul. Axoo has a good soul," she whispered to herself, pressing her head against Mala's shoulder as the floor continued to rumble and sway.

The movement finally stopped. The room went silent again.

"Here we go!" Axoo shouted.

Lirah swore she heard Mala squeak in desperation, followed by the sound of another knob being handled by Axoo.

The crystal slab lit up.

Startled by the flash of bright light, Lirah squeezed her eyes shut again.

She heard Axoo chuckle, followed by a loud gasp from Mala.

"Woah ... that's ..." Au's said.

"What?!" Lirah asked.

"Amazing." Au sighed dreamily.

Lirah took a deep breath and forced her eyes open.

CHAPTER 24

What had once been a transparent wrapping of crystal was now a divine projection, an abstract art piece, illuminating the whole room. Floating lights, shimmering colors, cloudlike giants, and speckles of glitter filled up the slab like cosmic liquid.

Except this display wasn't a still image like Axoo's wall art downstairs; the glitter and swirling masses were constantly in motion. Some sparkles rapidly flashed in place while others soared across the entirety of the curved crystal and out of sight, fleeting trails of light following in their wake. Their variety of colors dazzled Lirah—lilac, indigo, teal, orange, red, brown, cream—and that was just for the masses of mist. The incalculable quantities of sparkling dots gleamed in their own assortments of reds, yellows, oranges, blues, and whites. They floated effortlessly, endlessly ... somewhere. The projection looked like an explosion that had never evaporated away, like smoke and sparks that grew and drifted farther and farther out, giving color and light to a previously black abyss.

Lirah recognized the way the sparkling dots flickered before her. They looked like more distinguished versions of the same lights she had seen while gazing up into the sky each night in the grasslands. Except here, the depth of the scene was exquisitely unsettling. She could make out their dense layers rather than viewing them all across the same flat plain.

Here, the twinkling lights grew noticeably smaller the farther back they went, until Lirah could hardly make out the minuscule gleams in the distance. She bet if she could step through the glass right now, she would keep falling through the black backdrop forever. She imagined herself crashing through bodies of rainbow mist, soaring past twinkling flecks of light, occasionally bracing herself for a ground that would never come. Whatever this was, wherever this was, it was limitless.

Axoo twisted another knob behind his desk. and the projection started rotating, bringing more colorful gleams of light and incredible swirls of formations into view. "Told ya' I had somethin' special to show ya, didn't I?" he said proudly.

Lirah broke her focus from the scene and looked over at Axoo, nodding. Swirls and sparkles reflected against his eye coverings, twirling around as he adjusted the view back and forth with the knob. She didn't feel anxious or exhausted anymore, just wonderstruck. She looked at Mala and Au and couldn't help but smile at their reactions. Beside her, both their mouths were hanging wide open, and their pupils were taking up the entirety of their eyes.

"What ... what is this, Axoo?" Lirah waved at the illuminated slab of crystal.

"Well, well. That's an interestin' question." Axoo chuckled once, then dropped his voice down into a gruffer, more serious tone. "There are lots of names to describe the same thing, but I like to call this the Universe of *Everythin' Ever Known*!" He spread his arms out wide above his head for dramatic effect. "It goes on fer'ever. Those dreamlike clouds ya see are called *nebulae*. And every single shimmer ya see is called a *star*. Just like the one outside here, givin' us light in the day and takin' it away at night, cyclin' over and over again, all the time."

"Wait … *what*?" Au asked. "You mean we're a part of *this*?"

Axoo bobbed up and down on the balls of his feet, hardly able to contain himself. "Yes! *Yes*! Every shimmer ya see here is just like our star. Well, some bigger, some smaller, some growin', others dyin'. Which can only mean there's tons of planets out there, like the one yer feet are standin' on right now! With creatures like us livin' on it, along with lots of other kinds too."

Mala collapsed on the floor.

Lirah and Au jolted themselves up from the bedside to help her, still trying to grasp what Axoo had told them. They each grabbed a shaking arm and pulled up Mala, her head dangling, her tears dripping to the floor.

"Mala, you have to lift your head!" Lirah was suddenly terrified. "Are you alright? What happened?"

Mala, still gripping onto their arms, lifted her head high. In the light of the crystal, Lirah could see her mother smiling hard. Tears streamed down into her mouth and over her beaming, crooked teeth.

A wave of relief rushed over Lirah. She wiped at Mala's current stream of tears and exhaled.

"Don't worry. Totally normal to be overwhelmed yer first time seein' this," Axoo said.

"Is this too overwhelming, Mala? Is that why you're crying?" Au asked as he and Lirah pulled her back up on the bed. "We can help you back downstairs if it's too much."

"No, Au. I want to stay right here." Mala cupped her hands to her heart and gazed at the crystal. "My spirit guides are out there. My Bue is *Out There*."

Lirah smiled as the falling tears from Mala's eyes reflected the light and sparkles, shining fluorescently like miniature kaleidoscopes on her cheeks.

Axoo let out a loud sniffle. "That's just too sweet."

Lirah rubbed Mala's back and rested her head on her shoulder.

"How are we able to see all of this, Axoo?" Au asked quietly.

"I was hopin' someone would ask." Axoo flashed Au his jaunty smirk. "I live in an observatory, ya see? And that there is a telescope." He pointed up at the tube that was aimed straight through the opening in the roof.

"A telescope intensely magnifies the sky, and this powerful one projects what it sees down on this here crystal screen. It uses filters to show us images in more light spectrums than our eyes can see naturally, like ultraviolet and infrared. And right now, we're lookin' at places so far away that we'll never be able to step foot on 'em … even if we traveled as fast as we could fer a lifetime." He paused, taking in Au's staggered facial expression with delight. "I'm not lyin' either. Ask anyone else here; we all observe the sky. That's why our grandparents and great-grandparents came here in the first place. Great place to observe the universe, the desert is. And a great place to pretend yer on another planet yer'self. I watch the stars every night, see what's goin on, and write down what patterns I see. Some stars I've even named myself."

"Woah," Au breathed.

Lirah could tell, as Axoo witnessed their reactions to something he had seen every night for years, that they had given him back a certain novelty to the experience. Lirah knew Axoo genuinely enjoyed their company. She felt welcomed here.

Axoo chucked. "If ya want, tomorrow I can introduce ya to some folks who live here. I'm sure they'd love some new minds to share their own findings with. Some of 'em could talk fer'ever, seriously fer'*ev'er*, 'bout the universe. We're all just as fascinated by this stuff even after years and years of studyin' it."

Lirah, Mala, and Au nodded in unison.

"Alright then, I'll set up the introductions." Axoo smiled, then yawned. "That's enough star gazin' fer tonight. There's always tomorrow."

He pushed a button, and the floor started to vibrate and

rumble again, lowering them back down to reality. Then he pulled down on a large lever. At first, nothing seemed to happen, until it became apparent that the projection was shutting down and the opening in the roof was closing up. The sparkles and mist—or as Axoo had called them, the stars and nebulae—were slowly starting to vanish, traveling farther and farther away, while the black backdrop was lightening to a shade of indigo.

"Sometimes the projection lags after I shut the telescope down." Axoo pointed at the crystal and shrugged. He passed by the trio sitting in a row on his bed. "I'm gonna get some water, and then I'm goin' to bed."

"Okay, we're heading down now too," Au said.

But Lirah wasn't about to move yet. She was stuck in a trance, watching the dying crystal and its lingering images of stars slowly sink into the indigo background. The remaining nebulae followed, floating down and catching the backdrop as if it was thick muck. The background swallowed up the last of the stars and nebulae, then gradually continued to lighten, transitioning into a solid color like a dull morning sky. That's when blackness poured in.

Lirah shivered. The crystal had fully restored itself back to its translucent form, taking all of the magic along with it and leaving the room in total darkness. She was left with a hauntingly familiar feeling of nothingness. It settled deep within her chest.

So, this had been her vision.

* * *

The following morning Lirah woke to the sound of clattering pots and pans.

After the star show had ended last night, the trio fell asleep instantly on the cushions in the living room, where remarkably, Lirah experienced nothing but pleasant dreams for the first time in ages.

She dreamt of zooming around on the back of a flying star and riding it through nebula mist before landing on soft ground. She sprawled out beneath sublime skies in the grasslands, except these grasslands were on a different planet. A young woman who looked just like her was there too, musing on about endless possibilities and combinations for life in the universe. They laughed together and breathed in the sweet air.

After she woke up, Lirah was disappointed she couldn't remember any secrets the woman had told her about the universe. But instead of allowing her desire for answers to rhetorical questions to drive her crazy, Lirah thought of it all as a game now. The telescope's projection only baffled her more about life and its mysterious meanings, adding layers to the already complex maze in her head. So, of course, she dreamt up explanations.

The idea that all those stars in the sky were providing light for other forms of life had her head buzzing. There could be others ... others just like her, and Au, and Mala ... *Out There.* Could this other Lirah look up, within her own bubble of sky, and see the same stars that she could? Entertain the same ideas that she did? Did this other Lirah wonder if life had a purpose besides living itself? Did she gaze through telescopes and wonder if there were others like her so far away that she'd never be able to have an actual conversation with them?

At least I can meet with her in my dreams, Lirah thought. *And more information has to be thrown my way at the Scope Settlement. It's filled with more technology than the Treetop Society could've ever dreamt up. Surely,* she reasoned, *residents here will have their own musings about life's purposes.*

Yet, she didn't understand how this upgraded lifestyle existed out in such a barren environment, rather than in a place teaming with life and resources like the jungle. Axoo had said the desert was a good place to look at the sky ... that everyone here was a *scientist.* Well, that sounded fancy and smart enough to Lirah. Anyway, she didn't need to worry about that right now; she just got here.

She exhaled deeply to clear her head and sat up. There was Mala, waking up beside her, yawning.

Au was already up. He was standing in the kitchen, trying to decipher the new stove technology.

He's the one making all the noise. Lirah stood and stretched.

She watched him turn a knob and jump back at the sight of a flame, bumping into a cabinet behind him. She giggled.

When she started feeling lightheaded, she realized she was still very dehydrated. She walked to the kitchen and searched the cabinets for two cups, stopping to give Au a good morning nose rub. She stepped outside to fill them in the river and found Axoo scrubbing Josie, who was covered in a bubbly foam that Lirah had never seen before.

"Hi, Axoo. What's that stuff on Josie?"

"Well, well. Look who's finally awake!" Axoo bellowed, rattling Lirah's weary eardrums. "This here is *soap*. Ya never used soap before?! I guess I forgot to give ya some last night to rinse with, huh? Well, it's great fer cleaning. You can use some when I'm all done here. Tell Mala and Au too."

"Okay, I will." Lirah laughed when he flung the bubbly substance at her as she filled up the cups in the river.

When she walked back indoors, she found Mala peering out the window at Josie and Axoo.

"What's that foam on Josie?" Mala asked sleepily.

Lirah handed her a cup of water. "Soap. Axoo said we can use some to clean ourselves after he's done bathing her."

"Hmm, interesting," Mala said in a dreamy voice, staring out the window, lost in thought again.

"Mala, what are you thinking about?" Lirah tried her best not to sound annoyed. She'd nearly forgotten how her mother behaved around Josie yesterday, but now Mala was acting weird again. "You can tell me anything. You know, no matter how bad."

"Oh, my light ... it's not bad." Mala sighed., "It's almost too good that ... I'm afraid if I speak of it ... it will become undone."

Lirah had no idea where she was going with this. "Please just tell me."

Mala opened her mouth to speak right as Au dropped a pan. It crashed loudly on the floor.

"Oh my, Au. I know you're listening," said Mala. "Fine, you two. Au, come over here, and I'll tell you both."

Au tossed some ingredients into the pot and bashfully tottered over, giving Lirah a weak smile as he stopped beside her.

Mala took a sip of her water, swallowing uneasily. "You might think this is crazy, but here it goes ... I think a spirit is currently inhabiting Josie's body, and I think that spirit is being controlled by Bue. Or it could be Bue himself ... somehow."

She sighed when neither Lirah nor Au responded.

But Lirah had no idea what to say. She looked out the window and intensely analyzed the bulla, as if squinting hard enough would reveal her father's spirit inside. She took a sip of water, keeping her eyes narrowed over the brim of her cup and locked onto Josie as she did so. Now Lirah understood why her mother had been acting so weird yesterday, because here she was, doing the *exact* same thing.

All three of them were huddled by the window staring Josie down as she got her bath. They watched Axoo pour bucket after bucket of water over her as she shook and jumped up and down, spraying the water everywhere.

If Axoo looks over at us right now, he'll think we're all deranged stalkers, Lirah thought.

She took a step back towards the circle of cushions so she wouldn't look like a creep anymore.

"It's probably temporary," Mala said, unconsciously following Lirah over to the cushions, Au trailing right behind her. "But I sensed Bue's presence very strongly when we first encountered Josie yesterday, and it hasn't gone away since. Every time I look at her, I feel like I'm looking at *him*."

"I believe you," Lirah said. Of course, she did believe her

mother, but she had never heard of Pride members turning into bullas after they died before either. "How did he, *um*, get inside of Josie's body, or ... er ... how is he *controlling* her?"

Mala laughed. "That's what *I've* been trying to figure out. I'd imagine that Bue became a spirit guide. After spiritual beings die in the physical world, they can still make some contact with us while inhabiting the spirit world. He always had connections to both worlds, so that idea makes the most sense. But I've never witnessed any spiritual contact quite like this before."

Lirah tried to figure out what that meant, how some beings could be spiritual and not others.

"Honestly, none of this speculating even matters much. Bue wouldn't be able to communicate with us using words or in any way that would give away it's really him in there." Mala's voice cracked. "But ... I wouldn't be surprised if your father knew we were going to die out there in the open desert, even before we did, so he guided Josie in our direction to rescue us."

"Wow," Lirah said. "So, the bulla running towards us at the perfect time ... wasn't just a coincidence after all."

"Wasn't Axoo the one guiding Josie to us?" Au spoke up.

Mala smiled dryly. "Owners like to think they have more control over their beasts than they really do. If Josie wanted to wander off in that direction of the desert, Axoo probably trusted that she picked up the scent of food when she was actually tracking us."

"That's amazing," Au said right as a harsh sizzling sound came from the kitchen.

The contents in his pot were boiling over. He ran over to save the meal. It smelt like he had been experimenting with fish and spices. It seemed similar to Axoo's broth from last night except even more pungent, somehow.

Lirah considered Mala's theory. It did explain why Josie had stared into Lirah's eyes and teared up when she was leaning against her after they arrived at the Scope Settlement yesterday. Would that mean Josie's true colors were also Bue's true colors? Could Lirah sense her father like her mother could? A lump formed in her throat.

Mala rested a hand on her daughter's shoulder and whispered in her ear, "My Always and Forever mate. Bue really embodies that phrase, huh?" She pulled Lirah in for a hug. Lirah nodded into her mother's warm shoulder.

Then, silently knowing there was nothing left to talk about regarding Josie or Bue, they went to observe Au's attempts at cooking.

"What are you making?" Lirah asked him, leaning over the counter.

Au was sweating, deep in concentration.

Apparently, he was not only trying his hand at mixing things together in a pot, but he also had a pan with eggs frying on top. They were blackened, smoking, and sticking to the pan unremorsefully.

"I was *trying* to make fish stew and eggs." Au groaned. "But I don't know how long to keep eggs on this contraption. I thought they'd take longer to cook on this than over a real fire, but apparently *not*." He turned his attention away from his burnt eggs and over to his broth, which started bubbling over again. A hissing sound pierced their ears as the liquid coursed down the sides of the pot and onto the heat source.

Axoo swung open the door. "Well, well! It sure does smell amazin' in here."

Lirah wondered if his sense of smell was working quite right. It smelt like sour fish smoke.

"Thanks fer makin' breakfast Au."

"Yeah, anytime," Au said, sweating over his steaming broth. "Thanks for letting me use your appliances and meat. I hope I didn't ruin anything."

"Oh, it'll be fine, I'm sure! Took me awhile to perfect my cookin' skills myself. Anyway, I've been up long before the light has, and I *still* haven't eaten a *thing*. I could eat anything right now. 'Course I meant to eat earlier, but I got caught up talkin' with some friends of mine, tellin' 'em 'bout rescuin' ya and all. Now they're dyin' to meet ya. Just as I expected." Axoo chuckled. "Yer all in fer another treat this afternoon. We're goin' to the library!"

Lirah scrunched her nose. A library? What was that? Before today, she thought she'd be excited to meet a whole new community, but now that it was actually going to happen, a prickly sense of nervousness rushed over her.

Mala and Au's faces looked unsettled too. Or maybe Au was just frustrated because of his burning meal, and maybe Mala was just lost in thought about Bue and Josie again. They did look like they were only half listening.

Lirah huffed. She wanted to banish these negative emotions. She had nothing to be afraid of. She had the ability to see others' true colors now. They couldn't be manipulated as they had been in Airis. She *wanted* to meet Axoo's friends. She forced her facial muscles into a large grin. "Great!"

"I told em' we'd be there around three o'clock," Axoo said. "But I always like to be early, so let's aim fer two. That way I can show ya 'round the library, and you can get comfortable before the other settlers show up. Today's an off day for workin' and takin' classes, so we'll have our own space at first. They're all comin' just to meet ya; nice, huh? Say, have you ever been to a library before?"

Lirah shook her head.

"Au? Mala?"

"*Hmm*, no," Mala said, her tone distant.

Au looked up from the smoking pan, "Huh? Library? Never heard of it."

"Well then, even better! You'll just have to wait and see then. I won't spoil it."

CHAPTER 25

After eating Au's experimental breakfast, which actually wasn't half bad, Axoo handed over a bar of soap. Lirah, Mala, and Au lined up and took turns bathing in one of the large silver buckets out front. Lirah scrubbed the soft bubbly bar over her skin, pushing off the rest of the orange grime she missed during her rinse last night.

Josie seemed quite amused while she watched them from her hut, and so did a few onlookers who casually passed by.

Lirah made eye contact with a petite, purple-skinned woman across the river who was clunking by in a long white shirt and large boots. Then she quickly turned her head the other way.

Why did I look away? Lirah scolded herself after the woman passed.

After bathing, the trio slipped on their original dress cloths that had dried overnight on Josie's gate, using them as undergarments. Then they threw their new, oversized white shirts on top. Lirah tussled her auburn hair around, which stopped past her hips now, and brushed up her long eyelashes with her fingertips, trying to make herself look most presentable.

Lirah hoped they would all ride Josie over to the library. She figured time with Bue's spirit would help settle her nerves and allow her to make a good first impression with the other settlers instead of shying away. But on their way out, Axoo rushed them right past Josie. Lirah sighed.

Even though the walk to the library turned out to be fairly short—crossing three bridges each spaced about a thousand feet apart—Lirah's sore legs were practically begging her to stop when they approached the high doors. She couldn't believe that just yesterday Axoo and Josie had rescued them. Before that, the trio was on their feet for entire days at a time. Lirah cringed at the thought of ever travelling like that again.

Rather than shaped like a mushroom, the library was one of the two structures shaped like a rectangular box. It looked like twenty mushroom homes had been melted together and smoothed out. Lirah, upon approaching its arched, looming doors and windows, gulped.

Axoo confidently pushed the towering door open. Cold air hit them in the face.

When the door creaked closed behind them, stillness took over.

At first, the lack of noise creeped Lirah out. It reminded her of when the grasslands had gotten too quiet and they were being stalked by that enormous, translucent snake. But when she breathed in the aged wood, which she had assumed was nonexistent in the desert, she calmed down and began to admire the massive room.

Several circular tables, with four wooden chairs apiece, sat in a short line by the entrance. Behind them, the rest of the room was filled with rows and rows of stacked wooden shelves that rose taller than trees, nearly brushing against the ceiling of fluorescent lights. Lirah couldn't tell how far back the rows of shelves ran. There were so many of them that it looked like an organized jungle.

Most peculiarly, the identical shelves were stacked with nothing but rectangular boxes, mimicking the exterior of the library itself. They came in different colors and thicknesses, but Lirah couldn't help thinking that only one stack of shelves was real while the rest were mere reflections of the one before it.

"What are all those things on the shelves?" Au asked. "With the colorful wrappings?"

"Books!" Axoo said, happily. "They're bonded papers with words written on 'em. The same words you speak out loud. But when ya write 'em down, they become more permanent. They can keep ideas around fer'ever."

"Can we look through them?" Lirah asked, curious to see how one felt. She wanted to make sure they were real.

"Sure! Just put 'em back in the same spot ya found em' in. They're organized by language and category, ya see, and they're in alphabetical order in those categories. Marg'd kill me if she knew we messed up her hard work. I'll stay here and come find ya when others start showin' up. Don't get lost now." Axoo chuckled. "Oh, and no shoutin'. Ya have to be quiet in a library. It's Marg's rule, and it's the polite thing to do."

The trio ambled towards the rows of shelves. They peered down each narrow path and chose one at random to walk down.

Skinny ladders on wheels were placed sporadically down the aisle. They were smartly attached to the wooden frames so you could reach the books that rose above your head, which the majority of them did, no matter how tall you were.

Au didn't hesitate to climb up to the very top of the first ladder he saw. He leaned forward and propped his elbows up against the highest shelf, giving himself an aerial view of the entire building.

"Woahhhh. This place is huge." His voice echoed from above.

Lirah shushed him.

Another "*shush*" came from a few rows down.

"Sorry," Au whispered, loudly.

Lirah giggled, lightly shaking her head as she pulled out a random book below him.

Mala looked on over Lirah's shoulder.

Lirah fanned through the entire book. Every page was covered in teeny black shapes. Lots of them. She had no idea what any of them meant.

"Words," Mala pointed out.

"They just look like lines and squiggles." Lirah had trouble comprehending how these black markings could possibly be combined together to symbolize ideas. She noticed that the same straight lines and looping curves repeated over and over again but in different orders, with spaces thin as fingernails dividing up groups of them. How was it that she could speak with Axoo so easily but couldn't understand the same ideas when they were written? Maybe some of these squiggles and lines even represented the thoughts that she was having right this second.

Lirah gazed up at Au. He was still perched against the top shelf, fanning through books and putting them back one by one. She hoped that he was having the same thoughts as her while he observed these odd, endless markings. Mala was farther down the row now, skimming through a fat red book, but she seemed more apathetic about the experience. Lirah wouldn't have been surprised if Mala had seen a book before. She somehow knew about everything. But one book couldn't come close to a library.

Everything was endless in a library, Lirah decided. The stacks of shelves, the books crammed together within them, the blocks of lines within each page of each book, the individual markings making up each of those lines. If someone spent every second of their entire life looking through these books, they would never finish them all. So how could you choose what was most important to start with? Did you start with the oldest ones and work your way forward? Or the other way around?

"Finding anything interesting?" A voice lined with curiosity came from behind Lirah's shoulder, making her jump and lose grip of the book in her hands.

She turned around to face a pile of shaggy black hair.

A stooped man gradually straightened up and handed Lirah her fallen book. He gave her the whitest, straightest smile she had ever seen, and a well-defined black mustache hovered above it. His clothes were also completely white—a fitted collared shirt, pressed pants, and shining boots—glowing against his blue skin. Three golden chains hung around his neck. The longest chain had a sparkling star dangling from its end, accenting his pristine look. Lirah was shocked that someone would put this much effort into their appearance.

"Do you speak Filigeze?" The blue man asked hesitantly. A grin still played on his lips, but it looked slightly forced now.

Lirah realized she probably looked wild from the way she was staring at him. She had registered the words he said but took in none of their meanings. "What did you say?"

"Oh, *good*. We do speak the same language. Well, actually, Zullus speaks five languages. But Filigeze is quite common here, and it's also the language that your book is written in." He pointed to the book in Lirah's hands. "Zullus just asked if you were finding anything interesting to read." His smile stretched out widely again.

"Well … I don't actually know what the symbols in this book mean." Lirah blushed. "And… who's *'Zullus'*?"

"Oh, how rude of Zullus. I haven't introduced myself. My name is Zullus, and I practically live in this library. Zullus teaches math and science classes here every day, except today. This is when Zullus prepares for classes. *And* I enjoy saying my name out loud." He grinned with pride. "Zullus has never seen you here before, but if you would like to come to a class, you are always welcome. Astronomy is my most popular one."

Lirah didn't know how she felt about this man. He seemed very friendly and charming, but artificial. He looked quite normal to her eyes, in regard to her true-color-spotting ability, but it was very strange that he referred to himself in the third person. She decided he was just very quirky.

"Hello, Zullus. I'm Lirah. I've never taken a ... *class* ... before. But maybe I can try one."

"My name is Au," Au whispered down harshly.

Lirah and Zullus jumped, then looked up.

Au was peering down at them, his narrowed eyes and furrowed brows peeking above a book he was clenching in his hands. He closed the book and shoved it back into its place.

Their eyes followed him as he swiftly climbed down the ladder and halted between the two of them.

"Hello!" Zullus said, enthusiastically. "Zullus didn't see you up there. Or ever before in my life. Really, Zullus has never seen anyone with your tone of skin before. It's *fascinating.* If you don't mind Zullus asking, where are you both from? Zullus presumes not far, seeing as we can communicate in the same language. Axoo was telling me about desert drifters he picked up just yesterday. Zullus assumes that he was referring to you. So, do you reside in this settlement now?"

Lirah didn't know what to say. She didn't know if they resided in this settlement now or not. Currently, she, Mala, and Au had no plans for their future whatsoever. Also, she didn't understand how they happened to know the same language as Zullus, or how their skin tones were so different from his.

"We're from the jungle," Au said.

"Does this jungle have a name?" Zullus asked.

Au shrugged and rolled his eyes.

After a long moment of awkward silence, Lirah let out a sigh of relief to see Axoo approaching from the back of the library, his arms weighted down with books. The row was so long that by the time he reached the group, he was out of breath.

"Hello ... Zullus," Axoo wheezed, "I'm happy ya met Lirah ... and Au." He breathed in, filled up his large stomach with air, and exhaled. "They're the ... drifters ... I was tellin' ya 'bout."

"Ah, yes Zullus has heard. This is very exciting news. Zullus really does hope you both consider coming to classes. There is much to learn."

"An endless amount," Lirah murmured.

Axoo's arms started to shake under his tower of books. "Here." he sighed. He split the stack and handed five books to Lirah and five to Au. "I was gettin' bored sittin' by the entrance. I decided to find some books that ya might like 'bout jungles and stars. Be careful though. They're mighty heavy." He chuckled.

Axoo stretched out his arms, twisted his plump torso around, and peered past the group, looking up and back down the empty row. "Where'd Mala go?"

"Hmm," Lirah said. "I'm not sure. She was skimming through a book on this row. She's probably checking out the rest of library now. I can't understand what any of these books say, but maybe she's able to."

"Aha! Zullus could teach you how to read. As a new, separate class each week," Zullus offered ecstatically. "It will be challenging and take lots of time, but Zullus is prepared to help."

"Well, well, that's a great idea!" Axoo bellowed.

Au and Lirah exchanged ambiguous looks. If learning to read required lots of time, then that implied they would be staying here awhile if they took these classes with Zullus.

Last night before dinner, Axoo did offer us a place to stay for as long as we liked, thought Lirah, *and this settlement really is nothing short of a dream. Especially compared to the brutal weeks leading up to being here. And where else would we go, anyway?*

Her heart started fluttering when she pictured herself living and learning in the Scope Settlement permanently. But she knew she had to speak with Mala and Au in private before she voiced these feelings, and she had to find Mala for that.

"Thank you for offering, Zullus," Lirah said politely. "I need to find my mother before accepting. I'll ask her if she'd like to take reading classes too."

"I'll come with you," Au said.

"Nice meeting you both," Zullus grinned.

Lirah and Au nodded to Axoo and Zullus and dismissed themselves, shuffling away with their arms piled with books.

* * *

Once Lirah and Au reached the center of the back hall, and after eyeing its plushy orange couches that faced glossy arched windows and a view of the striking blue river, they set their books down beside a couch.

"I'd like to sit right here and read ... if I ever learn how." Lirah ran her hand over the back of the plush fabric. "It's so peaceful."

"When we find Mala, we can all come back and lounge around. We can make up words and pretend like we can read." Au smiled and stroked a piece of her hair.

"Perfect." Lirah laughed. "Let's split up and make this quick. I'll look down all the rows on the right side of the library and you cover the left half."

Right away, Lirah thought she found Mala skimming through a book just one row over. She couldn't wait to whisper to her mother about the funny man she met and how he liked to say his own name out loud. She wanted to show Mala the nice couches and ask if she already knew how to read, and if so, how?

Lirah paced down the narrow hall of packed books, straight towards the back of Mala's black and messy hair, when Mala turned her head and Lirah realized the browsing woman wasn't her mother. It was the woman with purple skin and blue boots that Lirah had turned away from earlier.

Lirah lightly waved to the petite woman before spinning on her heel, still not wanting to make conversation with the stranger. She knew she would have time to speak with her at three, along with the rest of Axoo's friends when they showed up.

Lirah checked down the other rows on the right side of the building. No Mala.

The last barren row sent a shiver from her neck to her toes. This drafty, enclosed box made her feel hollow. Time passed differently in here than it did outside. She felt like she had already been looking for Mala for hours, when in reality, only minutes had passed.

She sighed, turned on her heel, and marched back to the middle of the hall. Au was already there leaning against the orange couch with their books piled beside it.

"Did you notice the doors all along the sides of the library?" he asked her. "I didn't think an indoor space could get any bigger! I opened one door and there were a bunch of small desks inside facing a board with a bunch of symbols written on it. I think that's where classes are held."

"Nice," Lirah said, looking around, preoccupied. "You didn't find Mala either?"

"No, I didn't see her."

Lirah felt her stomach tensing up, like a worm had wrapped itself around it and started pulling. Why would her mother suddenly leave her in this unfamiliar, *massive* place? And without telling her where she was going first?

"Maybe one of us missed her," Lirah said. "Let's search again but switch directions. And look inside all the side doors too."

Lirah peered down each row. She found Axoo and Zullus still talking on the same row as before, and a few more men in a small huddle down another ... but no Mala. She poked her head inside each of the five rooms along the far-left end of the library.

As the door clicked shut to the last empty room, the nervousness in her stomach doubled up. The worm yanked harder, forcing her to run slightly sideways as she went back to find Au, hoping Mala would be by his side. She tried picturing them both sitting on the plush couch, staring dreamily out the arching window, the reflection of the flowing river dancing in their eyes like the stars had last night ... when they were all together.

Lirah picked up speed, grunting through the pain knotting up in her stomach and coursing down her sore legs. Her imbalanced steps echoed down the drafty row. She tried her best to hold onto the peaceful image of Au and Mala sitting on the bright orange couch. But a wicked scene kept shoving its way past and beckoning her attention. A powerful scene that felt too real to banish after it worked its way to the front of her mind ... her vision of Mala dying.

No, that couldn't happen. Not here. Not yet.

We're finally in a safe place, Lirah tried convincing herself.

The bright couch was empty. No Mala. No Au.

She jogged by it without losing speed, the crisp wood-scented air smacking against her face, keeping her focused.

She found Au opening and closing the last door on the right side of the library. His forehead was creased with panic. "No sight of her. This place is way too big, don't you think?"

Lirah couldn't answer. She was busy heaving, faster and faster, as if the worm around her stomach had stretched out and yanked her lungs into its grasp too, pulling them shut so air couldn't travel in. She fought against it, but the faster she breathed, the more her anxiety built up. Anxiety bubbled up through her chest, into her throat, and straight to her buzzing head.

"Hey now," Au said, placing a hand on her back, centering her. "Slow your breathing. Yes. That's it. Slow."

Lirah placed a hand on her stomach and took deep breaths, but not without pain.

"Listen," Au said. "We have to spot her eventually. Don't forget we haven't checked the entrance yet. Let's go there. Then we can check outside. Maybe it got too cold for her in here."

Lirah rapidly nodded in an effort to jerk back her forming tears. Yes, it was freezing in here. Maybe the temperature was why she had chills running up her spine.

But that vision just kept replaying her mind, no matter how hard she tried to focus on her breathing. She needed her mother, very much. Mala couldn't die. Lirah refused to trust her vision. Her unstable, inadequate ability.

Au patted her back, "Let's go."

They barreled down the row and towards the entrance, colorful books blurring together in their peripherals. They decelerated near the front of the row. Lirah jerked her head towards the tables and the entrance door.

Nothing.

She walked closer, arching her neck to peer out the window. Nothing.

"Lirah, look!" Au pointed at a table.

Mala. There she was. Her head lying face down, her flat arms sprawled out on the tabletop.

CHAPTER 26

"*Mala*!" Lirah lurched forward, sprinting to reach her mother.

Why hadn't she checked here earlier? Why did she assume Mala would be standing and climbing ladders, looking through undecodable books, exploring the rest of the library? The anxious buzzing in Lirah's head suddenly plummeted. The worm curled up and dropped like a rock through her body and to her feet, weighing them down. This was *her* fault. She had been so stupid. She should have known Mala needed more rest, given how sore her own legs felt. She should have shouted her mother's name at the start, and ignored the *no-yelling-in-the-library* rule.

Lirah tripped as she took her final step for the table, knocking right into it when she steadied herself. But Mala didn't even notice; she lay completely limp.

Au skidded to a stop directly behind Lirah, gripping her shoulder for support. "Oh no. No. No. No. No." His hand was shaking as he spoke.

Lirah placed her palms against either side of her mother's

sagging head and slowly lifted it.

"Mala?" she choked, tilting her mother's head back to examine her face. Her eyes were closed, drool pouring out of her open mouth. "Mala! Open your eyes! Can you hear me?" She shook her mother's head in her hands like it was a jar full of insects.

Au reached out and clasped his hands over Lirah's, slowing her hand motion. But Lirah didn't care if she might be disturbing Mala, she just needed her to wake up. Tears grew in her eyes, blurring her vision, "Mala! Please. *Please*. Wake up!"

"Lirah, don't shake her head so hard!"

"Then what *should* we do, Au?" She didn't understand why no one in the library was coming to help, as surely their distressed voices were loud enough to hear. And weren't more of Axoo's friends supposed to be walking through the entrance any minute now? All of the fancy "scientists" and "doctors?"

"Mmm." Mala groaned.

Lirah loosened her grip on her mother's temples. "Mala? I'm here."

"My... *lighhhh*," Mala managed to squint her eyes open for a moment and glance up at her daughter. Then they rolled back into her head like white stones and her eyelids fell shut again.

"Oh no. Not good," Au said. He stepped back, brushed his hair out of his face, and sighed. "Okay. *Okay.* At least she spoke. We just need to keep her awake."

"Axoo!" Lirah screamed. He didn't respond. She swore she heard a few confused murmurs from a nearby shelf though. She cursed them under her breath. "I'll be right back," she said. "I'm a faster runner. Here, hold up her head."

Lirah ran as fast as she possibly could, adrenaline aiding her greatly, back to the row where she had last seen Axoo. Luckily, he was still standing there with Zullus. They were in the midst of a lengthy conversation.

"Axoo!" She ran at him full force.

In an instant, Axoo's magnified eyes grew three times larger. "What?! Why do I keep hearin' shoutin'? I told ya, yer not supposed to be yellin' in a library. Is everyone else here now? What'd they say to ya? I'm sorry I got lost in a conversation but ya don't have to be scared to meet anyone."

"Mala ... Mala ... she can't open her eyes ... or sit up." Lirah panted, wishing she could have gotten out the words faster.

"Where is she? Zullus can help. I have read books about the inner workings of the body and remedies for sicknesses," Zullus said, popping his shirt collar.

"So have I," Axoo said, as if this was some competition to see who was more knowledgeable.

"Great ... She's by the entrance." Lirah wheezed. "Slouched ... over a table. Au's there."

Axoo and Zullus started speed walking in that direction, talking in medical tongues all the way down the hall and correcting one another.

Lirah gave herself a moment to catch her breath. She felt like she was breathing through the hole of a small tube. She needed to calm herself down so she could properly assist her mother. She told herself that Mala would be okay, that Mala had spoken, which meant she was still conscious.

When Lirah rounded the corner to the entrance, she saw all of Axoo's friends there, surrounding Mala. It must be three o'clock.

"What's wrong with her?" Lirah demanded as she approached the table, trying her best to ignore the whispering residents all gawking around. Just earlier, she hoped to make a good first impression with them. Now, impressions were the least of her worries.

No one answered her question.

Axoo and Zullus stood hunched over Mala, their eyebrows furrowed in concentration, assessing her. Zullus was holding the back of Mala's head in one hand, slowly rocking it side to side. His other hand was shining a delicate light-device into each of her lulling eyes. Axoo had his fingers pressed against Mala's neck while he looked down at a bracelet ticking on his other outstretched wrist, counting out loud.

Au pulled out the chair next to his, "It's okay, Lirah. Just let Axoo and Zullus focus."

Lirah sat down stiffly, wishing she could block out the croaking murmurs of all the bystanders watching this scene unfold—

"Are these the strangers Axoo wanted us meet?"

"Yes. Axoo brought them here."

"Well, I have things to do."

"What happened to that one?"

"She's getting her pulse checked."

"Well, I know that."

"Does she have a sickness that's going to spread?"

Lirah could hardly take it, she wanted to scream at them all to go away if they weren't going to help.

She turned her head to the side and analyzed the group of them. Most of them were wrinkly and deflated, and the men had to outnumber the women ten to one. Lots of them had magnifying contraptions over their eyes like Axoo did. And short, frizzled hair. They looked like a pile of fuzzy, rainbow apricots. Some residents were orange, others pink, purple, or blue. A small amount of them looked healthier and younger, probably around Axoo and Mala's age, and Zullus was by far the youngest.

Lirah sighed hopelessly. She couldn't yell at these residents. Respect for elders was too engrained in her from growing up in the Pride. She squeezed her eyes shut and dropped her head down on the table.

"Oh no, that one dropped too."

Lirah groaned. She folded her arms and cradled her head in the pocket of dark space they created, pressing her arms firmly against her eardrums and embracing the warmth. She released her tears like a cage full of butterflies, letting them stream down her face and onto the table. She felt so helpless. There was nothing she could do for Mala.

Lirah felt a tap on her shoulder. She sniffled and lifted her head. It was Zullus.

"Zullus doesn't know the cause of this behavior. Zullus thinks the best thing to do is to bring her back to Axoo's. She needs plenty of water and food. And most importantly, sleep."

"That's what I said," Axoo mumbled. He cleared his throat and straightened up his squat stature, "Lirah, don't worry. She'll be alright. After all you've gone through, the travelin' and trauma and all, she's gotta be physically drained and mentally exhausted. Her body probably knows it's finally safe for it to give out." He reached in his pocket and pulled out something very thin and flat. It looked like a leaf. He peeled an artificial skin from the item and stuck it to Mala's arm. "Rehydration patch," he said. "This should help her until we can replenish her with more nutrients."

Lirah nodded and wiped her tears with her arm. Au gave her his hand and helped her to her feet. She was glad they were leaving.

Axoo and Zullus pulled Mala out of her chair and adjusted her arms so that each one rested across their neck and shoulders, supporting her weight as they walked.

Zullus flashed grins and apologies to the squinting bystanders on their way out. Axoo explained to them all that Mala was only exhausted, not sick or contagious.

So, Axoo heard their whispers too.

"... And thanks for comin' everyone! I'm sorry 'bout all this. We'll have to reschedule," Axoo said.

The door swung closed, cutting off the murmurs.

"She'll be alright, Lirah," Au said, more hesitantly than reassuringly, as they trudged through the plumes of orange dust.

The light above burned down hard, directly onto their skin.

Lirah was not convinced that her mother was "alright." From the way that Axoo and Zullus had behaved on their way out of the library—embarrassed, apologizing, explaining—it dawned on her that they just wanted to be out of the crowd. They didn't care about Mala. Angry sparks filled her chest. She wanted to explode.

She ran ahead and stood in front of Axoo and Zullus, blocking the bridge that they were about to cross. "What if she doesn't wake up again, *huh*? After you lay her down to rest? Then what? She's my mother! She's *never* acted like this before. She needs more than food and sleep. She needs some kind of medicinal tea or remedy. She would know how to make one! Do you *really* care? You don't even know her." Lirah looked down at her petite mother. Mala's head was slumped to the side, bobbing against Axoo's shirt, with drool spilling from the corners of her groaning mouth.

"Lirah, please move. Of course we care! Mala needs outta this harsh light, quick! Let's get her inside and then we'll talk more."

"Zullus knows remedial drink recipes, Lirah, don't worry. She is under the best care in the Scope Settlement. It's quite lucky that you ran into Zullus." He gave her a wide artificial smile, his bleached teeth nearly blinding her in the light.

Lirah stepped out of the way, letting them pass her. Suddenly, she was sobbing again. What was she thinking? She had no other choice but to trust them, the *scientists*, whether she wanted to or not. She looked straight down and watched as her falling tears made little rings when they crashed into the sizzling ground.

Really, this entire journey, that was all she had been doing—trusting others. Au used to tell her that she was overly trusting. But now, after everything they'd gone through, a shift must have taken place within her.

She realized that she had no control when she lived in the Treetop Society and she still had no control outside of it, even if it seemed like she did at times. Instances of control had been an illusion, and she felt herself breaking because of it. She squatted down and wrapped her arms around herself, continuing to watch her tears fall down to the sand.

Au's shadow came into view. He squatted down and released her wrapped arms from her thin body. He helped her stand, took hold of her open hand, and guided her over the bridge. He was the only stable part of this whole experience. Lirah gripped his hand harder and rubbed her thumb across the side of his rough palm as they walked to catch up with the others.

* * *

Axoo threw open the door of his observatory home. Cool air rushed over them as they stepped inside, relieving them from the midafternoon light.

Axoo and Zullus slowly settled Mala's limp body down onto a cot. Lirah flew to her side and grabbed her hand.

"She'll be alright," Axoo murmured from the kitchen, grabbing a cup for Mala and filling it from a metal pipe, rather than walking to the river.

"We can drink that water?" asked Lirah.

"Yeah. It's the same water that's in the river. There's pipes underground connectin' 'em. I use both." He shrugged and shuffled over to Lirah. "Get her to drink the whole cup."

Lirah nodded and pressed the cup up to her mother's red lips, which were blistered from the desert heat. With her other hand, Lirah attempted to steady Mala's dangling head, but her tangled hair kept getting stuck in Lirah's fingers.

"Can someone help?" Lirah arched her neck towards the kitchen.

Zullus was searching through Axoo's cabinets, grunting at certain jars of spices and returning them to their spots, and *ooo-ing* and *aaa-ing* at others and setting them down in a straight line on the counter.

In his cooling box, which he had called a "fridge" last night, Axoo was doing the same thing—pulling out ingredients, smelling them, tossing some next to Zullus's jars, and putting others back.

Whatever they planned to make for Mala, it looked like guesswork to Lirah.

Au made his way over to help Lirah. He steadied Mala's head while Lirah poured thin streams of water into her mouth. Mala accepted the water, swallowing it easily. That was a good sign.

But Lirah found it unsettling and awkward to force her mother to drink. Mala had always been the healthy one, taking care of Lirah and Bue when they were sick. She knew just what to mix together to make them feel better. Mala used to blend different herbs and boil them to make teas, filling the hive with smells of ginger and wildflowers, coaxing her loved ones to swallow every thick, bitter drop. Lirah wished she knew her mother's recipes now.

She whispered in her ear, "Bue saved us, Mala, and he's caring for you now. You're going to be just fine."

Once Mala drank the entire cup of water, Lirah hummed soft melodies and stroked her hair. She wanted to keep her mother awake until she ate and drank something substantial.

Besides the clinking and cutting in the kitchen, the only sounds in the room were Lirah's soft hums and sniffles.

CHAPTER 27

Zullus handed Lirah a cup full of lime green sludge. She took a sniff and nearly gagged. "Zullus thinks this should be strong enough. Try to get Mala to drink all of it," he said.

Just as they did with the water, Lirah and Au worked together to help Mala swallow the sludge. But it kept shooting up Mala's throat and splattering all over Lirah's arms like baby vomit. Not that the stew Axoo made was any better. Mala spit out the first few bites of that too. But eventually, Mala coaxed her stomach into keeping down most of the stew and half of the drink. She seemed to be perking up, and some of her color was returning.

Lirah smiled up at Au, Axoo, and Zullus. "Thank you for your help, all of you."

They nodded, mouths full, finishing up their own bowls of Axoo's stew.

Axoo dropped his bowl in the sink. "Anytime! I like the company anyhow. Now, I 'oughta go and see who's left at the library, to explain what's goin' on." He wiped his mouth with his shirt and marched towards the door.

"Zullus will come too. It was a pleasure meeting you all. Zullus knows you'll get better soon, Mala." Zullus smiled down at Mala, noticed she was sleeping, and shifted his gaze over to Lirah. His dark brown eyes pierced through her own as if he wanted to say something more. He opened his mouth, closed it again, cleared his throat, nodded to her, then strutted out the door behind Axoo.

Silence took over the room. Lirah found a blanket and spread it over Mala, then she finally made herself a bowl of stew. Her rumbling stomach was relieved when she took her first bite.

"Do you want to stay here and take classes at the library?" Au asked her. "I think that would make the most sense, especially given Mala's condition. We can talk to Axoo about it tonight. Even though I think he already assumes we're staying."

Lirah lifted her head from her half-eaten bowl. She had completely forgotten about Zulus's offer to teach them and Axoo's immediate approval of the idea.

"Oh, so now you trust our company, huh?" Lirah smirked. "I didn't like how those residents were treating us at the library. Maybe I won't talk to you for months and mope around if we stay." She playfully rolled her eyes at him.

The blood drained from Au's face. He looked at her like he had been wrongfully accused of a crime. "Lirah, I ... but I was right about the brutes—"

"Au, I'm kidding. I have abilities that I never had in Airis. We know this place is safe, and I'll warm up to Axoo's friends eventually. Also, we're in the middle of the desert. Where else would we go? I agree with you, staying here sounds nice." Lirah smiled and took a large bite of stew.

"*Uh-huh*, and if we stay that means you'll get to spend lots of time with Zullus. It seems like you two will get along just fine ... with the way he looks at you." Au sneered.

Lirah nearly spit out her mouthful of stew. "What is *that* supposed to mean, Au? *You* are my partner." She tried to sound annoyed, but secretly she felt flattered that Au was jealous. This had never happened before. "But even if you weren't, I don't like Zullus like *that*, and he cares a little too much about his image, wouldn't you say?"

Au shrugged. "I thought you would like how he dresses. He's ... you know ... clean."

Lirah couldn't help but laugh. "No. I prefer messy hair, and tattered dress cloths. Especially on you. Your body isn't all covered up that way; it's natural."

Au blushed and opened his mouth, but quickly clamped it shut again. He shook his tussled hair around.

What is it with men and not wanting to share their feelings?

"What is it?" she asked.

"Nothing, it doesn't matter anymore."

"I'm sure it matters. Tell me."

"Well..." Au paused. He twiddled with his fingers, staring at them as if they held all the answers. "You just mentioned that we're partners, and ... you know, if we were still part of the Pride ... we would have to officially announce who our Always and Forever mates are around this time. We're nearing that age ... you know?"

Lirah gazed at him. Her heart turned mushy and warm like her stew.

"Yes, I know," she said. "We are nearing that age, aren't we? I haven't thought much about my age since we fled the Pride ... but, you're right."

"Yeah." Au blushed down at his fingers.

"Do you think all of that still matters? Having an Always and Forever mate? Throwing a celebration? I know the Treetop Society got destroyed, but I actually always liked that tradition."

Au finally looked up from his hands and into Lirah's eyes. He stared at her longingly but uncertainly, like a wild animal being offered food from someone and trying to decide if it's safe. "Yeah, I liked going to those ceremonies too. When I was young, I always imagined ..." he paused and blushed his deepest shade of pink yet, then he dropped his head again.

Lirah grinned and placed her bowl down on the table. She stood and plopped herself down on his lap. "I always imagined getting our noses pricked together too." She wrapped her arms around his neck and tilted up his chin. She rubbed her nose against his. "I think it's amazing that we can focus on this now that we're finally out of danger. We could still have a ceremony, if you wanted."

Au's face lit up, like she wasn't a hunter after all, but his glorious guardian. "So, you'll be my Always and Forever mate?" His voice shook.

Lirah beamed. "Yes. After all that we've been through together? Getting locked in cages, escaping from the Treetop Society, running from brutes, trekking through those bizarre grasslands, and nearly dying out in the middle of the desert? I think the spirits want us together. Or the universe that Axoo told us about does ... or whatever else is *Out There*." Lirah's amber-brown eyes gleamed over with tears as she spoke, "I think we're Always and Forever mates already."

Au wiped away her tears, though had his own forming. "You're right. We just need a ceremony to make it feel more official."

They looked into each other's eyes, their faces only inches apart.

Lirah leaned in closer.

Au placed his hand on the back of her head and pulled her in.

They shared their first kiss.

PART 4: BOXES AND BEGINNINGS

CHAPTER 28

"Could you bring me some water?" Mala asked in a particularly raspy voice following her long nap.

"Hm? Oh yes. Of course." Lirah shook her head clear of her fantasies.

Ever since she and Au shared their first kiss, they dozed and let Mala sleep in peace. Lirah had been replaying her own perfect rendition of their Always and Forever mate ceremony in her head and flashing her eyes over at Au. Each time, she found him gazing lovingly back at her.

Lirah scooped up Mala's empty cup and rushed over to the sink to fill it. The idea of clean water streaming from a pipe at the turn of a knob still boggled her mind.

"Are you feeling better, Mala?" Au asked.

"Yes. I'm feeling alright now," Mala answered while attempting to sit up but failing. She wilted back down, her head flopping over the side of her petite neck. She looked like an old doll.

Au gently pulled Mala's shoulders forward so she could sit upright, and Lirah handed her the water.

Mala downed the entire cup in one slurp. She handed it back to Lirah asking for more.

"So … at the library," Lirah started slowly, her back facing Mala as she walked over to the sink, "I found you sprawled out over a table. Unconscious. I was able to shake you awake … kind of. But you couldn't move on your own or really even speak. Axoo and Zullus had to haul you back here. Do you remember any of this? Or what led up to your collapse?"

Only the sound of the running faucet offered Lirah a reply. She sighed.

"Could you *please* tell us what might have caused this? *Anything*." Lirah handed her mother the freshly filled cup. Mala chugged it in its entirety again.

Mala sighed tiredly, as if drinking water required the same amount of labor as sprinting did. "At the library, from what I remember, I started feeling lightheaded right when we walked through the library doors … after looking up at all those bookshelves … their endless repetition." She pressed her index finger and thumb against the bridge of her nose and crinkled her eyes shut. "I remember I started feeling even worse right when you two started talking with someone. I didn't want to interrupt so I left that row and decided to make my way back to the front tables and sit down. That's when my vision went black. I'm grateful that I even made it to a chair before I passed out."

Lirah pictured finding her mother lying unconscious on the library floor, warm blood pouring from her head and flowing down the slick floors. Yes, it could have been much worse.

"I wonder why that happened … the lightheadedness …" said Au.

"It must have been from our journey, right?" Lirah asked, her voice tinged with anxiety. "The lack of food, the hot desert sun, walking miles every day. But now that we're safe it won't happen again, right Mala?"

Mala shrugged. "I'm just getting old."

"What? What do you mean?" Lirah scrunched her brows.

"You're not *that* old."

"Old enough that I can't keep travelling like we have been."

Lirah quickly took the seat beside Mala and clutched her weathered hand anxiously in her own, smooth one. "You don't have to. Remember? Axoo said we could stay here for as long as we wanted."

Mala looked at Lirah like she had just eaten something disgusting. "You don't think you're really going to live here for the rest of your life, do you?"

Lirah was rattled, and it wasn't just because of the repulsed look Mala gave her. It was how her mother had used the term *"you're"* instead of *"we're"* in regard to living at the Scope Settlement.

Had Mala experienced a similar vision to Lirah's … one about her *own* death? Was that even possible? Lirah quickly shook the image out of her mind.

"Well," Lirah said. "Zullus offered to teach Au and me how to read, and Axoo thought it sounded like a good idea. Besides that, this is a safe community … full of knowledge, advanced technology, and plenty of food. So yes, *we're* going to stay."

"And after you've completed your reading classes?" Mala asked firmly.

Lirah looked to Au for some sort of input. He stood with his arms folded, already gazing intently back at her, but only shrugged.

"I—*we*—don't know what will come after that," Lirah sputtered helplessly, exasperated. "Where else is there to go? We're in the middle of nowhere and you know exactly what it took to get here. We nearly *died*."

"Exactly. We did *not* come all this way for you two to stop here," said Mala. "You don't belong in a metal box slowly cooking away in the desert. This is not your final destination."

"What else do you think is out there, Mala?" Au spoke up.

"I know there must be communities elsewhere, with generations of families, growth, and resources. Think about it …" Mala sighed, tired from talking so much. "How did all of these resources end up here to begin with? These contraptions weren't made here. They had to have been transferred over."

Lirah was momentarily dumbfounded. She tried envisioning where these homes, books, telescopes … all of it … may have been transferred from, when Mala gave her final order.

"There is no future here," she said. "You can take your classes, learn quickly, and then you need to leave. Meaning leave *me* here."

"But you'll recover," Lirah whined.

Mala shook her head. "My light." She sighed. "I'm done travelling. I only began this journey for you in the first place. You have a lot more to live for than I do. So, I ask that you continue on without me."

Then she closed her eyes.

Lirah stared at her mother's worn face. It was full of lines marking the years of her life, as if an artist added another brush stroke each time a crucial event had passed.

Deep down, she knew Mala was speaking the truth. Just because Lirah wanted so badly for this settlement to be the destination of her dreams, she knew it was not. There was no youth here. The youngest inhabitant she had seen was Zullus, and he must have been double her age.

But leaving without Mala was not an option. Lirah was going to be with her until she took her last breath. That was a fact. She couldn't look at her mother anymore. She wanted to be alone. She released her grip from Mala's hand and marched out the door to the edge of the river.

It had grown cool outside. It was around dusk now, but Axoo still hadn't returned. Lirah hoped he wasn't staying away because he didn't want to disturb Mala. It was his home after all.

Maybe there's an open structure we could move into for a while, Lirah thought as she gazed around at the other metal homes gently reflecting light beneath a sheet of faded pink clouds. She squinted through the spaces between them.

Flat, orange, desolate land was all that spanned in the distance. She didn't see how anything else could exist out there. She tried reminding herself that the jungle was *Out There*, and the grasslands were *Out There*, even if she couldn't see them now. So, what other environments might be there be?

She wished she could drift around like these pink clouds and leave her legs behind. She took a deep breath, tried filling herself up with air to grow light, then exhaled. She kicked at the dust beneath her, watching it rise and float off.

Heavy and defeated, Lirah turned to go back inside, but not before admiring Josie in her hut. She stroked her mane, and it softened her heart like melted wax. She didn't know why this simple action helped so much, but she felt a little better. She turned her focus to more positive thoughts as she petted Josie. She decided that when she got inside, she would prepare food as a gesture of thanks to Axoo for when he returned. It was the least she could do. He had taken them in and genuinely wanted to help them in any way he could.

Inside, Au, her soon to be Always and Forever mate, had already beaten her to the task. He stood over a boiling pot, mixing yet another fish stew, while Mala slept soundly on her cot. Lirah's heart melted further. She joined Au in the pungent smelling kitchen. He smiled sleepily at her, his eyelids drooping. She leaned in and they shared their second kiss.

* * *

The next morning, Lirah woke to the sound of Axoo's boots stomping down the spiral staircase. She rubbed her eyes and stood from her cot, remembering that she never saw him come home last night. They had eaten without him, but made sure to leave him extra stew in the fridge.

She smiled at him when he passed by.

"G'mornin," Axoo whispered, tipping his head down as he slowly opened the front door. Au and Mala were still sound asleep.

"Wait," Lirah whispered loudly.

Axoo held the door open for her, and they stepped outside.

Light had just risen and the desert didn't feel nearly as hot as Lirah expected it to. And the sky was incredible. The clouds were a medley of reds, oranges, and purples, bending and swirling into each other like a moving art piece. No wonder Axoo always woke up right before dawn.

"What's up, Lirah?" Axoo asked. "How's Mala doin'?"

"She's a lot better. Thanks for helping her yesterday. I was really, really scared. I'm sorry that I jumped in front of you and started yelling on our walk back from the library. You didn't deserve that."

"It's okay. I understand. That happens under stress." Axoo shrugged with his hands stuffed in his pockets. He looked up at the beautiful sky.

Lirah nodded. "I wanted to tell you that, since I never noticed you come home last night, you really don't have to try and give us space while we stay with you. If anything, we should be giving *you* space. Is there another home we could move into at the settlement?"

"They're all full right now, until someone dies." Axoo snorted. "But how many times do I have to tell ya that I like havin' ya here? Actually, right now I was gonna borrow my friend Hubert's wagon, hook it up to Josie, and steer her over to the warehouse. Gonna get ya some proper beds there. And pillows, blankets, the whole works. Mala could sure use a better bed to sleep on than that small cot."

Once again, Axoo's hospitality stunned Lirah. "Do you want any help?" she asked.

"Well, sure!"

Lirah stared back at his door. She wondered if she should wake Au so that he could help too. Then again, someone had to stay back and monitor Mala's health, and Lirah wanted to witness this warehouse herself. She climbed onto Josie's back and Axoo steered them over to his friend's home.

CHAPTER 29

Hubert was a squat, middle-aged man who looked and spoke very much like Axoo. While Axoo hitched the empty wagon to Josie, Hubert asked Lirah a few questions about where she came from and said he was glad that she made it here safely. Then he started wheezing and said he needed to go lay down.

"What's a warehouse?" Lirah asked Axoo as they climbed up Josie and pulled away from Hubert's home. "And how do you have one filled with beds and stuff out here? Who made it?"

Axoo grunted. "The warehouse is a place that holds supplies and things for residents at the Scope Settlement, but I don't know who made it or nothin'. I was born here, ya see, and it got built long before then. But I do know it gets restocked once every five years or so. Everything I've ever needed has been in this here warehouse."

"Wow, that's really nice. Who has to restock it?" Lirah pried.

"I've never seen who does that exactly. But I've seen the cargo trucks that they travel over in to drop off the supplies."

"What's a cargo truck?"

"*Hmph* ... well, think of Josie and how we can get on her and travel around. A truck is like that except it's not livin' or breathin', which makes it a machine. It can hold a lot more weight and travel far without takin' breaks."

Lirah watched the back of Axoo's head sway back and forth as Josie trotted along. She had a perplexed look painted on her face that she was thankful he couldn't see. "Why do these strangers give you things?"

"All of us scientists give 'em our daily journals and research data. They give us materials and appliances. It's a trade, ya see?"

"You trade once every five years?"

"Yup."

Lirah's mind reeled. Did Axoo understand the significance of what he was telling her? Mala was right. This settlement didn't have the resources to build itself, it had all been *brought* here.

But why? Having everything handed to you in exchange for some journals didn't seem like a fair trade to Lirah. She wondered who brought over the materials to begin with. She pictured mysterious silhouettes seeking out this spot, building up the settlement, and leaving some scientists behind on their way out. She hardly noticed when Axoo pulled Josie to a halt and tossed the ladder down her side.

"You comin', Lirah?" Axoo's voice rose from the desert floor.

"Oh, coming!" Lirah turned to climb down the ladder. From here, she had a view of the entire collection of metal mushrooms reflecting in a hazy dust. She was surprised by how far out the warehouse sat from the rest of the settlement.

Everyone must borrow Hubert's wagon to take furniture from out here, she thought.

From the outside, the warehouse looked just like the library: an enormous, metal box. Lirah followed Axoo to the door, a fairly small one considering large items had to be lugged in and out of it.

"We'll be right back!" Axoo waved to Josie and stepped

inside.

He flipped up a switch. White, fluorescent lights flickered on one by one.

Piles and piles of musty cardboard boxes and damaged appliances came into Lirah's view. Messy didn't come close to describing it. Tall mounds of broken furniture sat rusting away with torn stained clothes thrown absentmindedly on top. Nuts and bolts were scattered all around like insects, and wires and broken glass covered half of the floor. It smelled like sweat and rust. Lirah sneezed from the dust.

"This way," Axoo said, leading her through the maze of torn up junk. "Watch yer step."

Eventually, the piles of clutter stopped, and the space opened up on the other side.

Lirah and Axoo stood on a faded red line painted across the floor, exactly where the mess ended. It looked like it marked the middle of the room. On the other side of the line, the boxes sat upright, nicely stacked and labeled with the same symbols Lirah had seen inside the library books.

"Kitchen utensils, blenders, spices, men's clothing size XL, men's clothing size L," Axoo pointed out the different labels as they passed each soaring stack of boxes, "Medium sheets, pillows, women's boots. Need any boots, Lirah? Let's grab some different sizes fer you and Mala. Hm, and let's find some men's boots fer Au."

Cradling the boots in his arms, Axoo went outside to put them in the wagon along with smaller clothes that he picked out for the trio. While he was gone, Lirah spun around under the fluorescent warehouse lights. She was in awe of the magnitude of modern furniture and equipment all around her.

"Hey, I'm back," Axoo's voice echoed from behind her as he waddled up. "If ya can, help me lift one of these mattresses. Then we'll come back fer two more, and some blankets and pillows." He pointed to a huge stack of white cots that looked like one thick rectangular tree trunk.

Lirah looked at the sign hanging above them. She wondered

if it said, "Matt – ress – es."

They lifted one and brought it to the wagon.

After the second one, Lirah's arms were already shaking. She almost regretted not waking Au up to come and help.

No, she thought. *If I woke him, I never would've gotten to come and ask Axoo all these questions about the warehouse.*

Still, she hoped Au and Mala weren't worrying about her like they had when Suki showed her around Airis for the first time. She shuddered at the memory of Mala's face across the fire, disappointed and hollow after Lirah's return. But this was different. Axoo wasn't a stranger.

"Axoo, I need a break," she said, resting against a box.

"Sure thing. I'll just get this last one on my own."

Lirah watched Axoo's squat body manage to lift an oversized mattress up and over his head like it was a barrel of water. He travelled across the organized section, through the jumbled maze, and out the door.

He came back in huffing and puffing. "I might need a break myself." He chuckled.

"Axoo?" Lirah asked, gazing around. "Why is one side of this place a mess, but the other side is full of brand-new things?"

"Because one side *is* the junk, and one side *is* new! Just like ya said." He smiled. "When those trucks come and give us new stuff like I told ya they did, I forgot to mention they also take all the trash. No food, though. We gotta compost that."

Axoo assessed the rolling hills of miscellaneous junk. "Guess it's been a while since they last came here, huh? The trash has really piled up. Maybe the five years are almost up. I sure hope they are. This is pretty ridiculous." He laughed. It reverberated throughout the whole metal warehouse and shook Lirah's chest.

"So, these cargo trucks not only bring the settlement new supplies, but they also handle your trash for you too? All in exchange for your research and journals?"

"Yeah! It's great, huh?"

"But *why*?" Lirah scrunched her face in confusion. "How did this all start? And where do these cargo trucks travel from?"

Axoo leaned against a sagging box. "I remember when I was yer age, so full of questions and all." He smiled. "Like I said, this whole arrangement started up before I was born. My great grandpa was part of the group that first came over. I don't know exactly where they came from, but my father told me when I was, *hmmm*," he scratched his chin, "'bout yer age, that we were actually descendants from a place so far away that they had to cross over a large body of water to get here. They used special floatin' machines called boats. My father said that when my great grandpa travelled here, he started doin' exactly what we're still doin' today. Collectin' data 'bout the universe." Axoo wiped his forehead. No air magically blew through this warehouse as it did inside his home or the library.

"And why did the travelers need to come right *here,* exactly?" asked Lirah.

"A group of all kinds of experts came to live out here. Mostly astronomers and astrophysicists, but also some biologists, chemists, engineers, architects, ya know, experts. They were all part of a program tryna see how to create a livable environment out on other planets in the best way possible."

"Uhhh ... what does that mean?"

Axoo chuckled. "Ya know, like bein' dropped in the middle of nowhere with a group and no way out. Then havin' to figure out how to work together and learn 'bout yer environment. That's why this place worked so well. It's desolate. Also, it has an amazin' view of the universe. Perfect fer astronomy."

Lirah nodded slowly and opened her mouth for clarification, but Axoo cut her off. Clearly, her facial expression gave away her massive lack of understanding.

"Wait, let me try and explain all of this in a simpler way," he said. "Basically, scientists came out here to get important information for the place they descended from. Today, we still do the same thing. We write daily journals 'bout our routines and feelings or whatever, along with collectin' data 'bout our areas of expertise. In exchange, we all get taken care of. We get metal, clothes, furniture, ingredients, new supplies. Heck, they even run this electricity fer us since we figured out how to work it."

"So, they give you all of this stuff in exchange for the data you have and to know what it'd be like to live on another planet?"

"Yer gettin' it!"

"But what if you wanted to quit the program and go back to the original place you descended from?"

Axoo let out a deep laugh, "Heck, nobody here wants to leave ... but I guess ya could. Well, that and nobody knows how to find the place we descended from."

"Why not? Aren't there books about it in the library?"

"No. No." Axoo shook his head. "Ya won't find nothin' 'bout that place in the library. Or 'bout any other place in the world."

"Why?" Lirah could feel her mouth going dry with anticipation.

Axoo's chuckles rumbled violently throughout the warehouse. "You got the mind of a scientist, Lirah. Always askin', 'why?' That's a good thing. Keep it up."

He wiped the sweat from his forehead again and leaned off the sagging box. He nearly flattened it. "Here. Come and help me pick out some pillows and blankets. When we're all done, I'll tell ya more 'bout what I remember. But we gotta keep movin' and get Josie out of that harsh light."

CHAPTER 30

Lirah followed Axoo over the faded red line and to the organized side of the warehouse. She speedily pulled pillows out from a large box, fell in, and climbed out again. She didn't care. She was focused on getting more answers.

Why were there no books in the library about other places in the world? Out of the *thousands* of books, there wasn't even *one* about the very place that the Scope Settlement descended from? The place that supplied their very *existence*? The place that the residents sent their personal journals and *life's research* to?

Lirah stumbled through the junky side of the warehouse and out into the natural midday light, her arms piled high with pillows. She tossed them in with the mattresses and clothes piled in Josie's wagon. Axoo dropped fresh blankets on top. They clapped their hands together in success, climbed up Josie, and started back toward the collection of metal mushrooms.

Axoo started whistling.

"So ..." Lirah probed him eagerly.

Axoo laughed. "So, what was I tellin' ya again?"

"You were going to tell me why there's no books in the library about other places, especially the place that supplies the Scope Settlement … with everything."

"Okay, sure. So, my great grandpa told his son, who told his son, who told me that the government, meanin' the people in charge of the place we descended from, took away every map, every book, and all technology to communicate with them from the settlement. I guess scientists were startin' to miss the city they came from. They got lonely out here, annoyed by the other residents." Axoo shrugged. "So the government took away the scientists' reminders and maps that could help 'em leave to navigate elsewhere. Then, sure enough, the scientists got over it. And now everyone from that original group of scientists has passed on. No one here ever thinks 'bout goin' anywhere else. I know I don't. I only think 'bout that place when we have to gather up our five years' worth of papers to be collected. Even then, we don't have to talk to anyone from that place."

Lirah was baffled. Her mind was reeling, and her mouth was so dry that she could hardly speak. She tried clearing her throat. "Doesn't it bother you that you've never been there or even seen pictures of where your life's work is going to?" She choked. "Or that you don't know what any other place in the world might be like?"

"I guess I never thought much of it. It's been this way my whole life. But to an outsider, I can see why this whole setup here might be very fascinatin'," Axoo said. "Also, I do know my data is gettin' put to good use. I know that *fer sure*. My father told me that the place we descended from has even more scientists and engineers over there than we have here. His father told him that. He said they've built vehicles that can travel through space, called spaceships. The scientists have flown in these spaceships past some of the very same stars you've seen in my telescope. Because of my data here, the scientists on those vehicles are able to land on other planets and settle down to make new civilizations. They're better prepared because of all the residents here, see?"

"That does sound pretty important," Lirah said, though her brain hadn't fully processed all of this information. A few days ago, she had no idea what space was, and now she was being told that vehicles could travel through it and land on other planets.

"I can only imagine what those scientists over there are doin' now," Axoo said. He let out a low whistle. "I'm proud to be a servin' such a cause."

Lirah could see Axoo's mushroom home now. Josie's large body wound through the shelters with the same precision and accuracy that a small malvor monkey ran over tree branches.

"Thanks for answering all of my questions, Axoo. The Scope Settlement's history is very interesting. Even though I'm still trying to process most of it," Lirah said.

"Of course! You think all the things that I'm so used to are so neat. My kitchen, my telescope, the warehouse, where it all came from! It's mighty refreshin' havin' ya around. So, thank *you*." He pulled back on Josie's reins, halting her beside her hut.

As she climbed down Josie, Lirah wondered why Axoo never found his own mate or had any children. He seemed like he would be a great father. She wondered if it had anything to do with the lack of women she saw yesterday. Maybe there just weren't enough mates to go around. She grabbed a few pillows from the wagon.

The front door swung open with a creak. She cringed, worried she might get condemned for leaving without any notice.

She turned around hesitantly. "Hey, Au. How's Mala?"

Au stood with his arms crossed rigidly across his chest, blocking the door. "She's fine. I gave her some water earlier, but other than that, she's been asleep. Where have you been?" He craned his neck towards the wagon to get a better look. "Pillows? Clothes? Oh. Nice." He uncrossed his arms. "Here, I'll help carry them in."

Lirah, Au, and Axoo hauled the new items inside as quietly

as possible. But after their third trip, the noise woke up Mala.

"What is all of this?" she asked groggily, watching Axoo slide a mattress propped on its side across the floor.

"We gotcha a proper bed!" Axoo said. "You'll be feelin' better in no time."

"Oh, well, thank you. But I'm just fine. Here, let me help out." Mala stood up, her legs wobbling.

Lirah wanted to protest, but she knew there was no point.

The four of them worked together and rearranged the space so that the low table and cots were closer to the kitchen area, and the new mattresses were positioned side by side on the far-left end of the home.

"Are you sure this setup is alright with you, Axoo?" Au asked. "We're kind of taking up your entire home now."

Axoo shook his head. "I don't wanna hear another comment about this *takin-up-my-space* non-sense. I got my bed and my telescope upstairs, and now ya got yer own bedroom down here. Seems perfect to me." He smiled. "Now, I gotta get this wagon back to Hubert's and stop by the library. I'll ask Zullus 'bout yer reading classes if I see him there." He tipped his head and marched out the door.

Mala climbed into her new bed, melting down into its plush. "Where did you get these?" She sighed. "This is the comfiest cot in the whole world."

"Axoo took me to a warehouse on the settlement outskirts," Lirah said, perching herself on the foot of Mala's bed. "It's this place piled high with boxes filled with anything you could ever need. I have *so* much to tell you. Au, come here! It's important."

"Okay. Hold on." He was in the kitchen pulling out breakfast ingredients even though it was practically lunchtime.

Lirah's stomach growled. She realized she hadn't eaten yet today, but she was too eager to tell Mala and Au about the mysterious place that supplied the settlement to care. She didn't know what this place was called or where it was located, but it sounded like an amazing place to live. Considering it could supply an entire settlement and continue to resupply it every five years. Plus, the mystery of it all only intrigued her further.

Once Au sat down beside Mala, Lirah leaned in with a keen grin and told them everything that Axoo had told her—how a government from a faraway place sent a group of scientists, including Axoo's great grandpa, to live here a long time ago. Their goal was to study what living in isolation on another planet would be like, along with gaining more data about the universe. Apparently, this desert was the perfect place for both of those endeavors. And after all these years, Axoo was here doing the same work that his family had done before him.

She told Au and Mala that, in exchange for the scientists' journals and data, the mysterious government sent cargo trucks over to resupply the warehouse once every five years, which provided the settlement with everything it could ever need.

She tried reiterating how Axoo had described cargo trucks and boats, but since she had never seen these machines, their descriptions felt made up as they flew from her mouth. She had merely taken Axoo's word for their existence.

"Are you making all of this up?" Au laughed.

"No. I *couldn't* make this up," Lirah said. "But I haven't even told you the weirdest part."

She leaned in even further and dropped her voice to a whisper, "This supplier government place took away every book in the library that might remind scientists of where they came from. Axoo said the government didn't want the scientists to get tired of living here or want to leave, so they cut off all communication and took away all reminders. There's not even *one* book about it. Axoo said he doesn't mind, though. The only time he thinks about this place is when the cargo trucks come to drop off more resources and pick up the residents' data and journals."

"See, I was right, wasn't I?" Mala's mouth lifted into an all-knowing smirk. "I told you all of this technology couldn't have been made out here from the dirt. I *knew* it came from somewhere else."

"You didn't have a vision about this, did you?" Lirah asked, scrunching her eyebrows together and examining her mother's eyes closely.

"No," Mala said, honestly. "But I hope I have one about this mysterious place. We should give it a name."

Lirah nearly slipped and said that she wanted to have a vision about this place too, but quickly remembered she still hadn't told Mala about her ability. She felt a tinge of guilt knock against her heart.

"Hmm," said Mala. "Let's name it RRS. Short for the 'Resources for Research Society.'"

"*Ha*, very clever. I like it," Au said. "So, Lirah, when do you think the RRS will come back and restock the settlement? One year? Two years?"

"Soon, I think," Lirah said. "The warehouse wasn't just packed with new items for residents. There was another side filled with old junk that residents threw out overtime, like ripped clothes and broken appliances. Axoo said the junk looked really piled up, which means the RRS will have to come and clean it out soon. The cargo trucks take the old boxes of trash with them when they bring new things."

"Really? Then do you think we could get there? I mean to the RRS itself?" Au asked, wide-eyed. "That's what you wanted, right Mala? And you could come too since no walking would be involved. We could sneak onto a cargo truck by hiding inside some old boxes. We could just take a bunch of food and water and sit around until we get there, right?"

Lirah's heart beamed. She jumped up and gave Au a huge hug. His ability to soak up this newly acquired information and predict where she was heading with it was incredible. She was grateful that he not only trusted this information but understood why it was useful to them, rather than finding the idea of sneaking over to this mysterious place absurd.

"I'll take that as a yes," he said.

"We think so much alike," Lirah said. "What do you think

Mala? Do you think we're crazy for wanting to do this?"

"No, I think it sounds like a great idea," Mala said. "You two should go to the RRS. It sounds like it's full of very powerful and intelligent beings. But not me. I'm going to stay here."

"Mala—"

"Lirah, I'm not travelling any further. I've told you this. And now I know you'll be on a direct path, travelling safely on trucks and boats instead of roaming aimlessly. This is the best scenario we could be in."

"I'm not leaving without you, Mala," Lirah said. "I won't."

Mala dug herself further down into her sheets and sighed. "My light, don't worry yourself about the finer details yet. We have no idea when the suppliers will be at the warehouse next. Also, you and Au have lots to learn before entering a society that I assume will be far more advanced than you're used to, even after seeing this settlement. Axoo said that Zullus is planning to teach you both to read, right? Focus on that for now."

Lirah huffed. "So not only are you refusing to come with us, but you're not going to learn how to read either? Or do you already know how to?"

Mala giggled ironically, "Of course I don't know how to read. But I have no use for it."

Au stood and silently walked back to the kitchen, continuing where he had left off with his meal preparations.

"Good idea Au," Mala said. "We could all use something to eat."

"I'll help." Lirah added, hoping to distract herself before she slipped up and yelled at her sick but endlessly stubborn mother. She reached the counter, which was topped with fresh eggs and spices. She didn't feel like eating. She pulled at her hair and turned back around to face Mala.

Mala had already fallen back asleep.

"She's never been this tired before." Lirah moaned, letting go of her hair and slumping over the counter, her stomach twisting in a knot.

"Are you thinking about the vision you had in the grasslands?" Au whispered in her ear, shaking some cheese into a bowl that was resting beside her elbows.

Lirah nodded.

"When should we tell her about our plans to have the ceremony?"

"Soon." Lirah tried to smile at him, then dropped her head into her palms.

"Hey, everything will work itself out," said Au. "Think of what we've already gone through together."

Resting his index finger beneath her chin, he titled her face up and kissed her.

CHAPTER 31

Lirah roamed through the towering rows of shelves at the library. She climbed up and down the ladders, picking up books and aimlessly flipping through them before placing them back where she found them. She hated being out here. When she walked down these endlessly narrow rows, her mind replayed Mala's tragic episode and nothing else. But she couldn't leave, as this was only her fourth reading class.

On her and Au's first day, when they arrived at the library, Axoo made sure they were early. Zullus was already there, his feet propped up on the same tabletop Mala had collapsed on. Lirah shuddered and turned around to leave, but Axoo enthusiastically spun her back around, and Zullus quickly escorted her and Au to a snug side room.

Lirah immediately felt more comfortable in the small room. A large window spanned across the back wall, and a table surrounded by six chairs rested in the center of the carpeted space. A metal supply cabinet was the only other object in the room.

"From now on, come straight to this room for class," Zullus

said. "Zullus will be meeting you here every other morning."

Then he dove right into the first lesson. He taught Lirah and Au the names and different pronunciations for each symbol that lived inside every book written in Filigeze. The symbols were called letters, and the Filigeze language had thirty-two of them. Zullus had them write down one letter over and over and over again. Then another.

They also studied the individual symbols throughout the second and third day of class. Zullus said this was important because once they mastered these thirty-two letters, they could grasp any combination of them. That was the ultimate goal. Their combinations were called words, and words gave books their meanings.

Today, on Lirah and Au's fourth day of class, Zullus told them each to go and search for a book to study with. And to choose wisely, because they would be using these books for many lessons to come.

When Lirah heard this, her heart dropped. She only wanted to stay in this cozy classroom. She stalled on her way out of the room by thanking Zullus for taking time out of his busy schedule to teach Au and her.

Zullus grinned and waved his hand as if shooing her comment away. "It's not a problem, Lirah. Teaching is Zullus' passion. This is what Zullus was made to do."

Lirah smiled at him, but frowned when she left the room.

Recently, she hadn't allowed herself to dive into the bottomless pool that was Life's Meaning ... until now, as she wandered the endless shelves, aimlessly climbing ladders and flipping through books too dense for her reading level of zero.

She blamed Zullus. He said that he was *made* to teach. The word "*made*" implied that life had a plan. That a purpose for Zullus had been arranged before his birth. How could someone be born to teach before they could even speak or navigate the world on their own?

Did everyone have a prearranged purpose? If so, Lirah wanted hers to be revealed to her by a spirit whispering gently in her ear. Or through an image made just for her, sculpted by clouds spanning across the whole sky. *"Do this..."*

Was she made to find the RRS? Or would she find her purpose when she got there?

Before now, she had only been concerned with finding out where she belonged and what the world could provide for *her*, whether that be the best community, technology, or resources. This was the first time she considered what *she* could provide for the world.

A soft feeling settled in her chest. She felt ... good, thinking about providing rather than receiving, like whisps of clouds were cradling her heart.

"Lirah?"

"Hmm?" Her eyes panned up, blinking away their dreamy haze to find Zullus standing with his arms crossed over his golden chain and his plucked eyebrows furrowed in concern.

"Have you not found a book that you would like to study with yet?" he asked. "Au and Zullus have been working together for quite some time now. Zullus was starting to worry you got lost."

"Oh, no ... I'm fine. I didn't realize how long I've been looking. I just ... *hmm* ..." Lirah dropped her gaze. She suddenly had the urge to leave, curl up in her soft bed, and think about her life's purpose.

"Lirah?"

"*Hmm* ... yes? Oh, right, picking a book." She looked up at all the books daunting her. "I still don't understand many combinations of letters. *Words*, I mean. So, does it really matter which book I choose? It's hard to pick when I don't know what to look for."

"Why don't you try our children's section? It is not used much, as you have probably sensed by the age of the settlement residents," Zullus said, giving her a half smile. "But children's books should hold easier, shorter vocabulary words for you to start with."

He led her down the rows of books, guiding her to the

children's section. "By the way, how is your mother doing?" he asked.

"She's doing much better. She stays inside and lays around most of the time, but she looks healthy. Her color has returned ... and her laughter." Lirah smiled to herself.

"That is great to hear. Also, Zullus has been meaning to tell you. After her collapse," Lirah cringed at those words, "Zullus conducted more research on the possible causes to see if it was due to anything serious, such as a previously unnoticed brain tumor that started bleeding. But Zullus thinks she passed out due to a common condition called 'syncope.'"

"Syncope? Is that *normal*?" Lirah asked, unable to think of a more appropriate adjective to use.

"It is fairly common, yes. Syncope is when there is a lack of blood flowing into the brain." He pointed to his head for reference as if she needed him to. "No underlying health conditions have to be present for it to occur."

Lirah couldn't tell if Zullus actually cared about her mother's health or if he just enjoyed knowing more than others did. He had a smile smeared across his face, looking pleased with himself and his research. Now she understood why Axoo rolled his eyes at Zullus but still got along with him. Zullus was a helpful, valuable colleague, but his reasons for being helpful seemed flawed.

Did intentions behind the action matter? Emotionally, yes. Especially if the intentions were evil. But, usually, evil intentions led to evil outcomes, and Zullus's color looked completely normal to Lirah's eyes. He could be trusted. He might be narcissistic, but not evil.

She smiled softly back at his bleached grin. "Thanks, Zullus. That information does make me feel a little better."

"Anytime! So, the children's section starts here and ends," he spread his arms wide like a bird flaunting its wingspan and walked forward, "about ... here."

Zullus dropped his arms, and Lirah thanked him for leading her over here. He bowed and sauntered away, but not before brushing against her side as he passed. She rolled her eyes, hidden beneath her fallen hair.

"*Great*," she muttered to herself. "Now I get to look through *more* words I won't understand but children half my age can read them."

Except, the first book she opened not only contained letters grouped like cliquey birds resting on invisible branches, but colorful images too. Her eyes fell on a picture of what she assumed represented the words written around it. The scene portrayed a young woman gazing at open wooden drawers, an index finger pressed against her chin. Her lips were scrunched together and pulled to the left side of her face. She was having trouble deciding what to wear.

Lirah grazed her fingertips over the woman's detailed face. Lirah liked pictures. Back in the Treetop Society, Pride members made paintings when they couldn't communicate verbally for whatever reason. She thought back to the painting she threw together for the Pride leaders to find. The warning about the looming brutes. That night felt ages away now.

"Concentrate, Lirah," she mumbled to herself, sliding the book back into place. She wanted to find a more gripping story instead of one about a woman selecting an outfit.

She drifted down the row, humming to herself, dragging her finger lightly across the book spines and over the many worlds pressed between bindings. She searched for the most vibrant one, hoping it might contain pictures of brilliant, foreign landscapes.

Then, just as her finger motioned over a deep blue book with golden letters trailing down its spine, her vision went dark. She gasped, leaned her back against the shelf, and closed her eyes tightly. She stood like this, motionless, with her spine unknowingly pressed against the deep blue book. She braced herself for what she expected to happen next.

Flashing crystalline lights materialized in her view, growing brighter and brighter every moment. If her eyes weren't already closed, she would have squinted them. She had no sense of what these lights could be. Nothing else was around to compare them to, though she could still feel her back pressed against a solid surface and her hands sweating.

She told herself to relax. She took a deep breath in, then let it go. Her vision panned out at the same speed the air exhaled from her nostrils. The lights suddenly blurred together, surrounded her, and then refocused themselves.

Structures towered above her, every inch gleaming with lights and chromatic colors. Gorgeous glowing women and men smiled down at her. They had striking skin tones embellished with intricate designs, perfect smiles, and metal-looking diamonds embedded into their necks and arms. Lirah waved up at three blissful-looking women, but they quickly faded into a pair of slick boots surrounded by neon words.

Embarrassed, Lirah dropped her hand and her gaze. She hadn't noticed before, but her ears hadn't been working. Now, sounds rushed towards her all at once. It was sensory overload. She heard what sounded like a million voices talking at once, in all different languages, in all different accents. She heard honking and beeping and stomping and whistling.

All around her, she saw what she assumed to be vehicles, like Axoo had talked about. They weren't living, and they moved quickly, hovering above the ground like bubbles with men and women encased inside. They zipped in straight lines across the perfectly straight land and made sharp turns around the perfectly edged structures. The men and women inside the vehicles and standing on the ground looked a lot like the ones shining down from the buildings. Many wore chains and had sparkling smiles like Zullus's. They were clean and happy, and they all had the metal diamonds implanted in different parts of their skin. Some had completely metal arms or legs altogether. Lirah stared at them with interest, but no one seemed to notice her.

She gazed up, curious to find where the tops of the structures might end. But far up, all she saw was glowing fog. It slowly trickled down and encircled her like a tube, blocking out all the sounds and lights until her mind returned to the Scope Settlement library.

Lirah opened her eyes, gasping with her back pressed against the bookshelf. When she regained her breath, she turned and stared intensely at the last book she touched before her mind had travelled away. The deep blue book with the golden words. She grabbed it from the shelf and speed-walked to the cozy classroom. She wanted to know everything that was written inside.

When she opened the door, she saw Au stacking papers neatly into the supply cabinet and shutting it. Zullus was packing up a bag and slinging it over his shoulder.

“Lirah, let’s hope you get used to the layout of this library. Zullus does not want you wandering the aisles each and every lesson, alright?” Zullus nodded, his eyebrows raised.

“Yes, of course. And I finally picked out a book, so it shouldn’t happen again.” Lirah raised the book in her hand and shook it around like she won a prize.

“No worries. But Zullus will have to ask you to bring it home. Practice reading the first chapter with Axoo so you will be prepared to read it aloud for Zullus during our next class. Au has already read through multiple pages of his book, so you will need to catch up.”

“Okay,” said Lirah, trying to hold back a giddy smile. She had been hoping Zullus would let her bring the book home.

“Zullus must attend to his astronomy students now. Thank you for cleaning up, Au, and great job today. See you both next time!” Zullus grinned and stroked Lirah’s back as he passed her in the doorway.

Au cringed. But when his eyes met Lirah’s faraway expression, his face turned quickly from annoyed to concerned. He cocked his chin, “What’s wrong?”

“I had a vision,” Lirah whispered. “When I picked this up.” She held up the blue book again.

Au reached over to inspect its cover. “What’d you see?”

“I’ll tell you on our way home. Let’s go.”

As they walked across the barren orange dirt, Lirah tried her best to recall what she had seen in her vision.

"I didn't see anyone I recognized," she said. "I didn't even hear my own voice. It was just this insane scene with a jumbled mix of loud sounds and glowing artificial lights everywhere. Like the kind Axoo has in his home, except there were millions of them. They covered structures that were so tall they stretched above the dense fog in the sky and made it glow! All of the vehicles were covered in lights too, and looked like floating bubbles. And everyone I saw had diamonds implanted in their arms or faces, or had fake legs or arms ... I don't know what they were for or how else to describe them. I've never seen anything like it. Everyone kept staring at me as they passed by like *I* was the crazy one without metal legs or diamonds in my skin. I think I was standing on some kind of walkway."

"Woah ..." said Au. "Do you think this place could be the RRS?"

"I do."

"That's good right? Doesn't that mean we'll make it there? Then we'll find out what all of that crazy technology is."

"I think so," Lirah said. "Every vision of Mala's ... that I know about ... has come true. Like when she was trying to *avoid* the brutes and the crashing hives from her vision, we saw them come falling down anyway." Lirah shivered. "I just wish I knew how visions worked ... and why Mala thought that situation was avoidable."

"I think it's time you told Mala about your visions." Au kicked at a small rock in their path.

Lirah shot him a dirty look. "I will not tell her that I saw her die."

"Then don't tell her about *all* of your visions. Maybe just this one. But it's important that you do it, and soon. Who else would you ask about visions? If we do ... you know ... lose her ..." Au trailed off.

They were silent as they crossed over a bridge, both looking out at the crystal blue streak below, with its rainbow fish and wavering plants.

"You're right." Lirah sighed as they stepped back onto the dirt. "I'll tell her."

She wanted to change the subject. They were approaching Axoo's metal mushroom, and she could see Mala's figure leaning against the gate of Josie's hut and petting her mane. "We have to tell her about our ceremony too!"

Au beamed at her. "Let's do it."

"We'll tell her about the ceremony first," Lirah said. She waved at Mala from a distance with one arm, her book tightly clutched in the other. She raised her voice, "Hey Mala! Hey Josie!"

CHAPTER 32

For the next hour, Mala would not stop sobbing. Every time she regained her composure, if she looked at Lirah or Au the tears would start up again. Even Axoo cried.

Lirah embraced her mother, cuddling up to her on her bed. "Don't cry," she stroked through Mala's hair.

"I'm just so happy. Let's start planning right away." Mala sniffled.

Lirah and Au had broken the news to Mala and Axoo over dinner. Of course, they had to explain to Axoo what an Always and Forever mate ceremony was, and describing it only made Lirah more excited. She pictured herself in a long dress in front of a cheering crowd, holding hands with Au, rubbing her nose against his beneath a beautiful archway. Axoo said he would make sure to invite everyone in the settlement.

Just a few weeks ago, Lirah never would've been able to ponder throwing a lavish ceremony with so many attendees. Out in the grasslands, her only focus was on survival. But now, she was in another world. A safe world. One with magical automatic lights, indoor cooking appliances called *stoves*, cooling boxes called *fridges*, and plushy cots called *mattresses*.

She felt guilty for planning to leave this place eventually, even though leaving hadn't been her original idea. It was Mala's *demand*. She worried Axoo would think she thought the settlement wasn't good enough for her. And Axoo still wouldn't stop saying how much he enjoyed their company.

Mala didn't want her daughter to settle, and at the bottom of her heart Lirah knew Mala was right. After all, the settlement was a science experiment. And its population wasn't growing.

Lirah also knew she needed to tell Mala about her vision of the RRS. And ask her if it was a sign that she would make it there safely.

She sighed deeply, patted Mala's beaded hair, and gazed over at her library book on the kitchen counter. She hoped it would give her more clues about the RSS ... even though Axoo said the library was wiped clean of every book mentioning it.

"Are ya ready to look through the telescope? It's 'bout time," Axoo said.

Lirah looked over at him. He was peering out the window at a star-filled sky.

"You all go ahead." Mala sniffled, her navy tear-filled eyes twinkling brightly. "I'm too tired from all of this crying."

"I'll stay here with Mala." Lirah winked and waved Au off. She wanted to have a serious talk with Mala. Alone.

Au nodded knowingly at Lirah and vanished up the winding staircase with Axoo.

Lirah's heart started pounding hard as she tried to think of how to start this conversation with her mother.

There's nothing to be worried about, she told herself. *Mala will be thrilled I have the ability to look into the future, just like she can. But what if she asks too many questions? What if I let it slip that I saw her die?*

Lirah stopped stroking Mala's hair and sat very still.

Mala giggled. She wiped at her dewy eyes. "What is it my light? My light who is about to be an Always and Forever mate."

Lirah couldn't help but smile. She turned towards Mala's beaming face, detecting the many laugh lines crinkled up around her cheerful eyes.

"So much is happening right now," Lirah said. "I'm so happy and so grateful ... but I'm sort of overwhelmed too. And I feel guilty for feeling overwhelmed." She sat up and stretched out her arms. "Considering we're cuddling in warm beds with an endless supply of food and water. You're recovering quickly, and a man who loves me more than anything is right up there." She pointed at the ceiling.

"I'm beyond happy for you, my light," Mala said. "Don't feel guilty. Happiness can feel overwhelming, or too good to be true, especially after a long phase of hardship."

"Well yes, but also ... something else happened today. I wanted to tell you about it alone, because ..." Lirah dropped her gaze down to the blanket covering her and fiddled with its fabric.

Mala leaned forward and brushed a stray hair out of Lirah's face, "Because?"

"Well, I had a ... vision ... today. I mean, I *think* it was a vision. I've... I've never experienced anything like it before." Lirah cringed. "It was like I stepped out of one world and into another. Like I was really there."

Lirah hated lying to her mother. Today was the third time she had this kind of experience. Her heart continued to pick up speed.

She peeked up at Mala, who appeared calm. Of course.

"That sounds like a vision to me. What did you see?"

Lirah locked her eyes back on the blanket. She analyzed its intricate woven patterns as she described the futuristic scene that she experienced earlier, including the sounds and feelings that came along with it. After she finished recalling the details the best that she could, Mala didn't say anything. She just sat there thoughtfully.

"That is quite a lot of detail to have in a first vision," Mala finally said. "My visions started out as snippets. Maybe three seconds long. They grew into longer scenes after quite some time. I had to train myself to hold onto them or the scene would slip away."

"Hmm," was all Lirah could say. Her actual first vision had been longer than three seconds too.

"Your ability must be much stronger than mine," Mala said. "It will only continue to flourish from here."

"You don't seem surprised that I had a vision," Lirah said, looking up at her mother.

"I had a feeling this was going to happen soon enough." Mala smiled, then yawned. "Well, my spirit guides had a feeling." She stretched her arms up to the ceiling then nestled back against her pillows.

"I have some questions about what I saw," Lirah said. "I told Au about it on our walk home from class today. He asked if the place from my vision was the RRS. What do you think?"

"It certainly could be," said Mala.

"So, does that mean we'll *definitely* make it there? And will that scene *definitely* become real? Or is there a chance that the future will turn out differently?"

Lirah secretly hoped her mother would say that visions weren't definite. That the future would always be unknown, even to those who could see glimpses of its possible outcomes. "I'm wondering because all of your visions have come true."

"Typically, yes, visions do become reality. But we can always try to change our future. From my experience, visions can only be predicted from the life path you're currently on. For example, *you* are currently interested in leaving this settlement and travelling onward."

"Mostly because of you," Lirah mumbled.

"I don't believe that," Mala said sharply. "But let's say that you *did* decide to stay here and never leave again. Then, *of course* you would never see your vision materialize into reality. But that isn't woven into your personality. You have a predisposition to explore. So, the vision will come true. Unless you go against who you are."

"Then why did you even bother trying to get away from the burning Treetop Society?" Lirah asked. "If you knew we'd see it fall anyway?"

"Firstly, my light, *you* were the one who took it upon yourself to leave the Pride," Mala said. "I joined you. And I would do it all over again too. There's nothing wrong with trying to change the outcome of the future. But it's hard. I'd be lying if I said I knew how visions fully worked. I simply experience them and learn more about them every time I have one. Same with living, right? I have no idea how I'm here, right now, sitting next to the most amazing daughter in the world. But I am. I'm experiencing life and learning more about it each day."

Lirah nodded. Her mother had a beautiful way of explaining abstract concepts to her. She would miss Mala so much when her spirit left her body. She wanted to cherish each and every moment she had left with her mother.

She snuggled up on Mala's shoulder and breathed in her scent. They had been out of the jungle for many weeks now, but Mala still smelled the same. Just like eucalyptus, mint, and something else ... her own sweet scent that couldn't be recreated anywhere else in nature. Lirah wished she could bottle up the smell. She knew she would subconsciously search for it for the rest of her life.

* * *

The following weeks went by in a blur of dust and sweat. Summer had begun and the desert wind picked up, howling and blowing so much that time sped up with it.

Lirah always had something to do. Whether she was learning to read, analyzing the stars, planning for her and Au's ceremony, riding Josie, or cooking meals, she didn't stop working until her eyes closed at night. And she always made time to talk with Mala. Each evening, they sat on Mala's bed and combed each other's hair while Lirah practiced reading aloud to her mother. Zullus had told her she was making significant reading progress, and Lirah could tell. She felt more comfortable reading the blue and gold book every night. She never returned it to the library, and she wasn't planning to. Axoo told her to tell Zullus that Josie ate it.

Lirah would never forget when she first showed Axoo the book. His hands shook as he flipped through its worn pages. She remembered how emersed he looked. Lost in a different reality, his eyes rapidly dodging back and forth, absorbing as many words as he could as quickly as possible. When he eventually closed the book, he was still lost in a daze. He dragged his hand over the raised golden letters on its cover, repeating its title a few times for Lirah, "*Ramona takes on the city.*"

Axoo said that even though the story itself was fictional, it was set in a very real place—the City of Flames. This book was the trigger his brain needed to remember. It was like a boulder had been blocking a stream of his memories and it was finally cracked open by a small drop of water, allowing a strong flood of memories to pour into the front of his mind all at once.

Axoo's family had descended from the City of Flames. He remembered his grandfather telling him about it. This book held meaning for him, and he wanted to keep its presence a secret so it wouldn't be confiscated or burned. "Settlement residents are such *goody-goody* rule followers," Axoo said. So, they kept it and studied with it in private. Lirah and Au learned about cars and jets, streets and buildings, neural implants and bionic limbs. All of the technical terms they might need to know before embarking on their journey to the City of Flames.

Though initially, when Lirah and Au told Axoo about their plan to sneak on a cargo truck whenever the suppliers returned, he laughed. He thought they were teasing, just being imaginative. Then his grin dropped like a rock.

Axoo stared, unblinking, at their tight lips flatter than desert ground. He started crying. He said he didn't want them to leave.

When Lirah tried telling him that he could come along, he refused. He said he would never leave his home. He loved Josie, and his telescope, and his friends. He didn't understand why they wanted to leave either. Until slowly, after delicate explaining, he finally agreed to help them sneak safely onto a cargo truck.

Planning for their escape to the City of Flames quickly became another addition to Lirah's busy to-do list. No one knew when the cargo trucks would come next, but Axoo said that when they did, it would be obvious. He said the suppliers always knocked on two residents' doors, requesting them to gather all the data and journals from every other home, stack them up, and bring them to the red line in the center of the warehouse. The process usually took a while, and many residents weren't very organized with their paperwork, especially five years' worth of it. So, there would be plenty of time for Au and Lirah to sneak to the warehouse and hide inside the boxes designated to be brought to the city for disposal.

Every day, Lirah focused on her future. But at night when she slept, dark distortions of her past crept back inside the unguarded holes of her mind.

Maybe the past chose to haunt her recently because she had consciously blocked it out for so long.

It wanted to be remembered.

Lirah always woke up sweating in the dead of night, cradling her hands in her head, elbows pressed against her kneecaps, rocking back and forth in the dark. She tried telling herself that her reoccurring nightmare was flawed, a sham, and it always changed slightly in detail. But she couldn't shake it off. Most nights she could expect roughly the same travesty to unfold after she drifted off …

A masked brute runs at Lirah through an open field, their arrow pointing skillfully at the back of her head. She can feel the deadly blow coming like the heat of fire. She's all alone. There's no one around to stop the brute. Then she hears a high-pitched cackle. The brute is pleased with their aim.

Suddenly, Suki appears in midair, leaping in between Lirah and the flying arrow. She falls to the ground. Lirah screams and reaches down to hug Suki's limp body, only to watch her figure fade away and rematerialize into a massive translucent serpent. Rearing up off the ground, it hisses in Lirah's face *"You killed me. How dare you move on with your life. How dare you think that you matter more than me."*

It lunges forward and binds itself around Lirah's body, pulling her up into the sky, hypnotizing her with its bright green eyes. Lirah doesn't resist. She accepts her fate. But then, she feels the snake loosen its grip. It's shrieking in Suki's voice.

Au, Riel, and Riggul are there, stabbing the serpent with spears from below. Lirah wants to tell them that it's okay, it's only Suki. But she can't speak. The snake falls flat to the ground, rolls around, and morphs into Mala. Weak, bloody, and dying on the grass. Au and the twins apologize profusely, trying to convince Mala that she had been a snake.

But it's too late. Mala is dead. They all huddle around her. Lirah brushes the hair out of her mother's face and kisses her forehead. Distracted and in mourning, none of them notice when three more brutes sneak up behind them gripping sharp daggers.

Two brutes are more eager than the third. They don't hesitate to stab the twins right through their backs. Riel and Riggul plunge into the thick grass as if it were smoke, falling elegantly downwards at the exact same speed, disappearing forever.

Au turns around in slow motion, just before the third dagger reaches his spine. Time speeds back up and he succeeds in killing two of the brutes. Then the final one stabs him through the heart. Lirah feels her legs shaking as she stands. She's sobbing as she wrenches the spear out of Au's lifeless chest.

She screams in rage, pulls back the dagger and pierces the final brute through the stomach. She looks around the field. It's void of life. She's all alone in the tall grass, shivering, surrounded by the dead bodies of her enemies and loved ones.

CHAPTER 33

Lirah thought about her nightmare a lot, but she never told anyone about it. She wanted to keep it trapped inside her head, unable to escape into the physical world.

One day in reading class, when she was spaced out, Zullus got angry with her for not paying him any attention. "Lirah, what have you been thinking about all of class? Certainly not about Zullus's lesson."

So, Lirah told him what she was thinking about. She wanted to know why terrible things happened to those who didn't deserve it. But mostly, she wanted to know what the purpose of pain and death was in general.

Zullus blinked once and told her that she'd have to learn how to read to find out. There were plenty of others who had asked the same questions. She could find plenty of musings about suffering and its purposes written somewhere in this library. But first she needed to read at a higher level. "So, let's continue with my lesson, shall we?" he said, and dropped the subject.

* * *

Last night, Lirah had the same nightmare. So, now, in the light of summer morning, she bathed herself in a cool bucket of soapy water, rinsing off the sweat and anguish. She needed to be clean. Mala had been sewing a ceremony dress for her and she finished it yesterday. Today, Lirah wanted to try it on.

"Could you pass out the ceremony invitations while we're finalizing Lirah's dress?" Mala asked Au, handing him the stack of invites as Lirah walked inside with dripping hair.

Lirah shivered as she wrung her hair out in the sink, butterflies filling her stomach. "Three days," she murmured.

She thought back to the four of them sitting around the table, filling out the invitations. They didn't know what date to hold the ceremony because they didn't know when their preparations would be complete. But with their minds already set on completing the cards, whose ruffled edges were all laid out before them mocking their uncertainty, Axoo came up with the idea to write *"in three days,"* instead of a date. That way, whenever they sent the invites out, it would be three days from then. Ingenious. Plus, no one could really argue because Axoo was the one filling out most of the invitations. Lirah and Au tried to copy examples of his to practice their writing skills, but their handwriting just looked like scribbles.

"Are you excited?" Au grinned at Lirah, giving her a kiss on his way out. His smile melted her butterflies away.

When the door snapped shut behind him, Mala urged Lirah over to her bedside. She whipped out a gorgeous white dress from beneath the covers like she had been waiting to awaken it for far too long now.

Lirah gasped at the intricate layers of lace and cloth laying before her. She fiddled with the long sheer sleeves and the beaded neckline.

Mala had pieced an assortment of cloth and blankets

together from the warehouse, just for Lirah. In the Pride, women passed down the same dress for generations. But here, Lirah would be the first to wear one.

"Mala …" Lirah mouthed. She was too choked up to speak.

"My light." Mala rubbed her daughter's back.

Lirah wiped her wet eyes. "You've been sleeping with my dress?" She laughed.

"Well, I didn't know where else to keep it hidden while you were here."

"It's gorgeous, Mala, beyond words. I don't know how you sewed this … or even thought up its design. Thank you."

"And thank *you*. For going to reading classes and giving me so much time to work on it." Mala admired her masterpiece and smoothed out its stitched fabric.

Lirah tried it on. Mala started crying.

Axoo walked through the door and he started crying too. He told Lirah that she had to see the dress for herself. "Go upstairs and look at yer reflection in my projection crystal."

Lirah climbed the staircase alone, carefully holding up the hem of her dress. She halted in front of the arched piece of crystal. The woman looking back at her took her breath away.

She could hardly recognize herself. The dress clung to her torso perfectly. And her hair tumbled down to her curved hips right where the fitted dress began to flow out like gentle waves. She lifted up the hem. Her long legs had filled out. She looked grown up. When had this happened?

She leaned forward, her nose nearly pressing against the crystal as she stroked her cheekbones, arched brows, and pouting lips. Her flaming auburn eyes glinted back at her.

She sauntered back downstairs with a newfound confidence radiating through her, and reluctantly changed out of the dress.

After Mala properly stored it back under her covers, Axoo urged them outside.

A tall shape, which looked like a thick arched window frame, loomed beneath a large sheet in Hubert's wagon bed.

"Look at this!" Axoo pointed at the shape with a big grin on his face. His magnified eyes eagerly waited for their reaction as he tore off the sheet.

An exquisite metal archway with detailed silver flowers fastened all around its brim gleamed brilliantly in the light. It reminded Lirah of how the Scope Settlement looked from far away, back when she was laying on her death bed. It looked like hope.

"I'm askin' everyone to try and supply chairs fer the event, and I went ahead and made this for ya to stand in front of. I know ya said ya needed an archway fer the ceremony. I thought this would pull the whole setup together. Hubert let me make it inside his garage."

"Axoo." Lirah pressed her hand to her mouth and closed her eyes, partially from the hot wind blowing in her face and partially from her amazement. "Thank you so much. I love it. And the flowers look so real. How did you make them?"

"I've been cuttin' up metal and heatin' and shapin' the little pieces together. Just makin' a few each day."

"You're both such artists. I'm so lucky to have you in my life." Lirah pulled Mala and Axoo in for a group hug.

* * *

That night, with a light heart, Lirah dreamt of her and Au's ceremony. Metal flowers, smiling faces, pink skies, love.

She was floating, vibrating too fast to experience her usual nightmare.

She woke up refreshed, realizing nightmares were actually quite weak, only choosing vulnerable targets to infiltrate. She had to laugh.

Later, during reading class, Lirah couldn't stop staring at Au. Today marked the last day they would see each other before their ceremony. The next time she looked into his eyes they would be pronounced Always and Forever mates.

Tradition rules stated that partners must stay separated the day before the ceremony. Au planned to drag his mattress upstairs and stay in Axoo's room all day and night.

Lirah laughed when she pictured Mala bringing food up for him as if he were a hostage. This had all come up so fast. But she felt ready. Very ready.

"Zullus believes we have done enough work for today." Zullus sighed and closed his book. "We will end class early."

Lirah and Au eagerly pushed in their chairs and stacked their books and papers in the supply cabinet.

"Zullus has received an invitation for *'Lirah and Au's Always and Forever Mate Ceremony.'* How very *exciting*." Zullus snorted, slinging his bag over his shoulder. "Zullus has never heard of such a ceremony, and with such a *long* title. Nevertheless, Zullus will be attending."

"It's a tradition from our Pride," said Au, his eyes narrowed like a chara cat about to pounce. "One that we wanted to hold on to. So, if you don't respect—"

"See you there, Zullus," Lirah interrupted. She put her hands over Au's shoulders and rushed him out of the room.

Out in the sweltering heat, Au scowled. "Zullus treated me differently today, did you notice? He was more overassertive and critical than usual. And did you see the way he was eyeing me? I think he ended class early because he couldn't stand to look at me anymore."

"Really? I didn't notice much of anything in class today. I was too busy looking at you and playing our ceremony over and over in my head." Lirah brushed her windswept hair out of her face and smiled up at him while they walked.

"Well, that's good." Au reached out his hand and interlaced his fingers with hers. "It probably annoyed him even more when you didn't notice his disapproval of me. I *know* he thought he had a chance to be with you, no matter how small ... until he read the invitation I dropped on his doorstep."

Lirah thought back to Zullus's subtle attempts to impress her, and how he would casually graze against her arm when he handed her a new book or passed by her in a row.

She grimaced, but at the same time, she pitied him. Zullus might never find a partner of his own. Not here, where every available woman had gone through menopause before he was born.

During her time here, Lirah had grown familiar with many of the residents, specifically Hubert, Gena, Earl, Faye, and Boog. They were all so sweet, but they made her nervous when they spoke to her. Their cautious voices always cracked like dying fire, and they all made the same joke about their uncontrollable coughs. "I've swallowed too much sand in my days. I'm surprised there's still this much around."

Au told her that when he was dropping off invitations, most of them declared, "Oh good, three days from now? I should still be alive by then."

At first it unnerved Lirah how all the residents said the same things, mimicking each other like squawking birds. But over time, she decided it was just the outcome of living in the same place for your whole life. When she compared the Scope Settlement residents to the Treetop Society elders, she decided the elders had all been equally like one another.

She tried to imagine her and Au as elders, with their own wrinkles, bad hearing, dark senses of humor, and stubborn beliefs. She couldn't help but burst out laughing. She had no idea where they would be, but they would be together, and it would be hilarious.

"What is it?" asked Au, looking disgusted. "Are you laughing at me for caring that Zullus is attracted to you? Or that he treats me worse because of it?"

"No Au." Lirah squeezed his hand in reassurance. "Well, I *was* thinking about that at first, and how the only reason he might show interest in me is because of how old everyone else here is. Then I started to picture *us* as Elders. Can you imagine?" She snickered. "That's why I laughed."

"I was not expecting that." Au chuckled.

They approached Axoo's home.

"What are you two giggling about?" Mala asked. Her hand was shading her face and her elbow was propped against Josie's gate, like usual.

"Growing old," Lirah said. "What are you are Josie talking about?"

Lirah knew it was Bue who Mala really wanted to spend time with in the midday heat, not Josie.

"Oh, you know, everything and nothing." Mala grinned.

That evening, Au made dinner for the household. His culinary skills had really improved. He never burned anything anymore.

Around the table, they toasted to the delicious meal. Lirah and Au's final meal together before their ceremony.

After their stomachs were full, Axoo, Mala, Lirah, and Au went upstairs to observe the universe.

To Lirah, the stars were shining brighter than usual, and the colorful nebulae were glowing brighter. She lost count of how many shooting stars she saw. Axoo said they brought good luck.

CHAPTER 34

"Lirah, Au, I hope you know how much I love you both. And to everyone else here," Mala waved out her arm as if she were casting sparkles over the crowd, "I would like to tell you all a story. In hopes that you'll grasp just an *inkling* of how much Lirah and Au truly love each other."

Lirah gazed out at the audience from her place beneath Axoo's beautiful archway, the morning light perfectly angled behind her like an aura. She had never felt as young and beautiful as she did now, in this dress that was made to fit her perfectly, with all eyes on her and Au.

Every resident in the Scope Settlement had shown up for the Always and Forever mate ceremony. They were leaning forward in seats that they dragged over from their homes, straining to hear Mala.

"Au left his home for Lirah. He left everything he ever knew for this troublemaker." Mala winked and motioned at Lirah. "We all ran away. And Au carried me, *much* farther than he should've had to."

Mala smiled and turned her gaze directly toward Au. "I

know that you love me," she said. "But I also know that you carried me for Lirah's sake."

Au shrugged, and beamed.

"You travelled to another jungle society with us even though you were absolutely opposed to the idea. You made that *very* clear, but, through the complaints, you stayed with us. Again, for Lirah." Mala flashed a smile. "Through years of observation, I have concluded that you make Lirah stronger. You give her the confidence to step out into the unknown. Because with you, she'll always be at home."

Lirah and Au faced each other with noses practically touching. Their hands were laced together, and their eyes were full of happy tears. The wind formed a net of hair around their faces, connecting them together.

Suddenly, only Mala, Au, and Lirah were there. The rest of the audience had disappeared as Mala continued her speech.

"No one will ever know *exactly* what will happen in the future," she said. "But I predict that no matter what happens to you both, your love will persevere. I have had the absolute honor of watching you both grow up. I have seen your bond continually change and strengthen over time. I have seen you progress as allies, best friends, and mentors for one another. Your strengths compliment one another and your weaknesses balance out one another. I have seen your heartbreaking days and your beautiful ones.

"Watching your love evolve has been the greatest, purest entity that I have ever witnessed. You have persevered through homelessness, starvation, and the death of loved ones, who I will name out of respect. Fia and Ruewai, Au's parents. Bue, my Always and Forever mate. Suki, a brave and moral accomplice. Riel and Riggul, fellow Pride members and skilled hunters. As well as many other Pride members of our fallen society in the jungle. They will all remain in our hearts forever."

Mala let the warm wind rush through the audience, allowing for a moment of silence. Then she inhaled deeply and continued, "Through everything, you two have managed to hold onto hope. This ceremony represents the unity of two partners, coming together as one, and creating an Always and Forever bond."

Mala looked away from Au and Lirah, addressing the audience again, "I dare to say that Lirah and Au have already formed this bond, when they were too young to comprehend the meaning of it, when they first chose each other many years ago during their first partnering process. So, let this ceremony be a *reinforcement* of their bond, and a way to announce it formally to the spirits, the universe, and this lovely audience."

The audience sniffled and wiped their noses as Mala reached for the metal shards placed on the stand beside her. On the end of the front row, with Josie tied off to the side of his chair, Axoo was sobbing the loudest.

Mala took one small shard and walked to Lirah's side, kissed her on the forehead, and nuzzled her nose with her own.

She pricked the tip of Lirah's nose with the shard before Lirah had time to brace herself.

Mala took the second shard and repeated the same process with Au, kissing him on the forehead and rubbing his nose with her own before quickly pricking it.

By the time Mala finished pricking Au's nose, the blood had already trickled down Lirah's nose and onto her chin.

Lirah's happy tears turned into a stream. She stared into Au's eyes, tears and blood streaked down his face too.

"Lirah, do you understand the commitment of an Always and Forever bond? And do you choose to share such a bond with Au?" Mala asked her.

"Yes," Lirah said.

"Au, do you understand the commitment of an Always and Forever bond? And do you choose to share such a bond with Lirah?"

"Yes," Au replied.

"Then please, solidify this bond. Mix the red liquid of life that drips from your face. Share this life force with your partner. Combine them."

Lirah and Au rubbed their noses together, crying and smiling.

They pulled apart, inspecting the blood covering each other's noses and lips, before leaning back in and sharing a kiss, further mixing the blood on their lips.

The crowd hooted and cheered, coughed and cleared their throats, then cheered some more.

The beautiful morning light had risen throughout the ceremony, climbing higher and higher as the sublime clouds in the sky morphed, brightened, then dispersed.

Now, the sky was completely clear. Light freely shined down on the new Always and Forever mates.

Lirah felt brand new.

* * *

After the ceremony, everyone brought a dish to the library to celebrate the new Always and Forever mates. Some residents mingled and ate around tables inside. Others went outside and blew bubbles into the wind using dandelion-shaped bubble blowers that Axoo twisted together with leftover metal from his archway project.

"Thank you, yes. *Mhm*, thank you," Lirah absently repeated, arching her neck, searching for where Au had gone.

Gena and Faye wouldn't stop complimenting her dress. They had Lirah cornered near the spread of food dishes in the library where they were nibbling on cream-filled crackers, egg slices topped with a tangy purple sauce, and crispy rainbow guppies on toothpicks.

"Oh dear! Yer food is slippin' off." Faye grabbed at Lirah's tilting plate.

"Oh no! Let me throw these away." Lirah stooped to pick up the dropped crackers and quickly walked off, happy to have an excuse to leave the conversation.

On her way to the library's propped open double doors, she

spotted Au and Hubert teetering inside.

She giggled at Au's distracted face. His eyes darted straight to hers.

He grinned and held up his index finger to Hubert. "Excuse me," he said. He marched over to Lirah and rubbed his nose against hers. "There you are."

"*Ow*, my nose is still sore." She giggled and reached for her nose.

"Mine too."

Through the open doors they heard a collective gasp.

"What was that?" asked Lirah.

"Let's look." Au rested his palm on the small of her back and escorted her out into the open air.

A group had formed a circle around a random spot on the dirt. They were staring down at the ground.

Lirah's heart dropped. She lifted the hem of her dress and pushed her way through the murmuring crowd.

She found Mala collapsed face down in the center.

Lirah went numb. It was like her brain instantly turned off its emotions so she could better focus on saving her mother.

"Back up!" Lirah waved her arms at the crowd. "Who's a doctor?"

The crowd grew louder. She heard names being called out to help as she knelt by her mother's side.

"Let's turn her over. Quickly!" Lirah said.

Au knelt down by Mala's legs and they flipped her over to face the sky. Her face was coated with orange dirt. Lirah tried wiping it off with her dress as Mala drooled and murmured incoherently with her eyes closed.

A wrinkled older man named Ryo shuffled up, handed his cane to an onlooker, and shakily knelt. He pressed his ear to Mala's chest and checked her pulse.

"Someone go get me my first-aid kit!" Ryo grumbled.

Axoo and Zullus pushed through the crowd.

"Mala!" Axoo said.

"Syncope." Zullus shook his head.

"Can you get everyone else to back up?" Lirah asked them, peering up from the orange dirt with her white dress spread out around her. She looked like a sad cloud in a pale orange sky.

Axoo and Zullus nodded. They thanked everyone in the crowd for caring as they waved them away. They told them that everything was under control and to wait inside the library for an update.

Someone else appeared at her side. Lirah was about to yell at them to stop staring at Mala when they dropped off Ryo's first-aid kit and walked away. Ryo pulled out his small pieces of equipment and started placing them on Mala.

Lirah and Au sat like stones while Ryo assessed her. Not moving much. Not thinking much. Not breathing much.

After a long time, Ryo sighed and said, "I'm sorry. Her heart is failing her and her body is slowing shutting down. I'm not sure if we have enough time to move her to my home. But we can try. That's where I store my proper medical equipment. I'd also need to sanitize my station. I'll let you decide what you want to do." Ryo stood and walked off, his shoulders more hunched than usual.

With Ryo's assessment over, Lirah's shell of numbness shattered. She pressed her head against Mala's chest and started sobbing.

Au started crying too.

This time, they both knew Lirah's vision would come true.

Axoo and Zullus slowly backed away, letting Lirah, Au, and Mala have this time for themselves.

A few straggling onlookers wiped their tears from afar.

"My light ..." Mala moaned.

"Yes?" Lirah tilted up her head and scooted behind Mala so she could be closer to her face. She needed to hang on to every last sound her mother made while she was still alive.

"It's okay to let me go," Mala whispered.

"You don't want Ryo to take you to his medical station?"

"I don't want to die inside." Mala sighed. "Let me feel the natural light on my cheeks."

Lirah cradled her mother's head in her hands and ran her fingers through her thick hair. Her insides felt weighted down. She wanted to collapse beside her mother, but forced herself to stay upright. She would look at her mother for as long as she had the chance.

Au scooted closer and gripped onto Mala's hand. "Mala, don't go," he sobbed. "We love you."

"I love you too," Mala whispered.

"I love you." Lirah heaved. Her sobs kept rolling in like waves.

She looked up at the cloudless sky. "Why today? Why now?"

She clenched her teeth and dropped her head back down. Her tears dripped onto her mother's calm forehead. "Mala ... *Mala* ... I love you, don't ... don't die."

Mala's eyelids opened. Her navy eyes were completely tranquil. "I won't be gone completely," she whispered. "I'll simply take on a new form ... It'll be alright, my light. It's my time to go."

Lirah moaned in defeat.

Mala's eyes fell shut and she smiled. "You will go on to the City of Flames and I will go on to be with my Bue," she whispered. "I've seen this day coming for a long time. Please be happy now. For me and for yourselves. On this lovely day."

Mala titled her head up to look at Au. "You both will take care of each other forever."

Au nodded at her, tears streaking down his face, "Yes. We will."

Axoo slowly made his way back over.

"Did you decide if Mala will go to Ryo's?" he asked.

Lirah shook her head. "Mala wants to stay here."

Axoo nodded once. He understood what that meant. He knelt and said his goodbyes to Mala as well.

* * *

Most residents went home right after they received the update that Mala wasn't going to Ryo's medical station. After a while, everyone cleared out except for Lirah, Au, and Axoo. They stayed and waited with Mala, watching the orange ball of light move across the sky and slowly fall away.

Lirah lost count of the number of times that she told Mala she loved her.

Mala said it back each time. Slower, and slower, until she stopped answering.

Au pressed his head against Mala's chest. He shook his head. He felt nothing. Her spirit had left her body right as dusk approached. Right when it was time for her to make a grand appearance up with the other stars. That's what Lirah hoped.

Through their tears, Lirah, Au, and Axoo pieced apart the ceremony archway. They rebuilt it as a casket for Mala, metal roses and all.

In the dark, they laid her inside the completed casket, closed its lid, and set it gently on the river. Lirah gave it a little push and sent Mala's body on its way.

"She'll eventually make her way out to sea," Axoo said.

All night, Lirah and Au laid out by the river looking up at the naked stars. They didn't want to watch them through the telescope's projection with Axoo tonight. They wanted the real experience.

The Always and Forever mates listened to the flowing river, glowing dimly with its bioluminescent life, and fell asleep resting in each other's arms, still in their ceremony apparel.

CHAPTER 35

Time slowed down. Silence took over.

Lirah wondered if time was trying to make up for moving so fast in the previous weeks. Or did time always slow down when someone suddenly left you? Someone that you saw and relied on every day for your whole life.

Lirah stopped going to reading lessons. She stopped eating much. She stayed in her bed most days. It was like metal blocks were pressing hard into her stomach and weighing her down, causing even her heartbeat to slow.

Lirah had known *the incident* was coming ... had known for so long. Mala had known too. And in her last living moments, Mala seemed quite at peace with dying. But now, nothing Lirah told her brain would change how her body felt. She never could've prepared for this gaping space that clawed at her chest, even if she had been notified of the *exact* moment her mother was expected to die. This gaping space would never be filled again. This space belonged only to her mother.

Sometimes, briefly, Au helped pull Lirah out of her sorrows. He'd come and sit on the foot of her bed and bring up a random memory of Mala for them to reminisce about. They'd joke together. He would tickle her or ruffle her unbrushed hair. Other days, he stayed away. But he never once tried to make her feel guilty for not speaking about their Always and Forever mate ceremony. They hadn't spoken about it since the day it occurred, before *the incident*. He told Lirah that he understood the tragedy of Mala's passing outweighed the happiness she felt for him and their bond right now. He understood, and that was that.

Lirah heard him crying outside at night often. Sometimes she would silently join him, and they would cry together. They would stargaze and try to find any sign of Mala *Out There*. But if Mala was a spirit, she refused to show herself.

The only clue Lirah noticed was in Josie. She behaved differently now that Mala was gone. The empathetic twinkle in her eye had faded, her tail had stopped happily swishing each time Lirah approached her, and her higher intelligence had left her. Lirah hoped Josie had changed because Bue's spirit left her body to be reunited with Mala's spirit. But Lirah would never know for sure. She hadn't experienced any other visions since her preview of the City of Flames either. She wasn't surprised. Visions couldn't occur if you were physically drained, so she doubted that you could experience one while mentally shattered either.

Mala's passing damaged Axoo too. Mala had planned to stay with him after Lirah and Au left for the City of Flames. Now, Axoo would be left to live alone again.

One night when Lirah was laying outside and stargazing (the only time she went outside anymore), she heard the shelter door open. A blade of light fanned out and covered her back in an orange glow before swinging closed again.

She expected to see Au. But it was Axoo who took a seat on the dirt next to her.

"Can I join ya?" he asked.

"Of course," Lirah said. She rested on her back and planted her hands behind her head with her elbows jutting out.

"Where's Au?"

"Sleepin'."

"You didn't want to look at the projection of your telescope tonight?"

"Nah. I was thinkin' you might have the right idea. Comin' out and lookin' at the real thing every now and then."

"It's just as beautiful out here, huh?" said Lirah.

"Yup. A different kind of beautiful."

Then they sat in silence, pointing out a shooting star every now and then.

It was such a clear night that there appeared to be more spots of light than pockets of darkness. Lirah could see every little crater and lake on the glowing golden sphere. Axoo told her the three glowing spheres were called moons.

Lirah laughed, thinking back to her happier memories with Mala.

"What is it?" Axoo asked, laying back with his arms propped behind his head too. They both looked like starfish resting on the bottom of the river.

"I'm just thinking about the first night I ever saw a sky full of stars like this. It was my first night out of the jungle too. I was predicting what they could be ... before I knew they were balls of gas billions of miles away."

"That's neat. I like that." Axoo chuckled. "I was taught all 'bout stars when I was little, so I never speculated on my own first."

"I feel like I had a spiritual awakening or something that night," Lirah said. "Ever since then, I've had so many questions flood into my head about the meaning of life. I remember, the day after that first night of stargazing, Au told me he thought the purpose of life was life itself ... just staying alive and keeping the ones he loves safe. But I don't know ... I don't think survival is enough. I feel like there *must* be a greater purpose for all of this." Lirah lifted her arms and spread them out wide. Then she hugged them back in as if she were pulling down an armful of stars to fill the space in her chest.

"Hmm," Axoo said.

"What do you think about all of that?" Lirah turned her head to the side to face Axoo.

"About the meanin' of life?"

"Yeah."

"Well, I think we *are* life. It's not a separate entity from us."

"So, you agree with Au?" Lirah sighed. "That nothing matters beyond surviving and staying alive right now?"

Another shooting star soared by.

"That's not what I'm sayin'," Axoo said. "I'm sayin' that you *are* the universe. Your individual experience is just one way the universe is expressin' itself. Every life is very important and unique. But at the same time ... I mean come on ..." Axoo chuckled. "Without new beings constantly comin' into the world and the old ones goin' out, everything would become stagnant. There would no longer be life. Change is necessary. So, death is necessary."

Lirah turned her head away from Axoo's dark silhouette and gave the sky a confused, irritated look.

"Think of it this way," Axoo said after a long pause. "You aren't even the same Lirah you were yesterday. You're constantly changin' and morphin' because of the events that are constantly happenin' in your life. You're always interactin' with whatever environment you're in, right?"

Lirah nodded, all choked up, but realized Axoo couldn't see her nonverbal response in the dark. She cleared her throat. "Yes. I think I understand. Because I can't really relate to who I used to be ... the *me* that lived in the Treetop Society. That Lirah is a totally different Lirah."

"There ya go. Every moment, yer old self is dyin' while a new self is bein' born," Axoo said. "So, don't worry yourself so much 'bout if anything really matters or not. You'll never get a straight answer 'bout the meaning of life from anybody. Because *nobody* knows the answer. But trust me, from my view, you matter. *And* yer the product of everything in the past. Think of all yer ancestors. Then think back before them. Yer here because of every event that happened in the past. Because *you* matter! You are the whole universe. A product of how it evolved up to this point. Isn't that neat?"

"Yes, it is. I like that point of view," Lirah said, still soaking in his words. After a few minutes she asked, "But if we all matter, why do some of us have to die earlier than others? Why do some beings get a longer life?"

"Because really ... death isn't bad. It's just another change."

Lirah sighed. "Death feels *really* bad when you're the one left behind."

"You got that right," Axoo said. "I miss Mala very much; don't think that I don't. This is just my general outlook on life and death, emotions aside."

"I like the way you look at life," Lirah said.

Then they let silence take over again.

Lirah breathed in, allowing Axoo's words to fan out into the air and hang around her head. Then she exhaled, letting his ideas plunge inside her mind for good.

Two more shooting stars flew by.

* * *

Summer turned to fall, and fall turned to winter.

On a particularly bright winter morning, Axoo burst through the door just as Lirah and Au were finishing breakfast. He told them that he'd been out riding Josie when he saw a group of strange objects coming at him from a distance. They were billowing up dust in their wake and emitting a constant roar. He said they were cargo trucks. *The* cargo trucks. Heading straight for the warehouse. They were practically here.

Lirah and Au dropped their bowls into the sink with sweating palms. They had been waiting on this moment's arrival for months. During those months, they formed a solid plan and reviewed it over and over:

1. Walk to the warehouse with packed bags and covered faces.
2. Enter quietly.
3. Pretend to be hoarders rummaging through piles of junk. (If anyone asks, we're searching for hidden gems among the garbage before it's taken away forever. Axoo's idea.)
4. When no one's around, climb into a box and hide out until destination is reached.

Simple.

But if they messed up, they would never get another chance to try again.

Lirah and Au rushed around the room collecting up their belongings into two brown backpacks. They crammed them full of water canteens, piles of dry food, flashlights, pocketknives, clothes, *Ramona and the City of Flames*, and a piece of Lirah's ceremony dress.

Lirah reminisced on the resources that Au, Mala, and her carried across the grasslands. Their sharpened rocks, wooden spears, flimsy waterskins, and one old sack stained with berry juice and rodent-worm guts, all still resting in the corner of Josie's hut. Lirah thought about how little they were able to prepare back in the jungle before they barreled through the wall of their makeshift cabin to escape the evil brutes. Back then, they didn't even know that canteens, flashlights, or pocketknives even existed.

There was a knock on Axoo's door.

Axoo peered through his curtain and turned around with a worried face. He put his index finger to his lips and waved at Lirah and Au to hurry upstairs.

They nodded and lightly ran up the stairs so no stomping could be heard.

From Axoo's room, they heard the front door open.

A deep and unfamiliar voice spoke. "Axal McAdoo?"

"That'd be me."

"I'm Eson Elvery. I'm here to collect data and journals from each resident in the Scope Settlement. Are you familiar with this collection process?"

"Yes I am."

"Great, because I'm relying on you to collect all the necessary documents from the east side of this settlement. Please bring all of the papers to the warehouse on the north end of the community by dusk. Do you think you can manage that, Axal McAdoo?"

He sounded friendly but straightforward. Strict.

"Yes, I do believe I can manage," said Axoo.

"Boogert Yeets is next on my list of suitable collectors. Before I speak with him about collecting from the west side of the settlement, do you believe he will be a good fit for this position? You two will have to coordinate."

"Yes. I sure think Boog would do a fine job."

"Great. Thank you for your service to science, Axal McAdoo. Lots of progress is being made in space thanks to this community. Here are brochures all about it. If you would hand one to each resident that you visit today, I would appreciate it." His voice boomed louder, "Each of you deserves to know your impact."

"Well, thank ya. I'll be sure to hand these out."

The door closed.

Lirah and Au heard Axoo muttering to himself and decided it was safe to go downstairs.

When they reached the foot of the staircase, he waved a brochure at them.

"Look here! I haven't received one of these in my whole life. I guess we're really makin' a difference. And look it says right here they're takin *Positive Psychology* more seriously." Axoo pointed at the bright glossy paper. "They want us residents to feel appreciated." He peeled a star-shaped sticker from the page and stuck it on his shirt.

"I made a difference," the sticker read.

Lirah looked over the words and pictures in the brochure, grateful she could read now. According to the brochure, years ago, the city's space program sent a brave group of astronauts to another planet in the solar system deemed suitable for life. So far, the program was a success. The team was faring well and successfully raised the planet's temperature in order to terraform it. After that, lots of civilians moved there and dozens of children had been born.

In the pictures, the planet looked a lot like a desert. In one picture, the large team was smiling next to a landed spaceship surrounded by dust and rock. The next picture showed metal boxes full of colorful plants and produce outside of a painted dome-shaped home. The last picture showed four children waving along with their beaming parents by a small pond. Lirah ran her thumb over their faces. Two of the kids looked about her age while the other two were much younger.

"This is incredible Axoo," Lirah whispered.

"Isn't it? And they couldn't have done it without us." Axoo chuckled his great big chuckle, making the room vibrate.

Lirah would miss that laugh so much.

"We'll miss you Axoo," she said.

Axoo's magnified eyes welled with tears. "Ya know, it's not too late to change yer minds. You can stay."

"We'll try to contact you when we're there," Au said. "Somehow ..."

Axoo nodded. They all knew no firm promises could be made about the future.

Lirah and Au continued their packing while Axoo shuffled around stacking up papers.

"Alright. It's time fer me to collect up the data and journals from other residents." Axoo sighed. "Good luck and feel free to take anything else ya might need fer yer trip." He hugged them each once more and left before anyone could get teary-eyed again.

Lirah's heart thumped wildly. She was filled with a mixture

of such intense emotions. Anxiety, wonder, fear, nostalgia, loss, doubt. The list went on. She took a deep breath and told herself that everything would work out. She and Au would make it to the City of Flames. She saw it in a vision.

"Ready to go?" Au asked her after they changed into the all-brown outfits they made to blend in with the warehouse boxes.

Lirah nodded. She sighed and gazed towards the three beds pushed against the left end of the room. From here on out, she would be part of a travelling duo, not a trio.

CHAPTER 36

Lirah slung one of the backpacks over her shoulder, tucked her hair beneath a large-brimmed, brown hat, and followed Au out the door. They stopped by Josie's hut and gave her goodbye pets.

A familiar voice rang out from behind them.

"Lirah! Au! Zullus is glad to see that you're finally outside. And at the zenith of light! Are you finally ready to continue with your reading lessons now that the initial shock of ... that day ... is well, *well* past us?" Zullus asked.

Lirah and Au rolled their eyes in unison and reluctantly turned to face him.

He sized them both from head to toe, his artificial smile spread wide. "New wardrobes, I see. And hats? For the library?"

"Would you mind keeping your voice down?" Au said through gritted teeth. "You probably know this already, but the data collectors are here and we don't want them to notice us. Since we weren't, you know, born here."

"Oh yes!" Zullus said.

Au clamped a hand over Zullus's mouth, *"Shh."*

Zullus pushed Au's hand away. "I know they're here," he whispered. "Zullus gave Boog many logs as well as a layout of all the classes he humbly provides."

Lirah nudged Au in his side.

Au nodded. "Alright, Zullus, we have to get going. Nice talking to you," he said. "For the last time," he added in a whisper after they started walking away. Lirah giggled.

"Where are you running off to?" Zullus said, following them in the opposite direction of the library.

This reminded Lirah of when the twins had trailed them through the jungle. They tried ignoring the twins just as they tried to ignore Zullus now. But Zullus kept following.

"Zullus orders you to stop!"

Au groaned. He walked up to Zullus and decked him across the face. It looked like he had been waiting to do that for a long time. Probably due to all those times Zullus had purposefully touched Lirah in the library.

"I told you to be quiet, twice. That's what happens on the third time." Au clamped his hand over Zullus's mouth and whispered fiercely, "You will not mess this up for us. Got that? We're going to the warehouse. You can come along if you'd like. We'll explain to you what it is that we're doing, *quietly*, on our way. But you must stay *silent*." Au forced Zullus to nod by gripping firmly onto the back of his hair and jerking his head up and down.

The odd trio continued walking towards the warehouse. Au had Zullus's hand gripped tightly in his own while Lirah stood on Zullus's other side whispering their plan to hide out in boxes. She told him that they wanted to be transported wherever the cargo trucks were heading, leaving out that she knew exactly where the trucks were heading to.

The only reason she told him anything was because she knew he would sell them out if she didn't. She had gotten to know Zullus pretty well. She knew that, above all, he liked to know everything. Sharing this information with him would satiate his biggest need. But what she *hadn't* expected was for

Zullus to trust in everything she told him. Then beg to come along.

Au flared his nostrils.

Again, Lirah's mind transported back to when Riel and Riggul had begged to join Au, Mala, and her on their journey into the unknown.

"Please. Zullus has always hoped for someplace else to go. Anywhere but this dreadful desert. Zullus cannot remain trapped here for his entire existence."

"You don't have a backpack of supplies to hide out with," Au said.

"There is dried food and bottled juice in the warehouse. Zullus will make do."

Au groaned. "I guess if you want to hide out in a box, I can't stop you. But hide away from us. I don't trust you to keep silent."

Zullus jumped for joy. He kept making excited comments along the way, and Lirah kept shushing him, telling him that he needed to settle down.

Au had to punch him again.

They approached the warehouse. Three cargo trucks waited far out in the distance for dusk to come.

She led the way through the side door. The bright lights were already on inside the warehouse. Two residents she didn't know very well were rummaging through boxes scattered around the floor.

Lirah assessed the boxes and rusted equipment stacked behind the scavenging men. She needed to find a box with soft clothes to hide in, and obviously not one with broken appliances or tools.

"Got anything in yer bags that yer gettin' rid of?" one of the hoarders half spat, half whistled at her. He had no teeth. "Could I take a look?"

"Actually, we're here for the same reason as you," Lirah said. "Collecting things to take back before it's all gone for good. Finding anything worthwhile?"

"Nah, not much. Just a few nuts an' bolts I might be able to use." He held out his rusty treasures. "I'll let ya three young'ins have at the rest. Good to see ya, Zullus."

The shriveled man smiled a toothless grin, then turned and shouted across the pile of trash, "Ernie! Let's get! I'm 'bouta lose ma bladder. I don't wanna be walkin' by Bertha's place with soaked pants!"

"I'm comin'! I'm comin'!" Ernie called back, limping around a box that was taller than he was. "Nothin' good anyways. Phooey."

"Lovely ceremony, by the way," the first man said, looking back at Lirah. "I knew I recognized ya. And that woman was a great speaker. A young'in too. She made me forget about Bertha fer 'bout ten minutes. What a shame she passed right after." He shook his head in disappointment.

"Alrigh', I'm here. Let's get!" Ernie shouted hoarsely. He shook violently with every step he took, hunched over his walking stick. "I don't wanna stop movin'. I'll lose all my momentum!"

The men walked out.

Au called out into the warehouse. The only response was his echo.

Lirah, Au, and Zullus were alone.

Au blocked off the side door in case more residents had the idea to come trash hunting. He said the wall at the far end of the warehouse was actually two pieces of metal that could be opened like a door, allowing the massive cargo trucks to drive right in.

"You're right. Nice. Well then, let's start picking out our temporary homes." Lirah smiled anxiously.

The three of them climbed the piles of boxes, opening and closing them depending on what they found inside. Once they found three boxes filled with old pillows and clothes, Au cut breathing holes in the bottom right corners of each of their sides. He did this to some of the other boxes too, so theirs wouldn't look suspicious.

Lirah and Au sipped from their canteens and munched on snacks while Zullus found his own snacks and juice, loading them into his box. They still had hours to wait until dusk and decided not to climb in the musty boxes until they had to.

Lirah paced up and down the red line dividing the warehouse, focusing on her steps and trying to calm her nerves as the time slowly passed.

* * *

The doorknob jiggled.

Lirah, Au, and Zullus crouched down behind their boxes and held their breath.

The side door banged and banged. Someone was kicking it.

"Who would need to come in this badly?" Lirah whispered.

"It's probably the collectors. Bringing in the data," said Zullus. Without hesitation, he walked over to the side door and unblocked it.

While Zullus was away, Au kicked Zullus's box away from Lirah's and his.

The door groaned open. Lirah peeked over the brim of her box and looked outside. Dusk was approaching quickly. The desert floor glowed with the day's final rays of light. She ducked back down.

"Zullus apologizes for the delay," he told Axoo and Boog.

"What are ya doin' here Zullus?" Axoo asked, concerned. "What happened to yer face? It's all bloodied up."

"Zullus was looking through boxes and slipped down a pile of screws and bolts."

Lirah could feel Zullus' fake smile from here. She wondered if she should wave to Axoo, to let him know she was alright. She decided not to. She didn't want Boog to see her.

"Zullus will take those."

"It's alright; I got it. Boog, ya can go on back. I'll wait on Zullus, and walk with him," Axoo said.

Lirah heard the door groan closed.

Footsteps approached the red dividing line. Lirah peered over her box again.

Zullus and Axoo were dropping the data and journals into two separate stacks on the center of the line. Boog wasn't there.

Lirah came out of hiding. "Hey, Axoo."

"Lirah!" Axoo hugged her.

"Zullus is coming along," Au said, standing up and rolling his eyes.

"Oh." Axoo paused. "Well ... I'll miss ya, Zullus. I'll miss you all so much. I'm happy I got the chance to say goodbye again."

"We'll miss you too," Lirah said. "Thank you, again, for everything."

Axoo wiped at his eyes, hugged each of them, and left. The door groaned closed behind him.

"I guess it's time to hunker down." Lirah patted her box.

"I guess so," Au said. He leaned over and rubbed Lirah's nose. Their scars from the ceremony had all but disappeared.

"Zullus wishes you both the best of luck on this journey," Zullus called from his box, holding the lid over his head.

"You too." Lirah and Au waved.

Zullus flashed them a final grin, squatted down, and planted the lid over himself.

Lirah turned and grinned at Au. She would miss his honey-brown eyes. She was happy they would be her final view before settling down into darkness. "Maybe after we're transferred to the boat, we can look for each other's boxes. I'll keep my eye out for boxes with holes in the bottom right corners," she whispered.

"Alright. But if not, I'll see you in the City of Flames," Au whispered back to her.

They shared their final kiss and settled down into their own boxes, closing up the lids.

Lirah heard lots of readjusting coming from Au and Zullus's boxes. She assessed her own tight space.: the pitch blackness, the clothes and blankets surrounding her, and her large pack firmly pressed against her back. She never thought of herself as claustrophobic before, but she felt more uncomfortable sitting here than she ever thought possible. She sighed. She would have to get used to it. The payoff would be worth the discomfort.

Lirah turned her thoughts to Mala, who was sealed in a small casket floating down a river, and wondered if she had made it to the sea by now. But that was just Mala's body.

Lirah hoped her mother's spirit was free somewhere in the vast sky with the twinkling stars.

* * *

Lirah didn't know how much time had passed. She fell asleep at some point, and an echoey, creaking noise woke her.

She heard the roar of a machine cut off, followed by voices speaking in a language she didn't understand.

She tensed up, scared to breathe now.

It was time. They were being loaded up.

She heard slamming. Boxes being moved.

The loaders weren't being very careful.

She heard more slamming, complaining, and irritated voices. When would she be moved to a truck?

Lirah considered all the boxes in the warehouse and sighed. She imagined the movers giving up, deciding it was too much trash to take at one time and leaving some behind. Including her box.

She heard more slamming and shoving and grunting.

Finally, her box was lifted.

She remembered when she was lifted in a cage and brought to receive her burn bracelet. This felt much different than that. She was nervous but so thankful to finally be in motion. She couldn't wait to get to the City of Flames, though she knew this journey was only just beginning.

Her box was dropped onto a new floor. Others were piled on

top of hers.

She tried to slow her breath. She was very trapped.

After counting the passing seconds, mostly to control her breathing, for what felt like many more hours, she heard the rev of an engine. She felt the floor vibrating, then a forward jolt. The push led to a smooth, continuous momentum.

Lirah let out a small shriek. Now their boxes just had to make it safely onto the boat. She thought about Axoo's brochure and the astronauts who relocated from the City of Flames to a different planet. It seemed like no one was ever satisfied with where they were.

No matter what society you happen to live in, she thought, *there will always be new places to travel. But maybe it's less about being dissatisfied with where you are and more about curiosity of the unknown.*

Lirah fell asleep visualizing the picture of the spaceship and its crew from Axoo's brochure. She pictured herself soaring through space. The nebulae, the stars. She waved to Mala, who didn't look anything like herself, but Lirah instantly recognized the sensation of her mother's spirit.

Then she woke up again.

More banging. A metal shaft sliding up. Footsteps. Bickering in another language.

She heard boxes sliding across a smooth surface.

This time, she understood what was going on. She knew they were being transferred to the boat, and she knew this process would take a while. As long as she didn't focus on what it would feel like to stretch her legs or see light, she felt used to being in this tight space. Keeping her eyes closed helped too.

As Lirah's box lifted, so did her heart. She could get through this. The next time her box was lifted it would be dropped on solid ground in her new home—the City of Flames.

She felt her box being planted on another. She could tell she wasn't resting on solid ground this time.

Then she felt herself swaying.

Boats travelled across water, she reminded herself. But she

wasn't sure if she liked this feeling.

She thought she might be sick.

She could *not* throw up inside this box. She scrunched up her eyes and swallowed hard, refusing to give in to her body's commands.

She thought of Au. How was he handling this? Probably better than she was. She imagined what her mother would tell her, "*My light, be brave.*"

"Almost there," Lirah whispered to herself. "I'll be brave, Mala." She smiled through her seasickness and transported her mind elsewhere.

She pictured herself bobbing side by side with Au on a crystal-clear river. She dove underwater and resurfaced, splashing cool water droplets into the warm light beams above. Au's laugh broke out, and the fragrance of the fresh greenery lining the river filled her nose.

Inside her cramped and gloomy box, as the boat slowly started accelerating forward, Lirah realized that her mind was more powerful than her surroundings.

In the darkness, she was the light. At least, her mother thought so. So why couldn't it be true?

Lirah had no idea what obstacles and opportunities the City of Flames would hold for herself and Au. Her vision of the city was only a snippet of what they would endure. But whatever happened, they would persevere and thrive if she believed they could. She held the power to bring light with her wherever she went. She mattered. The entire universe progressed in order to bring her up to this point. She was an elemental force. She was drifting light.

ABOUT THE AUTHOR

Kendall Clarke

Like Lirah, Kendall is somewhat of a drifter herself. She grew up in sunny Tampa, Florida and received her Bachelor's in Psychology from Florida State University in 2020. Since graduating, she has travelled around and explored many of America's natural wonders by working in different service occupations along her way, from teaching remotely in North Carolina to managing surf shop inventory in California. Currently, Kendall calls Steamboat Springs, Colorado her home. She enjoys hiking in the warm months and snowboarding during the winter.

Find her elsewhere:

Instagram- @thoughtsofkendall
Email- kendallclarkewrites@gmail.com

Made in the USA
Monee, IL
20 June 2023

36310461R00184